Naked Feminism

For all women – modest, or otherwise

Naked Feminism
Breaking the Cult of Female Modesty

VICTORIA BATEMAN

polity

First published in 2023 by Polity Press

Polity Press
65 Bridge Street
Cambridge CB2 1UR, UK

Polity Press
101 Station Landing
Suite 300
Medford, MA 02155, USA

ISBN-13: 978-1-5095-5606-9

A catalogue record for this book is available from the British Library.

Library of Congress Control Number: 2022946838

Typeset in 11 on 14pt Warnock Pro
by Cheshire Typesetting Ltd, Cuddington, Cheshire
Printed and bound in Great Britain by CPI Group (UK) Ltd, Croydon

The publisher has used its best endeavours to ensure that the URLs for external
websites referred to in this book are correct and active at the time of going to
press. However, the publisher has no responsibility for the websites and can
make no guarantee that a site will remain live or that the content is or will
remain appropriate.

Every effort has been made to trace all copyright holders, but if any have been
overlooked the publisher will be pleased to include any necessary credits in any
subsequent reprint or edition.

For further information on Polity, visit our website:
politybooks.com

Contents

Figures and Tables

Figures

Tables

Acknowledgements

This book is personal and political. It fuses academic work with the experience of placing my own naked body in the public sphere. It provides a response to all those who have questioned whether being naked can be feminist. And it is a reaction to the numerous times I have been called 'trashy', a 'whore' and an 'idiot'. It tells the story of when, how and why societies became obsessed with women's bodily modesty – whether their virginity or their state of dress – and explores the many adverse consequences that have resulted. It lifts the lid on the battle that has long taken place within feminism: between those who regard modesty as a necessary tool of liberation, and those, like me, who argue that a woman's respect and worth should not depend on something as superficial as either her state of dress or whether her hymen is intact.

Much of the book was inspired by observation: observing the way 'scantily clad' women, as well as those dressing modestly, are stereotyped; observing the way strippers and sex workers are disparaged and talked down to; and observing the way people reacted with judgement towards my own naked endeavours. Throughout the associated judgement, I have been extremely fortunate to have received support from friends and colleagues, including Ruth Scurr, Karenjit Clare, Carolina Alves, Clive Lawson, Lucy Delap, Michelle Baddeley, Avner Offer, Arif Ahmed, Alan Fersht and Natasha Devon, along with my sister Stephanie. I have benefited not only from the published work but also the camaraderie of Deborah Oxley, Emma Rees, Bina Agarwal, Keon West, Philippa Levine, Kate Lister, Erin Hengel and Belinda Brooks-Gordon: all of these, and so many more, deserve a big thank you. I have also been touched by the support offered to me by those who have reached out online (and by post) and have been forever moved by the kindness offered by both the sex worker and the nudist communities.

Polity Press deserves a particular thank you, most notably my editor, Louise Knight, along with Inès Boxman, Emma Longstaff, Susan Beer, Anne Sullivan, Emma Nash, Jim Caunter, George Owers and Pascal Porcheron, and two anonymous readers, who offered not only helpful suggestions but also support when the project was in its first stages. Emma Rees read the full manuscript in great detail and injected punch into the final stage of the project, for which I am very grateful.

The unfailing and unconditional love of my husband of seventeen years (and counting) is something I never take for granted and goes to show that immodest women can – and should – be treated with love and respect.

Preface

This book isn't a feminist manifesto for nudity – even though I would happily write one. And it isn't an invitation for every reader to strip layer-by-layer with each passing chapter, though I certainly have no objection if you do so. Its aim is broader: to place in full view what I call the 'cult of female modesty' – the way in which, in many societies across the world, a woman's worth, value and respect depend on her bodily modesty. It draws not only on the personal – the private and public criticism I have received for my own acts of bodily immodesty – but also on the experiences of women who face a much tougher culture of modesty, from forced veiling to virginity testing and honour killings.

As I hope will be clear, my objection is not to modesty – in the sense of what people wear or how they choose to live their sex lives – but, instead, to societal attitudes: to those who think that women's uncovered or promiscuous bodies are 'the problem', and who in turn deem immodest women a threat to themselves, a danger to other women and a disruptive force in wider society. Challenging the modesty cult does not therefore mean that we should all shed our veils or bikini tops, it means that we should respect modest and immodest women alike, resting a woman's value and respect on much more important things than bodily modesty.

Throughout, I reflect on how modesty culture is affecting women's lives today, and consider how the past has shaped the present. To provide vital perspective, Chapter 1 offers some historical background, revealing the way in which the modesty cult is deeply rooted not only in the Middle East but also in South Asia, the Far East and parts of Europe. While not all world regions have historically been as tightly within its grip – including parts of Australasia, South East Asia, Western and Southern Africa, and the Americas – we'll see how colonisation, international trade and religion acted to spread the cult of female modesty into these areas, with serious consequences for women. For the sake of brevity, our historical journey is necessarily a speedy one, meaning that my focus is on covering major trends across large geographical areas rather than providing detailed analysis of an individual society or a specific period. And, precisely because modesty culture is multi-faceted, I try to give a taste of not only clothing customs but also attitudes to women's sexual activity, including those towards the most 'immodest' of all women: sex workers.

Since my focus is on breadth, for a reader who has more time to explore history in greater depth, I would recommend Philip Carr-Gomm's *A Brief History of Nakedness*, Ruth Barcan's *Nudity: A Cultural Anatomy*, Annebella Pollen's *Nudism in a Cold Climate*, Hanne Blank's *Virgin: The Untouched History*, Kate Lister's *Harlots, Whores and Hackabouts*, Ruth Mazo Karras's *Common Women*, Emma Rees's *The Vagina: A Literary and Cultural History*, Stephanie Cronin's (ed.) *Anti-Veiling Campaigns in the Muslim World*, Nikki Keddie's *Women in the Middle East*, Barbara Molony et al.'s *Gender in Modern East Asia*, and Faramerz Dabhoiwala's *The Origins of Sex*, amongst many others.

Much of the book is what could be defined as heteronormative: it discusses policies and practices that are constructed on the assumption that men are attracted to women who are in turn attracted to men. This is because the modesty cult itself is predicated on heteronormative assumptions – that we are cisgendered and heterosexual.[1] The feminist critics of 'immodest' women, who we similarly encounter in this book, also tend to deploy their armoury (including concepts such as 'the male gaze' and 'objectification') in a heteronormative way. As the journalist Zoe Williams points out, '[t]he rhetoric of objectification relies on the idea that it's one-way traffic, that only men objectify, and only women are objectified'.[2] Since I do not support the modesty cult, it may not come as a surprise that I also do not support the – explicit or otherwise – homophobia and transphobia that almost without exception accompanies it.

As becomes clear in the course of this book, women can themselves be complicit in the cult of female modesty – judging and looking down on those who are either insufficiently covered or deemed sexually 'promiscuous'. Why this is the case – and whether modesty culture is truly in women's collective best interest – is the topic of Chapter 4. With it, I consider numerous strands of feminist thought – including the feminism of the suffragettes, socialist feminism, Islamic feminism and radical feminism – to uncover the degree to which they do or do not embrace aspects of the modesty cult. The lines are rarely either clear-cut or consistent. Some feminists reject naked protest, while others support protesting naked but oppose glamour modelling; similarly, some feminists question casual sex, while others view it as a sign of liberation, but condemn those who sell sex; and, some object to compulsory hijab abroad while also disapproving of short skirts and revealing tops at home – ironically, using the same logic as those imposing the compulsory hijab.

It is certainly common for people to 'pick and choose', approving or being tolerant of some behaviours which could be deemed 'immodest' but not others: for example, life models are commonly seen as more acceptable than glamour models; women who have premarital sex in a long-term relationship are typically seen as more 'respectable' than those who also engage in casual sex; strippers are often judged less disapprovingly than women who have sex for money; and, women who have lots of casual sex are judged much more favourably than those who choose to sell sex.

I frequently, however, find myself questioning the divisions that are commonly constructed in our minds between different aspects of immodesty. For example, if I was ever to be paid for delivering a naked performance on the topic of feminism, would that have any overlap with stripping? If a life model sells naked images of herself to artists for artistic purposes, does what she is doing have any degree of overlap with glamour modelling (after all, some of her images may well be bought for pornographic use)? If you model underwear for a high street chain, is there any overlap with posing for a 'Lads' Mag'? While there are certainly differences between each of these activities – which many are of course keen to point out – there is also some degree of commonality, and acknowledging this is, I believe, vital to breaking down the divisions between women.

The feminist Robin Morgan worried that 'the erosion of the virgin/whore stereotype' would erase 'the last vestige of (even corrupted) respect for women'.[3] But, surely, we can build respect for women on the basis of something other than bodily modesty? Rather than erecting a wall between women, we can – and should – be setting a wrecking ball loose on the very idea of division.

If we truly object to the modesty culture that drives compulsory hijab, virginity testing and honour killings, we should not be slut-shaming scantily clad women and stigmatising glamour models, strippers or sex workers. By breaking the cult of female modesty we have the power to solve a whole host of problems that plague women's lives across the world – problems that have so far proved intractable. Our ultimate aim must be to ensure that every woman is respected and valued, irrespective of her state of bodily coverage or the degree to which her hymen is intact.

Introduction

What determines a woman's worth? Is it her achievements, her personality, her beliefs? Is it her conscientiousness, her open-mindedness, how kind and generous she is to others? Or is it what she shows, or doesn't show, of her body that determines whether a woman is valued and respected by society?

I pose these questions not only as a woman but also as a 'naked feminist', someone who views my body, alongside my brain, as a means of advancing feminism. Rather than being afraid of the female body, and keen to repress femininity and sexuality, naked feminists respect those who make use of their body, their brain, or both. As someone who has, among other things, delivered public lectures, attended a Royal Economic Society gala, and appeared on national television, all while wearing no more than shoes and a smile (albeit accompanied by my trusty handbag), there is little doubting my commitment to the naked feminist cause. Yet not everyone agrees with my approach; below are a select few (of the many thousands) of comments I have received:

Good God she single-handedly took feminism back to the Stone Age!

There's nothing more anti-feminist than having to strip naked desperate for a man's attention.

A woman's body is a work of art . . . a gift from God to man. My wife would wholeheartedly disagree with you on flaunting it for this purpose. Thanks for sullying the sanctity of women whose bodies are private to them and their significant other.

Being trashy is never classy and you certainly are quite trashy.

You're a disgrace to all women!

One person even reported me, via Twitter, to the Cambridge police department. Unfortunately for them, they were foiled by their poor understanding of geography: as they discovered, the Cambridge P.D. in Massachusetts has no jurisdiction over Cambridge, England (not that I had, in fact, committed any crime).

You might of course be questioning why it matters if I receive a torrent of abuse for revealing my body. After all, haven't I asked for it with my actions? Don't I deserve my comeuppance? Yet it is this 'asking for it' mentality that sometimes on a more subconscious level pervades so much of society's attitude towards women. Explicitly or implicitly, and inside as well as outside feminism, women's respect still hangs on their bodily modesty – on the degree to which their body is 'unseen' and 'untouched'. As a result, crimes and inappropriate behaviour committed against what society judges to be 'immodest' women are trivialised, with women who 'show off' their bodies, along with those who are deemed 'promiscuous', being seen as 'fair game', and deserving of punishment.

By imposing bodily modesty as a perceived virtue on women, society actively prevents the equality of the sexes. In other words, what I will call 'the cult of female modesty', the belief that a woman's worth, value and respect depend on her bodily modesty, inhibits equality, rather than furthering the cause of women. As we will see, this modesty cult not only shuns and devalues the women it categorises as 'whores', it hurts all women – modest as well as immodest. No one escapes its wrath.

In some countries, the modesty cult could not be more clear. In Egypt, Morocco and Palestine, more than eight in ten men think that their honour depends on how their female relatives dress and behave, and more than a third think that the victims of honour killings 'usually deserve such punishment'.[1] A study of male preferences in regard to female partners found that 'sexual inexperience' was valued highly by men in Indonesia, Iran, India, China and Taiwan.[2] Measured in terms of attitudes to virginity, Indonesia, Jordan, Pakistan, Palestine, Turkey and Egypt, where 90 per cent or more of people consider premarital sex unacceptable, would surely top any modesty ranking. Other countries that also display high levels of disapproval of premarital sex include Nigeria (77%), India (67%) and China (58%).[3] As Tang et al. write, '[n]owadays, Chinese people typically hold more open and positive attitudes towards sex than in previous decades, but its citizens are still not as open as Westerners'.[4] In the West, the proportion of people who deem premarital sex unacceptable stands at 30 per cent in the United States, a mere 13 per cent in the UK and only six per cent in France and Germany, which rank as the most 'promiscuous', or least judgemental, of all countries. Attitudes towards birth control, which capture the degree to which people think that sex can and should be divorced from reproduction, also help us to reveal where the modesty cult is most apparent.[5] The countries that rank highest in these terms are Pakistan, where 65 per cent find birth control unacceptable, Nigeria (54%), Ghana (52%) and Malaysia (40%). In the United States only seven per cent of people take the view that birth control is morally unacceptable; in the UK it is even lower at three per cent and in Germany it is a mere one per cent.

But, on a personal level, the reaction that I have faced to my naked feminism has made clear to me that, even in supposedly liberal countries, too many of us still judge women based on their bodily modesty. Delving deeper into embedded societal attitudes and behaviours only confirms this fact and, worryingly, the evidence is that modesty culture is now on the rise. And this is why I am writing this book. I want to explore the history of female modesty; to examine the situations of the women whose lives are most blighted by the modesty cult today; to bring to light the way in which modesty culture is gathering steam; and to raise the alarm as to what lies ahead. I want to make clear that the modern-day modesty resurgence isn't only associated with clerics, conservatives and nationalists; it is also at risk of polluting feminism itself, particularly as we react to the issues raised by the ubiquitous presence of sex and women's bodies in today's 'striptease culture'.[6] I end with a plea to all my fellow feminists and liberals – a plea to reject, rather than to embrace, the modesty cult. While today's 'raunch culture' might be far from perfect, we should be careful not to throw the baby out with the bathwater; as we will see, the modesty cult cannot be our saviour.

For too long, and in too many places, the cult of female modesty has gone under the radar, and that is in large part because modesty culture possesses a secret weapon; it is exceptionally evasive. The line between modesty and immodesty is drawn in a different place in different time periods and in different societies. What one person judges to be modest, another might judge to be immodest, depending on where they live, and in which century. In parts of the Middle East, a woman without a headscarf is considered 'naked', whereas a European woman wearing a bikini would not, in general, be described as such. Indeed, as Monique Mulholland notes in her book *Negotiating Pornification*, a scantily clad woman can still be considered 'respectable' in Western culture, so long as she behaves in a 'controlled' way in terms of her sexuality. Moreover, within the nudist community, nakedness itself is not perceived as immodest but as humbling, innocent and without vanity, whereas the 'sexualisation' of the body is considered more of a taboo. Bodily coverage (and the acceptance or otherwise of nudity) is, therefore, neither necessary nor sufficient as a metric of modesty culture; attitudes towards women's sexuality also need to be considered. Indeed, history tells us that societies often seek to control not only how women dress, but, more specifically, their sexual behaviour, creating not only an obsession with virginity, but also, at the opposite end of the spectrum, a demonisation of those who might profit from their bodies, such as glamour models and sex workers.

The fact that bodily modesty is multi-faceted, and that there are no universal rules, might make the modesty cult elusive, but that does not mean that we should be fooled into thinking that we have escaped its torment. Any society in which the word 'whore' acts as an insult to women should be considered to a greater or lesser extent to be within its grip. This is because, at its heart, the modesty cult divides women up into 'good girls' and 'whores' and anyone who is on the wrong side of this line is deemed lacking in respect and worth. Whorephobia and slut-shaming are the inequitable, and damaging, consequence.

I admit that I once subscribed to the modesty cult. As a young teenager, while other girls were rolling down their socks and rolling up their skirts, I was doing the reverse: my favourite attire consisted of an almost Victorian-era style of dress, with long socks and a skirt that reached to my ankles. While I was being mocked for my 'prudish' state of dress, I could see how others elsewhere in society were laughing at my boob-tube-wearing peers. They were deemed 'silly tarts' and 'pieces of meat'. When they were harassed or abused, well-mannered society would respond: 'well, weren't they asking for it?' And that is, of course, one of the reasons I covered up. I didn't want to be written off as 'trashy' or 'common', or to be seen as 'fair game'. But, the more I thought about it, and the more

I collected my badges of academic achievement, the more I wondered whether I was myself complicit in society's attempt to divide women up into good girls and whores. I started to notice the way in which my body increasingly felt like a liability, one that risked sullying what I had achieved with my brain. Not only was I left feeling uncomfortable with my sexuality, I felt under pressure to choose between my body and my brain. I began to ask myself: why should I be categorised as a brain and by implication not have a body? And why should other women, from models to strippers, be classified as bodies, with their brain ignored? By shedding my own clothes I wanted to question the dangerous societal divisions women face; I wanted to show that behind every body is a brain, and behind every brain is a body and we should celebrate both, and fear neither. I wanted to take charge of both my body and my brain, something that every woman should be free to do.

As I started to realise, not only do we still have further to travel until women are in full control of their bodies, but it is the cult of female modesty that stands in the way. Despite the supposed ubiquity of women's bodies, body-phobia remains. When Janet Jackson accidentally exposed her breast during the 2004 Super Bowl there was an uproar – along with a $550,000 fine for the network that televised it.[7] Around the same time, the topless Spirit of Justice statue housed in the Justice Department of the USA was being draped in fabric at taxpayers' expense, all so as to avoid embarrassment for the officials photographed or filmed nearby.[8] In 2014, Leena McCall's painting 'Ruby May, Standing' was removed from the Society of Women Artists' Annual Exhibition in London after complaints from visitors that it was 'pornographic'. The subject was, in fact, mostly covered, but with pubic hair protruding above her trousers. While full female nudes were on display at the same gallery, Ruby May's more sexually knowing and confident pose was clearly too much for some visitors to handle.[9] Even more recently, in May 2022, Adidas launched a sports-bra campaign filled with non-sexualised bare breasts of infinite variety. After complaints from the British public, the Advertising Standards Authority banned the advertisements. Women's bodies are, apparently, too offensive for public eyes.

Even when it comes to holidays, which should be our period of peak relaxation, the modesty cult rears its ugly head. Going topless for comfort remains taboo for women. Interestingly, according to a 2020 YouGov poll, women are more likely than men to object to other women being topless on the beach. Less than half of British women think that topless sunbathing is 'acceptable for both men and women' compared with 70 per cent of men.[10] Similarly, a half of British women think that non-sexualised naked protest is completely unacceptable compared with only 38 per cent of men.[11] Many women take the attitude that too much female flesh on show serves the 'male gaze'. To them, what other people, predominantly heterosexual men, might think or feel in response to a woman's body is more important than a woman being free to use her body as she chooses.

Alongside the body-phobia, whorephobia is ever present. Women still face numerous sexual double standards. The words 'slut', 'slag' and 'whore' are still considered to be some of the greatest insults that can be directed at women, precisely because society deems bodily virtue, or the lack of it, to be a central determinant of a woman's worth. From a young age, women walk a fine line between being called 'prudes' and 'whores' and, once that line is crossed, their reputation may never recover. While nowadays, being 'hot' can command respect, being 'slutty' does not; and, of course, only women can be sluts.[12] Revenge porn has, sadly, become a growing phenomenon, used to shame and embarrass women. Adolescent girls are well aware that their reputation is on the line when it comes to sexual encounters and, in the words of two sexual health experts, simultaneously 'feel less entitled to sexual pleasure from masturbation'.[13] Even when it's solo, erotic

pleasure is shameful. Furthermore, women experience higher
levels of guilt than men following their first sexual encounter.[14]
And, while casual sex is a status symbol for men it remains 'a
sign of being a slut for a woman'.[15] More generally, women's
sexual pleasure and desire are neglected relative to men's.[16] We
rarely confront the fact that one in ten British women experience pain during sex,[17] something that can in turn be linked to
sex-guilt and to a fear of appearing unladylike or immodest.[18]
Cindy Meston reveals her struggles in accessing funding for
research on female sexual pleasure: '[y]ou can talk about wellbeing or marital satisfaction, but talking about sexual arousal
or orgasm as an ultimate end point will diminish your chances
of getting funded'.[19] In the words of Emily Maguire, '[y]ou can
have orgasms or respect', not both.[20]

Slut-shaming is not only common, it has become institu-
tionalised, to the point that it is considered an acceptable
form of punishment for girls. In the last few years, stories
have circulated of American high schools recommending
the distribution of 'modesty ponchos' for prom nights, while
in September 2019 a high-school swimmer was initially disqualified from winning a swimming competition because
her school-issued swimsuit rode up her backside as she
climbed out of the pool.[21] In their interviews with parents
and young people in Scotland, researchers spoke to a teacher
who 'recounted how he had challenged colleagues in his
(Catholic) school for their readiness to describe female students as "sluts" on the basis of their clothing'.[22] In Ireland in
November 2020, students at a Carlow Secondary School were
brought together in the school hall and instructed on what
was and was not appropriate wear for gym classes. According
to one parent, her daughter was told that she and other young
women 'should have more respect for themselves [than to]
be showing off their bodies'.[23] In protest, a group of students
began pasting posters to the school walls with the message
'[s]top teaching women how to dress. Instead, teach men how

to respect women.'[24] The school responded publicly by saying that gym days were becoming 'fashion shows' and that the talks were nothing more than a reminder of the school's gym uniform rules.[25]

The model and actress Emily Ratajkowski reflects on her own treatment as a young woman and how it left her feeling uncomfortable in her own body:

> [M]en and women had told me that if I dressed a certain way I wouldn't be taken seriously and could even be put in danger. A middle school teacher's comment, 'You can't expect anyone to respect you' echoed through my head.[26]

In 2018, when Ratajkowski was reportedly detained on Capitol Hill while protesting the Supreme Court nomination of Brett Kavanaugh, headlines were soon circulating about what she was wearing. In her own words, '[e]ven women from the Left, who fully supported the purpose of my protest, made comments about my missing bra underneath my white tank and jeans. In their minds, the fact that my body was at all visible had somehow discredited me and my political action.'[27] The body is assumed to detract from the brain, and, in turn, being 'sexy' is also assumed to detract from being 'smart': '[w]omen with brains and beauty are not allowed to use both'.[28] Not only are women expected to choose between being smart and being sexy, if they do choose the latter, their choice is seen as somehow damaging to womankind. As Ratajkowski notes, 'we look down so much on women who like to play with what it means to be sexy'.[29]

Modesty culture is therefore deeply ingrained, but more worryingly, and despite some feminists arguing that 'raunch culture' is now the status quo, it is also experiencing a resurgence, and in more places than one.[30] In Israel, gender segregation on modesty grounds has been growing since the 1990s. It aims to '"clean" the public sphere from any manifestation, real or perceived, of female sexuality'.[31] Elsewhere in the Middle East, the veil has descended, a phenomenon that has become known as 're-veiling'[32] and, while for many women it is a personal symbol of piety and of religious identity, for others it is a collective tool to fight sexism.[33] Gabby Aossey, for example, claims that Muslim women who dress modestly are the true feminists, and that other women should embrace modest dress if they want to be respected in life.[34] But the modesty branch of Islamic feminism is not alone. In the United States, 'purity culture' has been taking hold in Christian circles. Evangelical Christianity, with its virginity pledges and purity balls, is the 'fastest-growing segment of the global Christian Church',[35] and it is armed with advice books for women, encouraging them to embrace bodily modesty in all its forms. Lookadoo and DiMarco's *Dateable* compares women who lose their virginity before marriage with used cars, asking '[w]ould you buy a beat-up, old, used car at a new car price?'[36] They claim that 'every new sexual experience when you are not married puts another ding, another scratch, another scar on who you are. You keep running your car into other people, and then you wonder why no one treats you special.'[37] Another best-selling advice book *And the Bride Wore White: Seven Secrets to Sexual Purity* categorises women as 'styrofoam, ceramic, or teacup in value' and goes on to suggest that '[g]irls who are teacups do not dress in sexy clothes, because they are more valuable, and girls who are sexy are not valuable'.[38]

This sort of advice has also crept into sex education. As one author argues, the American government has an 'official virginity policy'.[39] In 1981, it passed the Adolescent Family Life Act, known to some as the Chastity Act. The Act compelled all organisations that were receiving state funding to tackle teenage pregnancy to teach only abstinence-based sex education. This chaste agenda went even further, both with Bill Clinton,[40] and, subsequently, with the expansion in programme funding that occurred under the Bush administration.[41] As a result, between 1988 and 1999, abstinence-only sex education expanded from representing just two per cent of American sex education to almost a quarter.[42] By 2003, almost a third of sex educators in the USA taught abstinence-only, with no discussion of contraception,[43] and in 2022 the Roe vs. Wade ruling, which protected a woman's right to abortion, was overturned.

As we will see in Chapter 1, far from revealing an upward march towards bodily and sexual liberty, history tells us that the pendulum has swung back and forth across the centuries. Today's resurgence in modesty is on cue; having witnessed the sexual liberalisation of the twentieth century, the puritans are now overdue a comeback.

The first major swing in the modesty pendulum took place four thousand years ago, when an obsession with women's bodily modesty first descended across the Middle East, North Africa and the eastern Mediterranean. By Roman times, however, women were not only unveiling their carefully manicured hair, they were also visible in public. The modesty-loving strands of Christianity, Islam and neo-Confucianism soon, though, stamped on this public display. And then, just as modesty culture was spreading from China across East Asia, Europeans were embracing the bawdiness of Chaucer and Shakespeare. The Puritans soon put an end to the parties, the illegitimacy, and the 'whoredom': immodest women were burned, imprisoned in Magdalen homes, or whipped by order of the state. And, thanks to the colonial adventures of the Spanish and Portuguese, not to mention the Puritans themselves, this modesty cult was shipped far and wide. Soon the Victorian moralists were 'saving souls' at home and abroad, teaching people to feel shame and embarrassment about their bodies in parts of the world that had, until then, no concept of 'nakedness'. In an effort to inflate the virtue of white European women, whole continents-worth of women were labelled 'whores', in turn contributing to widespread rape and abuse.[44]

And, where colonialists faced women who dressed particularly modestly, then so as not to bump European women down the modesty rankings, they were automatically labelled backward and oppressed.

As we will see in Chapter 2, the cult of female modesty continues to impact the lives of millions of women today, causing harm in multiple ways, all of which are ignored by those who claim that what we need in the West is a 'return to modesty'. Across the world, government policies and social practices are implemented as a means of protecting women's all-important bodily 'virtue'. This 'protection' can include banning women from travelling alone, restricting where they can work and rest, regulating their dress, performing intimate virginity tests, or removing their genitals. In extreme cases, women are tortured and killed by their family if their bodily modesty is brought into question: in Nangarhar, Afghanistan, it is estimated that one in sixteen families have perpetrated an honour killing.[45] Despite the beliefs of its adherents, the modesty cult does not make women's lives safer, it leaves them exposed to harm, as the high levels of street-based harassment in countries such as Egypt, Morocco and Lebanon reveal.[46] As we will see, the modesty cult also harms women and girls in more subtle ways: in the reluctance of families to send their daughters to school or university for fear of mixing with men, restricting their opportunities; in a woman's reluctance to report sexual abuse, for fear of her reputation; in the embarrassment a teenage girl feels when asking for contraception, something that might cause her just to 'take the risk'; in the vaginismus that can so easily result when women are raised by society to feel that sex is sinful; and in a reluctance to attend smear tests and mammograms, which can have a serious effect on the chances of surviving cancer. Questioning the idea that a woman's value and respect rest on her bodily modesty is vital to challenging the policies and practices that harm women's lives across the globe. Rather than welcoming modesty culture, we should be doing everything within our power to break it.

Of course, if the modesty cult is to be broken, we also need to understand what lies behind it. Chapter 3 therefore delves into the effects of religion, biology, geography, climate, warfare, politics and economics. While the modesty cult has existed across time and across place, it has done so to very different degrees. This variation allows us to uncover why modesty culture exists, and what needs to be done to release ourselves from its grip. As we will see, as early agriculture developed in the direction of the plough and pastoralism, as private property replaced a communal existence, and as inequality grew, virginity became increasingly prized and policed. Warfare and population pressure further added to the policing of women's bodies. All of this helps us to explain the strength of the modesty cult in parts of the world such as the Middle East and North Africa, north-west India, and the eastern Mediterranean. In contrast, western Europe, the Americas, south-east Asia, and western and southern Africa initially escaped some of the worst ravages of modesty culture. But, in Africa, as nomadic pastoralism spread outwards, women's sexual and bodily freedoms were increasingly regulated. In western Europe, following the population collapse of the Black Death, which decimated the wealth of landowners, society became in many ways more sexually permissive, but, by the late sixteenth and seventeenth centuries, once population had rebuilt and inequality had returned, the Puritans were on the march. By the nineteenth century, industrialisation brought the extremes of both wealth and poverty, a rapidly expanding population, and a growth in heavy industry favouring male labour, leaving women competing with one another for the wealthiest husbands on the basis of their 'purity'. At this point, even feminists were embracing the purity agenda, for men as well as for women, culminating in Christabel Pankhurst's demand for 'votes for women, chastity for men'.[47] Today, the same pressures that have in the past precipitated a return to modesty are once again building: inequality, population growth and religious fervour. Unless it is nipped in the bud, modesty culture is on course to expand.

John Stuart Mill, author of the nineteenth-century classic *On Liberty*, recognised that 'the despotism of custom is everywhere the standing hindrance to human advancement'. When it comes to the modesty cult, this 'despotism' ensures that modesty is drummed into us from a young age, and that those who transgress modesty norms face punishment from the state and society. Precisely because of this 'socialisation', immodesty can bring with it intense feelings of embarrassment and shame, along with disgust from onlookers. This explains the visceral and impassioned response I often receive to my naked feminism, based not on logic but on deep-seated and subconsciously driven moral feelings. As Kira Jumet notes, 'emotions are tied to moral values; therefore shock and/or outrage may arise when there is a perceived infraction of moral rules'.[48] Rather than prompting a reasoned response, the violation of our modesty norms elicits an almost instinctive emotional response. But, when emotions run high, we need to stop and question, rather than to dig in our heels. We can, so long as we place logic ahead of emotion, unlearn the shame, disgust and embarrassment that we relate to women's bodies.[49] Resisting the modesty cult, and placing women's freedom on stronger foundations, requires us to question feelings and assumptions that are so deep within us that they are taken as truths.

In particular, I would ask that every reader stops and asks themselves:

Why should our respect for another woman be conditional on something as superficial as a piece of cloth?

Is it right that women who are scantily clad or who make money from their bodies are judged as worth less than other women?

Should we really be referring to immodest women as 'disrespecting themselves' (after all, can't your self-respect hang on much more important things than your bodily modesty)?[50]

Does it really make sense to deem 'promiscuous' women 'cheap'?

By asking these questions we have the power not only to change the way we think about ourselves, but to challenge attitudes that affect the lives of millions of women across the world.

In Chapter 4 I argue that, more than any other group, feminists themselves need to be asking these questions. Breaking the modesty cult will involve doing more than tackling religious extremists and social conservatives; it also requires us to rethink feminism. Feminism is in need of a revolution, one which purges it of whorephobia and replaces it with a broad and tolerant interpretation of the mantra 'my body, my choice'. As we will see, an uncomfortable battle has long been taking place within feminism: a battle between what I term naked feminists and those of a more puritanical variety. In bringing this battle to light, I unpick feminist reactions to women's bodies – to the scantily clad, to strippers, and to naked artists and protesters – exploring the arguments commonly used by feminists to justify more modest dress and behaviour. While, as we will see, there certainly are valid concerns when it comes to women who are forced, coerced or 'socialised' into revealing or monetising their bodies, we must also be careful not to fall into the trap of unthinkingly imposing our own particular modesty norms on other women. According to Yasmin Alibhai-Brown, both a 'half-naked woman' and 'a veiled female' represent 'an affront to female dignity, autonomy and potential . . . Both are

marionettes, and have internalised messages about female-
ness.'[51] While I myself prefer to rest a woman's dignity on
something other than a piece of cloth, according to Alibhai-
Brown, you can only be 'feminist', and only have dignity and
autonomy, if you follow her personal dress code (not too little,
not too much). This Goldilocks-style approach to modesty,
which condemns any deviation from the personal preferences
of a supposed feminist intellectual, is in reality no different
to modesty requirements imposed through religious fervour
or government diktat, and should be railed against by all true
feminists.

A similar contempt towards immodest women is apparent
throughout feminist writing. Joan Smith's *The Public Woman*
opens with a multi-page description of the appearance and
activities of Katie Price, describing her life's goals as 'artificial',[52] and criticising the 'narcissistic'[53] culture she represents.
Natasha Walter condemns modern-day women who dress
sexily and who turn to cosmetic procedures as 'living dolls',
while Ariel Levy coins the term 'female chauvinist pigs' for
women she derogatorily refers to as 'bimbos'.[54] Levy seems
disturbed by the best-seller status of Pamela Anderson's book
Star, that the author of *Diary of a Manhattan Call Girl*, Tracy
Quan, spoke at an author event alongside a Chief Justice, that
'Paris Hilton isn't some disgraced exile of our society . . . she
is our mascot', and that a senior award-winning TV executive, Sheila Nevins, makes documentaries about strippers, as
well as about the holocaust and war orphans.[55] The notion
that women they view as less intelligent than themselves can
succeed through their looks seems to fill some feminists with
fear.

Bernadette Barton, taking a cue from Levy, argues that
raunch culture is 'ruining our society'.[56] Her book is filled with
images of big-breasted and scantily clad women, taken from
bill boards, film, television, and music videos, including everyone from Red Hot Riding Hood and Jessica Rabbit to Pamela

Anderson and Miley Cyrus. She writes that '[p]eople are having sex before they date, and women make their own personal porn to share on social media . . . Instagram users measure their self-worth by chili pepper emojis . . . Hordes of young women prefer the quasi-sex work of being a sugar baby to dating'.[57] Emily Channell notes that '[m]ainstream women's organisations and many academic feminists see Femen's topless actions as simply giving men more of what they want – easily accessible women's bodies'.[58] Muslim feminist Gabby Aossey seems to agree, writing that '[h]ip Feminist campaigns like Free the Nipple only encourage a gullible behavior of disrespect for our own bodies, leading to everyone else around us disrespecting our bodies as well'.[59] According to Naheed Mustafa, women who protest topless do 'a huge disservice to the difficult, persistent, long-term work in which feminists are engaged the world over'.[60] She instructs naked protesters to put their clothes back on, as if to win feminist arguments a woman has to pretend that she doesn't have a body. It is clear that feminism has internalised the concept that a woman's own respect and that of women more generally hangs on bodily modesty.

While these feminist fans of bodily covering claim to be challenging the 'male gaze', offering critiques of the constant presence of women's bodies in society, they are in fact facilitating its dominance: in their view, a woman's freedom to uncover her body comes second to how men might think or feel in response. In other words, if men risk being sexually stimulated, women must cover up. Naked feminism is, according to this internalised modesty cult, not only illogical, it is oxymoronic; it is sacrilegious to feminism. Theo Hobson, writing in *The Spectator*, declared my own naked protests 'unfeminist', while The *Telegraph* columnist Juliet Samuel argued that nudity 'strips my arguments of force', and is 'meaningless and hackneyed'.[61] One might expect such a response from social conservatives, but to find feminists adopting the same view is more troubling. After all, why shouldn't women be free to uncover or monetise their bodies as well as their brains? Why should what some men might think or feel in response dictate what we can or cannot do with our bodies? And why should a feminist intellectual elite – able to succeed with an 'all brains, no body' mentality – constrain all womankind? Too often, feminism comes across as body-phobic, femme-phobic and whore-phobic.

For millennia, the state and society have policed and regulated what women can do with both their bodies and their brains. Over the last century, women have become increasingly free to make the most of their brains and, while we are a long way from full equality, they can now be found among the educated elite, working as politicians, academics and doctors. But, sadly, women's bodies remain constrained, judged and controlled. For women to take control of their bodies as well as their brains, feminism will need to break the cult of female modesty. At the moment, by casting immodest women as problematic, feminists are instead encouraging the growth of the modesty cult. My message here is simple: beware puritanical feminism!

As we see throughout this book, challenging the modesty cult helps all women, whether they are modest or immodest. But ultimately this book stands up for any woman who is judged 'immodest', objecting to the notion that she is lacking in self-respect and dispelling the idea that she causes harm to other women. Whether or not women cover their bodies in line with the ever-changing norms of time and place, and whether they choose to monetise their body or their brain (or both), women deserve respect. To hang this respect on bodily modesty is not only superficial, it favours the intellectual elite, and it panders to the patriarchy.

In her book *The Pornification of America*, Bernadette Barton quotes the advice offered to a victim of revenge porn by a group of female peers:

We've told her if you want people to look at you differently you have to change what you do. You have to excel academically, you have to excel at everything you do because every time they look at you, every time they think about you, they're going to think about this video. You have to give them something more positive to think about you.[62]

For Barton, such advice is empowering and represents the future of feminism. For me, it is deeply depressing, regressive, and steeped in modesty culture. While there is nothing wrong with advising the young woman to excel academically, why not also suggest to her that her worth does not depend on her bodily modesty, and that anyone who thinks it does, anyone sneering or laughing at her, is shallow and misguided? The woman is, after all, the victim of a crime, yet the advice from her peers portrays her as a guilty party. Every woman should be able to hold her head high, rather than live in fear. Feminism will only have succeeded, and women will only be truly free, once we confront and challenge the cult of female modesty.

Chapter 1

The Modesty Cult: A History

Housed in Berlin's National Gallery is a dark and haunting painting that, despite its moderate size, catches visitors' attention from quite some distance. You don't have to search high and low for the title – it is engraved on the frame itself. It is, quite simply, *The Sin*. Painted by the artist Franz von Stuck, there are at least twelve known versions of the painting, the first dating back to 1893, housed in galleries as distant as Palermo and Seattle. The subject is a semi-nude Eve with a serpent scaling vertically upwards along the left-hand side of her chest, its upper body circling around her neck. From the centre of its head, on top of Eve's shoulder, the serpent's eyes stare outwards at the viewer. Eve's own eyes also look towards us, but in a more alluring manner. It is a dark painting, both literally and metaphorically, aside from a golden light in one corner. The fact that there are multiple versions of the painting speaks to the popularity of the subject: the association of women's bodies with sin.

For millennia, women have been expected to cover up and to repress their sexuality, their bodies being seen as a danger both to their souls and to social stability. This chapter delves into this long history to explore where and when women's bodily modesty came to be regarded with such importance, and how the pendulum has swung across both place and time. As we will see, ancient civilisations such as Egypt and Babylonia, once known for their liberal attitudes towards women's bodies, are now some of the most ardent adherents of the modesty cult. And, in those in which we tend to take women's freedom for granted, a modesty revival is underway, backed up by religious zealotry, including in the USA. Rather than representing an onward and upward march towards bodily and sexual liberalism, history is filled with attempts by the modesty cult to reassert itself: it happened in the ancient world, it happened in Song Dynasty China, it happened in seventeenth-century Europe, it happened in Victorian Britain, and, as we will see, it is happening again today.

When the Nude was not Rude

For thirty thousand years of human history, before humans first began farming the land, fleshy and naked female figurines proved popular. The oldest example, the Venus of Hohle Fels, is a mere six centimetres tall and was carved from the tooth of a mammoth. Discovered in 2008, it is the first known image of a human being in history, and dates to around 38,000 BCE. From then until around 9,000 BCE, many more such three-dimensional miniature figures were produced in what would have been a significant investment of time for foraging and hunter-gatherer societies.[1] Perhaps the most famous is the Willendorf Venus, unearthed in Austria, and thought to be about 25,000 years old. While many archaeologists have assumed an overtly sexual status for these little ladies, even describing them as 'pornographic', others point to their affinity with female experience, including pregnancy and stillbirth, and even suggest that they could have been used as dolls.[2]

Of course, for a long time, human beings didn't wear clothes
at all. In a sense, it wasn't the act of removing clothes that first
rendered our bodies naked; it was instead the act of wearing them. Ian Gilligan explains the rise of clothing as being a
response to the climate change of the Pleistocene era (ending
about 12,000 years ago) which left all naked primates vulnerable to cold and wet weather.[3] This was particularly so for those
of us who had 'migrated beyond the tropics'.[4] The invention of
fire was one solution, as was occupying caves and building
shelter, but so too was the creation of clothing. According to
Gilligan, the Neolithic Revolution, when human beings first
started to farm the land, was as much about cloth as it was
about food. Crops were cultivated for their fibres, not just to
fill our bellies.

The apparent lack of shame surrounding the female body
in Palaeolithic society remained alive and well in at least some
of the societies to emerge from the subsequent Neolithic
Revolution. The 'licentious manners' of the Ancient Egyptians
and of Ancient Babylon (in present-day Iraq) proved shocking
to future historians, who, by comparison, considered themselves 'civilised'.[5] One Victorian writer seems aghast at the
idea that there was no such thing as 'illegitimacy' in Ancient
Egypt, and that 'chastity does not appear to have been the
capital virtue' of Egyptian women. He recants in prurient tones
the Festival of Bubastis, in which barges filled with music and
laughter sailed along the Nile, containing women who 'flung off
their garments'.[6] While in Egypt at this time nudity sometimes
represented vulnerability and a lack of rank, it equally signi-
fied rebirth and a heavenly status. Ancient Egyptian artists,
who commonly depicted defeated enemies in a naked state and
portrayed workers hard at work in the sun with little bodily
coverage, also represented gods and goddesses in the nude.[7]
And, despite being surrounded by flesh, sex was not something
with which Egyptians were obsessed. Unlike more repressive
societies, eroticism featured little in Egyptian literature.[8] And,

since sex was not a particular obsession, neither was chastity. Virginity was not a cult and sex work did not bring shame.

Early Babylon, more so than Egypt, seems to have acquired a reputation for 'whoredom'. The Greek historian Heroditus claimed that every Babylonian woman had at some point prostituted herself in the Temple of Venus. While such claims have recently been questioned,[9] as it appears that historians had simply confused the Babylonian word for an unmarried women with that of a sex worker, Babylon was hardly a haven of modesty. Unlike the women of later eras, married women in Babylon were 'permitted to go out in the street unveiled' and were not secluded within the home.[10] Women worked as weavers, they ran taverns, and they towed boats and cut reed.[11]

In the broader area of Mesopotamia, married women were free to mix in public, without a veil, and were not secluded within the home.[12] They could also divorce and remarry.[13] In fact, women's sexual pleasure was the topic of poetry and love songs, which spoke of the vulva tasting 'sweet like beer'. Women who were left sexually unfulfilled were said to turn into 'maleficent ghosts who broke into homes to terrorise young women and men'.[14] In parts of the neighbouring territory of present-day Iran, Elamite women were active and visible and they were paid at the same rate as men. Ancient Persian women such as these are thought to have mingled with men at feasts and banquets, something that caused shock among the latter-day Ancient Greeks.[15] Ancient Elamite art depicts women with uncovered bobbed hair[16] – and even in the nude. Archaeological finds dating to the second millennium BCE include mould-made female figurines adorned in jewellery, with curly and abundant pubic hair, cupping their uncovered breasts.[17] This liberalism towards women and their bodies was not, however, to last; the pendulum of modesty was about to take its first swing.

The First Modesty Mongers

In 2003, as American soldiers were invading Iraq, looters found easy pickings in the museums that housed the region's ancient relics. Their booty included the metre-high Warka Vase, originating in Uruk in the fourth millennium BCE, which weighed a hefty six-hundred pounds. Having been dropped and smashed into a dozen pieces, the vase was later returned to the museum, which painstakingly reassembled it in time for the museum's reopening more than a decade later. The disappointment following its disappearance and the jubilation following its return speaks to the importance of the vase.

The vase depicts the Venus of the day: the Sumerian goddess Inanna, the goddess of sex, love, fertility and beauty, and the precursor to Ishtar and Aphrodite. Unlike the Venus whose pinkish flesh graces the canvases of the renaissance, Inanna is depicted fully clothed on the vase, with only her face showing, albeit while being served by nude men.[18] In mythology, Inanna descends to the underworld, where she must strip off her crown and clothing, and is subsequently condemned to a death from which she is reborn, but not without consequences for others. Shame and vulnerability feature highly in the interpretations of this myth, and it is difficult to escape the fact that Inanna's naked body is, as the mythological tale goes, turned into a literal piece of meat, left rotting and covered in flies.

In light of the Warka vase, whether the heady days of early Babylon and Ancient Egypt were the exception or the rule for the Middle East is, of course, open to debate. But, one thing that is clear is that where it did exist, the liberalism did not last. While Egyptian goddesses had historically been represented in the nude, whether in the form of statues, or painted naked on the ceilings of temples and tombs, by the Late Egyptian Period (525–332 BCE) they had also acquired clothes.[19] More generally, in parts of the Middle East where women had not previously

been expected to seclude themselves or to cover from head to
toe, the pendulum was swinging in a more modest direction.

Evidence of women being secluded and veiled in the Near
and Middle East is particularly strong from around the second
millennium BCE, at which point it is apparent in literary
sources, in art and artefacts, and in legal codes.[20] One of the
earliest legal references to veiling can be found in the Assyrian
Law Codes of the second millennium BCE. Article 40 of the
twelfth-century BCE code describes in detail which women
should and should not veil, and assigns punishments for those
transgressing the rules. In sum, all women were legally obliged
to veil with the exception of 'harlots' and 'slave girls', along
with daughters who lacked status. In order to maintain the
distinction between these groups of women, any 'harlot' who
was caught veiled was to be stripped of her clothing, caned
fifty times, and to have 'pitch poured on her head'. Any slave
girl caught doing the same was to have her ears chopped off.
If a man failed to report a veiled harlot or slave, he was also
to be stripped and caned, and would have his ears 'pierced
threaded with a cord tied behind him' while doing a month
of 'hard labour for the king'.[21] Unveiling was also used as a
form of punishment for women in the 'respectable' camp. An
Old Babylonian legal judgement from eighteenth-century BCE
Nippur, a Sumerian centre in southern Mesopotamia, instructs
two women to remove their head covering as a punishment for
giving false witness.[22] According to a literary text from the
Middle Assyrian era (which began in the 14th century BCE), a
woman who does not veil has no shame, indicating that only by
being veiled could a woman command respect.[23]

Veiling was, however, not the only aspect of this ancient
modesty cult. Even more important, and, indeed, a key driver
of veiling, was the emphasis placed on virginity. As Eric
Berkowitz notes, '[f]emale virginity was a commodity in the
ancient world, with a price, a market, and laws to protect its
male owners'.[24] So important was a woman's reputation for

virginity that gossip could be brought before a court. Laws in Sumeria dating from around 1900 BCE 'required a man making . . . an accusation [of non-virginity] to pay a fine if proven wrong'. By the Middle Assyrian era, rape victims were expected to marry their rapist so as to maintain their honour.[25] And, while female infidelity had long been dealt with harshly, including through death by drowning or the chopping off of a woman's nose, such punishment was becoming increasingly refined, and with much clearer double standards that placed the blame and punishment squarely on women.[26] While previously a cuckholded Babylonian husband could spare his wife, in return for which the king would spare a slave, by the New Babylonian era (in the seventh to sixth century BCE, spanning either side of the reign of Nebuchadnezzar the Great) she was to be killed with an iron dagger. In some cases, such a punishment was written into marriage contracts.[27] An adulterous husband, by contrast, was dealt with far more lightly, often with the simple payment of a fine.[28]

As Ancient Greece emerged and, under Alexander the Great, expanded its rule into and beyond the Middle East (which included defeating Darius to take the Persian Empire, the founding of Alexandria in Egypt, and conquests as far as India), one could be forgiven for thinking that things took a turn for the better. After all, the Greeks have gone down in history as being the fathers of modernity, with a 'civilised' reputation and a penchant for democracy. But, for the Greeks, and for those who ply them with praise, nothing was more civilised than a chaste and modest woman. Not only were the Ancient Greeks just as obsessed with the cult of female modesty as the societies they unseated, in some ways they helped the pendulum to swing in an even more modest direction and all in the name of 'civilisation'.

Modesty Matters: The Greeks vs. the Romans

In the middle of the fourth century BCE, an Ancient Greek woman was dragged before a court on the charge of impiety. She had, among her other antics, walked naked into the sea, casting off her clothes as her hair trailed down her back, at a festival in honour of Poseidon. While nudity was, at this time, a symbol of athleticism and strength for men, it was out of bounds for women. Facing the death penalty, Phryne was in serious trouble.

The injustice could not have been more blatant. Not only was Ancient Greece filled with nude statues of men but, soon, Alexander the Great was to come face-to-face with the naked Sadhus of the Jhelum river in the Punjab. While Alexander believed in conquest, as a former student of Aristotle he also had an appreciation of philosophy. So enchanted was Alexander with the 'naked wisdom' of the Sadhus that he invited one of them to become his personal philosopher.[29] Still today, following in the same tradition, Jain temples are adorned with naked saints 'designed to demonstrate their renunciation of physical attachments and pleasures'.[30] And, unlike elsewhere, this nakedness wasn't purely reserved for men. Akka Mahadevi, who lived sometime later, was a beautiful long-haired poet who had abandoned her old life and walked off naked into nature to start a new life.[31] She is celebrated today for her 'songs for freedom'.

But, in Ancient Greece, double standards certainly were rife, meaning that women's naked bodies were largely absent in public until, that was, Phryne attempted to fill the gap. Not only did she walk naked into the ocean, inspiring an epic painting by the artist Apelles, she also posed for the first full-size nude statue of Aphrodite, which was sculpted by Praxiteles. While her sculpted body, placed in Knidos, became an instant tourist attraction, it shocked moral authorities. Aphrodite had, after all, previously been depicted not only clothed but veiled.[32]

Even the goddess of sex and beauty was expected to abide by the modesty norms of the day.

In Ancient Greece, female respectability rested on bodily modesty in all of its forms. Women's sexual relations were viewed with greater 'suspicion and even condemnation' than many of the societies that had come before.[33] Unlike the sexually promiscuous Greek gods, the majority of Greek goddesses were virgins.[34] In order to overcome the obvious practical difficulty, the Gods could themselves, in theory, bring about new life. Aphrodite was the product of the severed genitals of Uranus, and Athena was born from the head of Zeus. Back on earth, where women were most certainly needed when it came to the creation of new life, men needed wives. Nevertheless, a wife was expected to display little interest in sex 'for she might otherwise be led to commit adultery and make her cuckolded husband the laughing stock of his neighbours'.[35] Women's sexual desire and fulfillment took a back seat; for the female citizens of Athens and, unlike some of the early Mesopotamian societies we've come across, sexual virtue was all-important.

Greek women were judged according to the twin concepts of *aidōs* (shame) and *sōphrosynē* (modesty).[36] In order to preserve her respectability, an elite woman had to avert her eyes from men, could not mix with men who were not her kin, and had to veil herself when in public.[37] There is, in fact, evidence that the Greeks took veiling to a whole new level; while Assyrian art depicted women who covered their hair but not their face, women on Greek vases and reliefs from the fifth to fourth century BCE were typically depicted with their heads fully veiled, including their face.[38] The Gynaikonomoi, a civic body, policed women's dress to ensure that it was sufficiently modest, and could even force entry to private property and punish those who were not sufficiently concealed.[39] Greek modesty culture meant two things: that only men could be 'free' and respectable, and that only women could be sexually unvirtuous.

In the sixth century BCE, Solon, an Athenian lawmaker, had put in place a plan to help maintain the virtue of respectable women. According to the poet Philemon, 'seeing that the state was full of randy young men whose natural appetites were leading them where they had no right to be', Solon made the decision to set up state-owned brothels, offering sex cheaply and in abundance.[40] Part of the proceeds were used to erect a temple to the Public Venus.[41] While sex work was legitimate in Ancient Greece to the point that it was taxed, there were clear boundaries between sex workers and 'respectable' women, and the existence of the former was used as a means of controlling the latter.[42] Sex workers were accepted but at the same time 'devalued and denigrated', and this meant that all women 'had to watch their behavior so as not to be confused with sex labourers'.[43] Any woman who lost her virginity before marriage was condemned to slavery (often sexual slavery), thereby preventing her from polluting the pool of 'respectable' women.

Modesty and chastity were also central to the lives of Roman women. Vestal Virgins, chosen from a young age, dedicated themselves to the city of Rome, with prime responsibility for keeping the flame burning at the Temple of Vesta. If they broke their vow of chastity, they were entombed alive.[44] Funery inscriptions provide an insight into what was expected of married Roman women: one famously refers to a wife who is 'pious, modest, frugal and chaste' and another to one 'who never wanted to go out in public without me, either to the baths or anywhere else'. Artistic depictions showed women in 'voluminous layers of cloth'.[45] There was, however, a clear and visible difference between Ancient Greece and Ancient Rome: Roman women were not expected to veil, with some becoming renowned for their hairstyle and clothing. Even elite women could 'show off' their hair, only donning a veil where it 'enhanced rather than covered their looks'.[46] Statues of women of renown depict curls, braided hair and knots.[47] While some women continued to veil based on custom, it was not a necessity, and certainly not a legal matter. Roman women also mixed publicly, much more so than Ancient Greek women. Elite wives were responsible for receiving guests, attending social events with their husbands, and keeping their husbands informed when they were working abroad, while also tending to their business interests at home.[48]

One Victorian writer, reflecting back, seemed unimpressed by the way that the pendulum appeared to move in a more liberal direction as the Roman period wore on, noting that 'during the more flourishing period of the [R]oman state, the prostitutes formed a class, to which the principal immorality of the female society was confined, while in the later or imperial age, profligacy ran loose among the people, so that the distinction between the regular harlot and the unrecognised prostitute was all but lost'.[49] The Fall of the Roman Empire was, in the opinion of this Victorian writer, a result of the deterioration in female morals.

Needless to say, once the Romans stopped persecuting them, Christians would be ready to rescue modesty from immorality. In the early fourth century CE, the Emperor Constantine established a new centre for the Roman world, Constantinople, where, on his deathbed, he was baptised a Christian. It ushered in a new era.

No Sex Please, We're Christian!

In 527 CE, the daughter of a bear-trainer, Theodora (c.495–548), a former actress and courtesan, was crowned the Empress of Byzantium. Her husband, Justinian I, had gone to extreme lengths – literally ripping up the law book – in order to marry her. The eastern Roman Empire had long outlawed any marriage between elites and former actresses, on the assumption that acting was tantamount to sex work. The preamble to the new law had a clearly Christian flavour, filled with both judgement and forgiveness: 'The errors of women, through which they may ... turn from honor through the weakness of their sex, may be corrected through proper moderation and ... they should in no way be deprived of the hope of a better condition.'[50]

Within Christianity, immodest women could be forgiven, on earth as well as in heaven, so long as they repented. Not only did Theodora repent her past life, she built a whole House of Repentance. Said to have been the first of its kind in the Roman world,[51] and housed in a former palace, just across the Bosporus Strait from Constantinople, it provided space for up to five-hundred former sex workers. As summed up by the Orthodox Church in America, Theodora 'was at first a notorious harlot and actress ... but then she repented ... After becoming empress, she led a virtuous life, maintaining purity of both soul and body.'[52]

Much like Theodora, women in general had 'led the way in converting to Christianity' during Roman times, particularly poorer women.[53] According to a former Pope, John Paul II, 'Jesus ... was sensitive to female suffering. Going beyond the social and religious barriers of the time, Jesus reestablished woman in her full dignity as a human person before God and before men ... Christ's way of acting, the Gospel of his words and deeds, is a consistent protest against whatever offends the dignity of women.'[54] Christianity preached monogamy and fidelity, and stood up to infanticide, all of which appealed to women who were frustrated by society's double standards. Women also featured prominently among the early Catholic saints and, while the original apostles were all men, it was women who witnessed the resurrection of Christ. Subsequently, however, men dominated religious authority and channelled Christianity in a direction that worked to their own benefit, placing 'continuing emphasis ... on charging Eve, and with her all women, with moral guilt for the fall of mankind'.[55] Hence, according to apostle Paul (1 Timothy 2:11–15):

A woman should learn in quietness and full submission. I do
not permit a woman to teach or to assume authority over a
man; she must be quiet. For Adam was formed first, then Eve.
And Adam was not the one deceived; it was the woman who
was deceived and became a sinner. But women will be saved
through childbearing if they continue in faith, love and holiness
with propriety.

Obeying your husband and living a modest and pure life was
the clear message (1 Peter 3:1–3:4):

Wives . . . accept the authority of your husbands, so that, even
if some of them do not obey the word, they may be won over
without a word by their wives' conduct, when they see the
purity and reverence of your lives. Do not adorn yourselves
outwardly by braiding your hair, and by wearing gold ornaments or fine clothing; rather, let your adornment be the inner
self with the lasting beauty of a gentle and quiet spirit, which is
very precious in God's sight.

In his sermon in Roman Corinth in the first century CE, Paul
had castigated women who prayed with their hair uncovered,
suggesting that if a married woman does not wish to cover her
head, she should cut her hair off first (1 Corinthians 11:6).[56]
Tertullian's treatise 'On the Veiling of Virgins', written a
century later, further encouraged veiling. For Tertullian, an
uncovered woman was not only dishonouring her husband,
she was violating and corrupting herself: 'Every public exposure of an honourable virgin is (to her) a suffering of rape', he
wrote. It was, therefore, not simply for the good of others that
she must cover, but also for her own benefit. Whenever she
appears attractive to or arouses a man, she was, apparently,
sullying her soul. Not only did Tertullian lambast women who
uncovered their hair in church, he also criticised the use of cosmetics, hairpins and hair dyes.[57] Following Paul and Tertullian,

the third member of our Christian modesty trio, Augustine, famously took modesty a step further, introducing the idea of seclusion for the most pious women.[58] For Augustine, an unveiled woman was not only a danger to herself, but a danger to all men. Women were deemed 'seductive stimuli'.[59] Sex was out of bounds even within marriage, as, for Augustine, the sexual act served to pass on the original sin to the next generation. The celibate marriage became the ideal marriage.

With these various Christian twists and turns, female bodies became tinged with a sin from which it was difficult to escape. Saint Alexandra built a tomb to enclose herself, explaining that '[a] man was distracted in mind because of me, and rather than scandalise a soul made in the image of God, I betook myself alive to a tomb, lest I seem to cause him suffering or reject him'.[60] It is of little surprise that of the seven deadly sins, the one that became most associated with women was lust.[61] While Christianity preached chastity as the ideal for men as well as for women, women were not only seen as the ultimate source of temptation, they were also held to a different standard. As Ruth Mazo Karras sums it up: 'Having had sex did not make a man permanently impure, because men in heterosexual intercourse were not penetrated.'[62]

As the Virgin Mary achieved iconic status, virginity became the 'virtual hallmark of the entire religion'.[63] While the Ancient Greeks solved the practical difficulties associated with virginity by giving the gods life-giving powers, the Christian solution came in the form of the immaculate conception, enabling a virginal birth. With modesty momentum building, the pendulum was swinging back to the pre-Roman world. While, as Eric Berkowitz writes, Christian teachings in regard to women and sex look like 'knockoffs of earlier regional laws', with a striking resemblance to those of the Sumerian King Ur-Nammu (21st century BCE) and the Babylonian King Hammurabi (18th century BCE), in some ways at least, Christianity was taking things to an even more extreme level. Now, not only was virginity to be maintained until marriage, it was, ideally, to be maintained for life. A virginal life in a monastery trumped that of a faithful wife.[64] The obsession with virginity was not just a matter of practicality, such as a means of avoiding premarital pregnancy and of guaranteeing paternity for a future husband, it was now an ideology. Venus, and all of her previous incarnations, were forever banished, replaced by the horrors of Eve. Statues, such as Phryne's Aphrodite, were torn down. Every woman was left with a binary choice: between the virginal Mary or Eve the temptress. In the words of one writer:

> The Madonna–Eve opposition institutionalised by the Church fathers turned the personal obsessions of a few troubled and probably sexually frustrated men into a monumental force that swept away all sense of reality and perspective, demonstrating the ability of culture to turn natural human inclinations, such as paternal uncertainty, into monsters . . . such monsters, once released, are very difficult to rein in.[65]

And soon, Christianity had a new competitor in the religious stakes, in the form of Islam.

Islamic Consolidation

In early Islam, much as in early Christianity, women did not take a back seat. Muhammad's first wife, Khadija, was a wealthy widow and businesswoman, who had employed the Prophet-to-be to take care of her caravans. Not only was she 'the boss', she initiated her marriage, proposing to Muhammad.[66] After Muhammad's death, Abu Bakr, the first of the 'pious caliphs' (632–4), faced numerous revolts from grand and notable women. Bakr defeated the female-led rebellions and took advantage of war between the Byzantine Empire and the Sasanian Empire of Iran to make territorial gains. His power, along with that of Islam, was growing, and women were on the back foot. The second caliph, Umar (634–44), continued the geographical expansion and instituted as law a combination of Islamic and non-Islamic practices, incorporating some practices from newly acquired territories. Modesty was high on the agenda. The new legal code included 'more stringent laws involving punishments for women and restrictions on their movements', such as preventing them from visiting mosques, together with death by stoning in the case of adultery.[67] By 656, at the end of the rule of the third caliph, Uthman (644–56), large parts of the Arabian peninsula and North Africa were under Islamic rule, including the Sasanian Empire, with its heartland in Iran, along with Syria and Egypt. But, when Uthman was murdered, civil war followed: as Ali, the son-in-law and cousin of the Prophet, took the reins of power, Aisha, the surviving wife of Muhammad, mounted her camel to lead a revolt against him. Aisha's revolt, which culminated in the 'Battle of the Camel', ultimately proved unsuccessful. She bravely battled on as others around her fell on the battlefield, but her camel was eventually hit, leaving her disarmed and captured. She became '[t]he last woman to play a major public role in the first centuries of Islam', and her 'failed leadership' was 'utilised as a warning against allowing women to take roles in politics or even to appear or speak in public'.[68] Islam was to take a patriarchal turn, but Aisha would live on as a feminist icon for future generations of Muslim women.

While the Quran offered numerous financial and social rights to women, the Hadith and Shariah pushed Islam in a different direction. The Quran was open to interpretation when it came to the question of women's clothing, but the Hadith settled the debate in favour of greater modesty. The Shariah pushed further: though the four schools of Shariah disagreed on the matter of facial coverings, they agreed that head covering was a necessity. The Adab, an Islamic literary collection from the ninth to thirteenth centuries covering society and culture, was dominated by male voices. Women were not only covered up, they existed only behind closed doors, albeit with one notable exception – war poetry. A common theme in Islamic war poetry was the uncovered helpless virgin, 'the ultimate symbol of defeat'.[69] One poet highlights, '[h]ow many a chaste maiden they carried into captivity, her face displayed without a veil'. The Cairo Geniza Manuscripts, which include more than ten thousand documents and letters relating to life in the ninth through to twelfth centuries, suggest that veiling had become the norm. Muslim, Christian and Jewish women were typically referenced with covered heads, and a wide variety of wraps, veils and mantles appear to have been worn. Mamluk Egypt housed the suq-al-bakhaniqiyan, a whole marketplace dedicated to women's head gear.[70] The Geniza Manuscripts also include pleas from poor women for financial help for the purchase of a veil or other head covering.[71]

While modesty was a common theme across religious groups, according to S.D. Goitein, the standards of modesty expected of Muslim women when it came to clothing exceeded those expected of Jewish and Christian women, fewer of whom covered their faces, and more of whom mixed in public.[72] Feminist Muslim scholars argue that women had moved backwards compared with the early days of Islam, and that this was in part a result of misogynistic interpretations of the Quran.[73] For El Guindi, the veil itself was not a symbol of backwardness, but, instead, represented a failure to apply the same modesty standards to men.[74] These same sexual double standards were even more visible in the infamous Harem and with the popularity of singing slave girls.

Life in the Islamic world was, at least in some regions, strikingly different to that beforehand. In the Egypt of old, women circulated in public with uncovered hair, as typified by Cleopatra's bobbed hair style, and goddesses were depicted in the nude. The Ancient Greeks and the Christians had already aligned themselves with modesty, and now Islam was doing

the same. Islamic scholars referred to the old era as Jahiliya:
the era of confusion and ignorance. In her classic study of
male–female dynamics in Muslim society, Fatema Mernissi
presents us with a pre-Islamic world of nakedness, where only
the rich could cover up and where women were so sexually
desirous and promiscuous that men did not know which children were their own.[75] She writes that Islam 'generalised the
aristocratic privilege of wearing clothes around the temple'[76]
and 'religion . . . came to help men become fathers and curb
womb-endowed, sexually aggressive females'.[77] She portrays
the Islamic veil as a 'symbol of the urge to control desire by
submitting one's narcissistic tendencies to the community's
demographic need'.[78] In other words, immodest women were,
according to the more patriarchal strand of Islam, a danger
to men, causing all kinds of temptations, and leaving them
insecure in their position as fathers. Islam, apparently, brought
women under control.

   As women were relegated to a life of modesty, Islam continued its spread, reaching much further than the Christianity
of the time. Large parts of Africa, Asia, the Middle East and
Europe came under Islamic control, resulting in the diffusion
of modesty practices. In the eighth century, Islamic forces had
conquered the Iberian peninsula, renaming it Al-Andalus.
Turning Eastwards, Islam reached central Asia in the ninth
century, which saw the rise of Islamic kingdoms such as the
Samanid Empire, and by the tenth century it had reached
as far as China. Part of this spread was a result of military
conquest throughout the Middle East, North Africa and in
parts of central Asia (Afghanistan, Pakistan, Uzbekistan and
Turkmenistan). But Islam also spread as a result of trade,
including along the Red Sea and Silk Road routes.[79] Islam
had a sophisticated trading code that greased the wheels of
trade, connecting distant lands with produce from far and
wide. Trade proved to be such a successful religious diffuser
because, rather than relying on intermediaries, Muslims

traded directly, which brought large numbers of people into direct contact with the religion. While the vast geographic expanse that came under Islamic control and influence, from Spain to the Far East, had once been a mixed bag of modesty practices, it had now become much more uniform, and with a religious backbone that in patriarchal hands proved intolerant of a return to diversity.

The Chinese Puritans

Thanks to the Ancient Greeks, together with the Christian and Islamic patriarchs, modesty culture had by now become deeply rooted in Europe and the Middle East. It was also spreading across East Asia, not only through Islam, but also in the form of neo-Confucianism. Starting in China in the Song Dynasty (960–1279), neo-Confucianism brought a form of seclusion for women that rivalled anything seen in Ancient Greece or the Islamic Middle East. Men and women were expected to inhabit separate domains. Even within the same household, they had to sit separately, could not pass food hand-to-hand, and could not share the same everyday necessities, from combs to wardrobes.[80] A woman's rightful sphere was, of course, considered to be the home. Ban Zhao's (c.45–115 CE) classic Confucian text 'Admonitions for Women', which was being repopularised, preached that women need not possess 'brilliant talents' but should instead be hard working, humble, yielding, modest and chaste.[81] Through the Ming (1368–1644) and then the Qing (1644–1912) dynasties, people were taught that 'there are 10,000 evils, and sexuality is the first one'.[82] Chastity was not only valued, it was rewarded, on earth and in heaven. Sex was increasingly taboo.[83] Against this backdrop, medieval China witnessed an explosion in chastity martyr biographies, and suicide came to be seen as a noble response to both widowhood and rape.[84]

Neo-Confucianism was also spreading beyond China, reaching Korea and Japan. In Japan, where sex before marriage, as well as remarriage, had previously been acceptable, the tide turned; by the fifteenth century, rape victims were being punished,[85] and by the seventeenth century women were no longer allowed to perform on stage.[86] In Korea's Chosŏn era (1392–1910), women were also increasingly confined to the home, and expected to maintain a pure and chaste body. While widows were not denied remarriage, by the fifteenth century any sons produced from a second or subsequent marriage were denied participation in the civil service.[87] Remarriage was actively discouraged.

In sartorial terms, Korean women faced even greater demands than in China. The Chosŏn ruling class claimed that 'women's lives in the [previous] Koryŏ dynasty were depraved due to their immodest public exposure and their participation in social activities with men'.[88] While headdresses were not entirely unknown beforehand, they were mostly worn by elites, either for protection from the weather or for the purposes of fashion, and, notably, were worn by men as well as women. By the eighteenth century, it had become a modesty-based requirement for women to cover their heads when leaving the home 'to avoid exposing their faces to strange men when they went out'.[89] To serve this purpose, the overcoat and the skirt were adapted into veils. The jangot, worn by lower and middle-class women, evolved from an overcoat to become a makeshift head covering and veil. The collar of the coat was placed on top of a woman's head rather than around the neck, allowing the hair to be covered and the two sides of the coat to close in over the face; the sleeves were left dangling and empty. The sue-gaechima, worn by aristocratic women, worked similarly, but instead developed out of the traditional voluminous Korean skirt, whose fabric was gathered around a thick waist-band. The waist-band could, like the collar of a coat, be worn on the head, with the fabric of the skirt providing coverage for the

hair and shoulders. This particular version of fashion evolution carried more prestige than the jangot-cum-veil, and was
easier to wear than the more traditional bamboo-framed head
covering used by court women, known as the neoul. Popular
colours for the skirt-cum-veil were white, jade and red, with
quilted varieties available for the colder seasons. Over time,
the sartorial class divisions began to fade, and so women of all
classes used the garments interchangeably.[90] The suegaechima
in particular lived on in rural regions well into the twentieth
century.

From Medieval Immoralities to Purity Wars

While Asia was in the middle of its modesty boom, Europe
initially seemed to be moving in the opposite direction. Since
the Fall of the Roman Empire, the power of the Church had
been expanding as Christianity stepped in to fill the numerous
gaps left by the Roman state. By about 1100, the Church had
a permanent system of courts to police and punish fornication and illicit sex, one which administered public beatings
for women engaging in premarital and extra-marital sex.
However, by the late Middle Ages, the extent and frequency
of punishment reveals the degree to which people commonly
departed from the types of behaviour the Church expected of
them.[91] Even the most modest woman of all, the Virgin Mary,
had by now become promiscuous, her virgin claim ridiculed
and mocked by writers from Chaucer to Malory.[92] The most
faithful followers of Christ, the pilgrims, might have defended
her virginity but, from the fourteenth century through to the
early sixteenth century, they also collected souvenir badges
that depicted female genitalia alongside 'walking phalluses
with tiny, wagging tails'.[93] Religious paintings showed Mary
topless, and theologians and preachers spread the story of her
seducing God with her innate beauty and sexual power.[94] In

sixteenth-century England, the illegitimate daughter of a King denounced by the Catholic Church took to the throne. This was the Elizabethan era: the bawdy age of Shakespeare, one in which the writer Pietro Aretino advised people to 'speak plainly, and say fuck, cunt and cock; otherwise thought wilt be understood by nobody'.[95]

The Fall of Rome had brought not only an expansion in the power of Christianity, it also gave rise to feudalism, with severe constraints on individual freedoms. But, by the late Middle Ages, feudal forces across much of Europe were being replaced by freer market relations. This meant that young people were able to move around, to create their own social spaces, and to enjoy what life had to offer: not just men but women as well.[96] Women were increasingly in charge of their own destiny, and that included deciding for themselves whether, who and when to marry. A sizeable proportion of women never married, while those who did tended to marry in their mid-twenties, especially in northern and western Europe. Alongside, Christianity appears to have been less successful than Islam when it came to ensuring virgin brides.[97] While premarital sexual activity was still frowned upon by Christians, given the protracted length of time between puberty and marriage, it was nevertheless common, and so the Church had to deal with it flexibly and pragmatically. If a couple went on to marry, which they were indeed encouraged to do, their children were deemed 'legitimate'.[98] If they did not, in northern and western Europe the authorities pursued the father for financial support on behalf of the mother and child.[99] In England, at least a fifth of all first conceptions were outside marriage.[100] Sex work, while also frowned upon, was tolerated. The Church not only supported but owned and made money from brothels, albeit regulating where and on what days of the year sex workers could practise their trade. The Bishop of Winchester's brothel in Southwark was the most notorious of the late Middle Ages.[101] Like many towns and cities, London housed a literal 'Gropecuntelane'.[102]

To quote Karras, the 'authorities judged it better to abandon a small group of women to sin and corruption in order to serve these men than to subject the whole of society to the disorder that would otherwise ensue'.[103]

While young people were enjoying greater freedom and in no small part because of it, economies grew. Alongside, so too did population, recovering from the decimation brought about by the Black Death in the middle of the fourteenth century.[104] While the strict social hierarchy of the past proved to be porous, allowing upward movement for some, not everyone made it to the top; many were left lingering at the bottom. By the late sixteenth and early seventeenth centuries, this combination of expanding population and growing inequality meant greater outgoings for charities, the church and official poor relief authorities, which started to take the view that society was getting out of control. The obvious scapegoat was, of course, sex – in its most literal sense. Sexual desire was seen not only as a threat to individual salvation, but also as 'destructive of social order'.[105] The Church had, apparently, let things get out of control and a new competing strand of Christianity was ready to stamp on the associated immoralities. The result was a battle for hearts and minds that took the form of 'purity wars'. With it, the pendulum was about to swing backwards.

The Catholic Church was challenged by new sects of Christianity, critical of what they saw as the opulence and hypocrisy of religious authorities. More than ever before, Catholics had to prove that they practised what they preached. In a fight for supremacy, Christians on both sides competed on the grounds of who could be the most pure,[106] and women came out squarely on the losing side. The Church became obsessed with rooting out and punishing 'promiscuous' behaviour. In England, parties and alcohol were increasingly off limits, low-cut dresses were 'filled in' with big white collars, and married women now covered their hair with a white linen cap. Bright colours were replaced with subdued tones, and flamboyant clothing was frowned upon. Puritanism was on the march and, while it aligned itself with long-existing Christian teachings, it nevertheless pursued them with much greater vigour, bringing more preaching and more punishment.[107] Local authority figures who had previously turned a blind eye to moral misdemeanours were replaced by 'men of a different stamp'[108] and 'disorderly popular culture',[109] in the form of dancing and drinking, was attacked. Not only were brothels on the radar, so too were alehouses. Opportunities for people to gather together outside the realms of the Church were being rooted out.[110] In 1609, English legislation ordered that mothers of 'bastards' who created a financial burden for local taxpayers be committed to a house of correction; by 1630, whipping was once again the order of the day.[111] And there was no safe way out: in 1624 abortion was made punishable by death in England.[112] Not only were newly unmarried mothers the target of harsher punishment, so too were those who had gone 'unsuitably' punished in the past. In January 1657, in Manchester, constables were ordered to 'apprehend . . . all such women . . . who have already had any bastard children and have not had punishment'.[113] By 1650, 'fornication' was illegal. The historical records capture the effect: while before 1600 one in three brides were pregnant upon marriage; by 1650 this had fallen to one in six.[114]

Across Europe, sex was increasingly regulated and controlled. Brothels were one of the first targets. According to Luther, sex workers were 'scabby, scratching, stinking' beings who should be 'broken on the wheel and flayed'.[115] London's Southwark brothels were closed down in 1546,[116] in Paris they closed their doors in 1556, and in Rome they were ordered to close in the decade that followed (albeit the order was quickly retracted when news came of thousands of people preparing to leave the city as a result).[117] The attack on sex workers was just the tip of the iceberg. By 1610, in Bologna, any woman in a public space after sunset could be arrested on the presumption of being a prostitute. This was similarly the case when it came to taverns. A 'respectable' woman would need to be accompanied by a male relative if she were to avoid stigma and punishment, which ranged from public whipping to exile.[118] Mary Magdalena, a Spanish nun who embraced the cult of female modesty in all of its senses, asked Philip II to establish a women's prison for the punishment of 'rebellious' and 'incorrigible' women who 'insult the honesty and virtue of the good ones with their corruption and evil'.[119] Magdalen Houses took hold across southern Europe, and explicitly focused on 'pretty or at least acceptable looking [women], for ugly women did not have to worry about their honour'.[120] According to Merry Wiesner-Hanks, 'imprisoning women for sexual crimes marks the first time that prison was used as punishment in Europe rather than simply as a place to hold people until their trial or before deportation'.[121] The most sinful of all sexual acts was, of course, sex with the devil. Women's bodies had long been associated with witchcraft, in possession of powers that men could not control, and now, as the anti-sex turn descended, they were being hunted out and murdered in their thousands.[122] Between 100,000 and 200,000 'witches' were tried and, of those, between 40,000 and 60,000 were killed.[123] Four-fifths were women.[124]

Just as the European witch trials were coming to an end, colonial New England embraced them with vigour. As Puritanism encountered growing resistance in Europe, perhaps unsurprisingly given the extremes that were reached, Puritans took to the seas, channelling their energies into building godly communities overseas, and punishing anyone whose behaviour threatened to bring damnation.[125] Between June 1692 and May 1693, two hundred people were charged with practising 'the devil's magic' in Salem, New England, with twenty of those ultimately losing their lives. In her book spanning the period from 1630 to 1725, Monica Fitzgerald tells the broader story of 'Puritans behaving badly', tracing the first three generations of

Puritans in colonial Massachusetts. She notes a marked change from an initial degree of equality between men and women to a belief that men and women occupied separate spheres, where women's misdemeanours were seen as sins against their inner soul, and men's were instead seen as skin deep. Women charged with illicit sex were, unlike men, seen as sinning against piety. Alongside a 'feminised piety', a double standard emerged in which women were held to a higher moral standard and, with it, faced much tougher judgement and punishment.[126] And the legacy lived on. Unlike in many European countries, US states 'continued to treat adultery and fornication as public crimes' well into the twentieth century.[127] Today's abstinence-only sex education along with bans on abortion speak for themselves.

By contrast with the United States, in eighteenth-century Europe the very same printing presses that had helped to bring about the Reformation were finding new purposes. Stories of infamous lawbreakers from the criminal underworld were big business, and the public appetite was insatiable 'even in elite social circles' and the racier the better.[128] It was against this backdrop that the novel emerged, penned in the style of revealing 'true' stories.[129] It was an opportunity to give modesty a grilling.

By George!

Hogarth's artistic depiction of a *A Harlot's Progress*, from innocence to experience followed by an untimely death, would have been familiar to any eighteenth-century reader. With it, defending 'fallen' women carried big reputational risks, as Mary Wollstonecraft found out when, upon her death, her work was deemed 'scripture, archly fram'd, for propagating w[hore]s'.[130] But, as is often said, 'art is power', and so it was by picking up their pens to write fiction that women could best critique the modesty cult. Female writers, including Jane

Austen and Elizabeth Gaskell, 'smuggled' their critical thinking into novels that could appeal on two very different levels to
conservatives and radicals alike.[131] This was subversion – sense
and sensibility style.

Not only can these women writers lay claim to being the
first generation of self-made women in modern history,[132]
they also single-handedly turned the eighteenth century into
the century of the novel.[133] As far as Virginia Woolf was concerned, Frances Burney was 'the mother of English fiction'.[134]
In Burney's 1778 novel, Reverend Villars warns his charge, the
young Evelina, that 'nothing is so delicate as the reputation
of a woman'.[135] But, despite being an illegitimate child whose
mother 'died in disgrace', Evelina marries a Lord. It was a story
that captured a changing society, and it posed big philosophical questions about a woman's worth.[136]

Perhaps more famous than *Evelina* was Samuel
Richardson's *Pamela*, which, when published in 1740, was an
'immediate best-seller' and placed novels in 'the respectable
mainstream'.[137] It told the story of a young servant fending
off the sexual advances of her Master, attempting to preserve
her virtue against all odds. It was such a success that the following year one of the writer's rivals published his own telling
of the story, under the title *Shamela*. It offered a less sympa-
thetic account, transforming Pamela into a con-artist, lacking
entirely in virtue, but faking a chaste reputation in order to
trick her Master into marriage. While the modesty cult was
under fire among women writers, the notion that a woman's
worth and respect depended on her bodily modesty, and that
immodest women were dangerous temptresses, would not die
quickly.

As the historian Vic Gatrell notes, 'female anxiety about
"reputation" could [still] be stifling', and so we should not
'overdo our sense of female liberty in this era' but, at the same
time, 'female culture was not monolithic'.[138] While upwardly
striving middle-class ladies had the most to lose from throwing

modesty to the wind, elite women could afford to be somewhat libertine. According to one lady of the land, female infidelity, albeit only after the first born, was a 'fashionable vice [rather] than a crime'.[139] On a much-talked-about occasion, the maid-of-honour to the queen was even said to have attended an ambassador's ball with no more than a transparent gauze to cover her bare breasts.[140] By the turn of the century, the fashion for the bosom to be 'covered with nothing more than transparent shawls that float and flutter over the bosom' was attracting the attention of the prurient press.[141] In 1794, the *Sporting Magazine* squirmed at the fact that 'the present fashion is, perhaps, the most indecent ever worn in this country'.[142] In 1803, the *Lady's Magazine* declared it a health hazard, as well as a 'trespass against modesty'.[143] The French influence on European fashion was already, controversially, in motion. The icon of the French Revolution was, of course, a bare-breasted woman.[144]

Across Europe, Puritans regrouped in an effort to resist this eighteenth-century 'sexual revolution'. Where they had pushed too far and ultimately lost parliamentary control, such as in the UK, they instead turned to establishing societies for the 'reformation of manners'. These societies acted as private police forces, actively hunting out and bringing to court anyone who infringed laws relating to prostitution, adultery or fornication. By 1700, more than twelve such societies existed in London alone, with the Tower Hamlets Society employing two full-time brothel-detectors, paid for by quarterly subscriptions by its members.[145] Each year, they proudly published a list of all those who had been brought to the attention of the law, naming and shaming 'fornicators', adulterers and sex workers. But, while initially popular, the societies soon lost support; their tribe of paid informants came to be seen as little better than pimps who profited from 'sin', and their high-profile members all too often escaped the kinds of punishment that their societies actively pursued in the case of the rest of society.[146] This hypocrisy left many feeling that the societies intentions were more prurient than pure. Daniel Defoe, among others, eventually cancelled his subscription to an Edinburgh-based society.[147]

As Faramerz Dabhoiwala notes, a further problem increasingly faced by the societies was expanding knowledge, along with a changing philosophy, of law. Sex workers were wise to the law, which made life all the more difficult for the brothel-hunters, while their muscle-powered clients, the expanding force of soldiers and sailors, were often at the ready to defend them. In 1711, Covent Garden sex workers faced a crack-down, which produced a battle between constables and soldiers, in which the former were squarely on the losing side. When East End sex workers found themselves in the local magistrates, a thousand sailors mobbed the building for their release.[148] By about 1730, sexual sin was increasingly perceived as being 'beyond the reach of criminal law'.[149] Historically, it had been thought of as folly to leave religion and morality to the individual, as human beings were presumed to be driven by animalistic passions, which, if left unchecked, would produce Sodom and Gomorrah. But Enlightenment thinkers, with their emphasis on reason and personal responsibility, challenged such thinking. The last English prosecution for the public crime of adultery came in 1746[150] and, across much of Europe, punishment for births outside marriage went into decline.[151]

Unsurprisingly, births outside marriage began to climb, trebling across the course of the eighteenth century in England. By 1840, around a quarter of first-born English children were 'illegitimate'.[152] Not only was illegitimacy on the rise across Europe,[153] it even began to increase in holier-than-thou New England, where, by the late eighteenth century, 17 per cent of first-born children entered the world within the first six months of marriage.[154] This was a demographic trend shared by economies at very different stages of economic advance,[155] meaning social, and not just economic, change was underway.

However, this particular sexual revolution was not to last. The pendulum of modesty was ready for another backward turn and those infamous societies would return under new names.

Victorian Virtue

Novels weren't the only books on offer in the eighteenth century. Between 1757 and 1795, a visitor to London could also purchase *Harris's List*, a guidebook to 'Covent Garden Ladies'. Compiled incognito by a waiter and a journalist,[156] it offered, quite literally, sex in the city. Not only did it serve as a practical guide for someone looking for female company, it also acted as erotic reading material. But, having been in publication for some forty years, *Harris's List* would become dead and buried in the century which followed. Just as the Puritans rescued our souls from Shakespearian bawdiness, Victorian prudery came to the rescue of Georgian harlotry. 'Immoral' women were the meat on which philanthropy cut its teeth in the Victorian age. Of the fifty 'reformative agencies' dealing with 'vice and crime' in London in the 1860s, twenty-one (more than 40%) devoted themselves entirely to the 'rescue and reformation' of 'fallen women'.[157] The oldest, The Magdalen Hospital, dated from 1758 and sought to 'save the hoary head' from 'shame, misery, and death'.[158] For fifty years it remained the only such institution but, by the 1850s, numerous missions, societies and 'hospitals' were opening up across the UK with the same goal in mind. As ever, sex workers were just the tip of the iceberg. By 1860, women's bodies and sexual desires were so off-limits that the word c*nt had become an insult, much as it remains today.[159]

Victorian Puritanism was strangling the flames of sexual revolt, and women were helping to lead the charge. Alongside the rapidly growing number of people, and the expanding slums that housed them, industrialisation also brought an expansion of the middle class, and there was no better way for a middle-class lady to mark herself out as 'respectable' than by judging other women. Instead of questioning the modesty cult, middle-class women both relished and propagated it. In the words of Beverley Skeggs, '[r]espectability became the property of middle-class individuals defined against the masses'.[160]

By the 1880s, these middle-class do-gooders had men in their sights. A social purity movement was gathering steam, questioning the 'double standards of sexual morality', with an eye to spreading chastity to the male, not just female, portion of the population.[161] The movement was not only part of a religious revival, it was also an outgrowth of the much-criticised Contagious Diseases Acts of the 1860s, which aimed to tackle the scourge of syphilis by allowing the authorities forcibly to remove and intimately examine any woman suspected of prostitution. Moralists had been outraged by the way the Acts appeared to be 'providing healthy women for profligate men', 'rendering safe indulgence in vicious pleasures', and offering 'protection and immunity to the sinner in the practice of his sin'.[162] Campaigners successfully brought about the abandonment of the Acts, and, having met with success, channelled their energies into wider moral reform.

Organisations such as the Social Purity Alliance (established in 1873) and the Moral Reform Union (1881–1897) sprang up with the aim of promoting chastity for men as well as women. Rather than, as in the past, seeing the male sexual urge as biological, in need of servicing by a small group of women for the wider protection of womankind, it was instead treated as a product of social influence, and so open to criticism.[163] No one was safe from moral judgement. Upper-class men were 'outed' for their bad behaviour and the Church was criticised for its apathy and hypocrisy. Jane Ellice Hopkins submitted 'A Plea for the Wider Action of the Church of England in the Prevention of the Degradation of Women', arguing that religious authorities needed to do more to 'protect' women, both by changing male sexual attitudes (reducing the demand for sex workers) and by acknowledging that poverty and lack of opportunity served to create a supply of sex workers. In contrast to the homes for 'fallen women', Hopkins had been busy initiating and supporting efforts that aimed to create homes and jobs for vulnerable women, with the hope of preventing them from 'falling into prostitution'.[164] This included the Ladies Association for Friendless Girls, which had associations in at least twelve towns and cities across the UK by 1879, expanding its reach further in the 1880s.[165] Hopkins went on to inspire the establishment of the Church of England Purity Society and the White Cross Army, whose 'purity pledge cards' committed men to 'Keep thyself pure.'[166] Laura Ormiston Chant can lay claim to similar successes within nonconformist Christianity. A frequent speaker at the Gospel Purity Association (established in 1884), she became the editor of the *Journal of the National Vigilance Association*. And, much as in the days of the Puritans, not only was sex off-limits, so too was alcohol. Those partial to a drink were now fending off a new temperance movement.

As part of the puritan arsenal, censorship laws were employed in an attempt to prevent 'dirty filthy' books about contraception reaching circulation.[167] In 1877, Annie Besant and Charles Bradlaugh had to defend themselves against the charge of 'obscene libel', all for publishing a forty-page pamphlet on contraception within marriage. While this did not stop many a middle-class woman from practising birth control,[168] eugenicists were soon holding their lack of reproduction responsible for the decline of the West, proposing subsidies to encourage white middle-class educated women to reproduce. One way or another, the fate of civilisation was felt to depend on women's intimate lives.

Of course, the Victorian era was not merely known for its moralism; it was also known for its inventiveness. But, where women were concerned, the promised 'objectivity' offered by scientific discovery was of little help. The medical profession was now acting in cahoots with moralists, happily making scientific case after scientific case in support of the suppression of sexual desire.[169] With their increasing tendency to measure and compare everything in sight, scientists were soon proposing that larger genitals came with a smaller brain, and that 'sexual excess' was the 'mark of inferiority'.[170] A French medic decided to test the hypothesis, examining the genitals of around five thousand Parisian sex workers, albeit reaching the conclusion that 'there is nothing remarkable either in the dimensions or the dispositions of the clitoris in the prostitutes of Paris'.[171] The implication was that all women were at risk of being overpowered by their bodies.

On both sides of the Atlantic, female masturbation was seen as a cause of 'over excitement' that led to hysteria and insanity. London-based Isaac Baker Brown, one of the first doctors to introduce pain relief into childbirth, and a pioneer of the surgical repair of the vagina, began an altogether less helpful and much more controversial practice: surgically removing women's clitorises as a 'cure' for all kinds of women's problems.[172] Not only was it touted as a solution for insanity, but also for nymphomania and for marital disharmony.[173] Fortunately, Baker Brown's 'craze' didn't last long; the year after the publication of his *On the Curability of Certain Forms of Insanity* he was expelled from the Obstetrical Society of London.[174] What particularly riled his gynaecological peers was his use of the media to spread word about his work. As far as they were concerned, this risked drawing too much attention to female masturbation, thereby spreading the practice and destroying the 'purity' of the 'fairer sex'.[175] While, not before time, this period of female genital mutilation was rather quickly put on ice, the notion that women's sexual desire was a threat was apparent on both sides of the Baker Brown case. Women who enjoyed clitoral stimulation 'became representative of women who behaved like men and denied their maternal obligations – behavior that led to neurosis, isolation, and social disintegration'.[176]

The American Dr John Harvey Kellogg, a nutritionist and purveyor of cereals, wrote chapter and verse on the benefits of chastity, marketing his cereals as a means of dialling down sexual desire.[177] In addition to eating his cornflakes, and for women prone to 'over excitement', he also recommended burning off the clitoris with acid.[178] Unsurprisingly, Kelloggs do not offer these suggestions in their present-day market-ing campaigns. Kellogg would, no doubt, have been happy about one thing though: illegitimacy rates were cut in three in America. Between 1841 and 1880, only six per cent of firstborns were born within the first six months of marriage – around a third of the level in the century beforehand.[179] Once again, American Puritans were leading the way.

Victorian Virtues Go Global

While women at home were squeezed into corsets, British imperialists were out and about stamping their values overseas. When Captain Cook first landed in Botany Bay he reported back that: 'No sort of clothing or ornaments were ever seen by any of us upon any one of them . . . from which I conclude they never wear any.'[180] What followed was 'the task of educating all those naked indigenous people around the world about the urgent moral need to cover themselves with decent clothes'.[181] They were taught to feel shame – and, conveniently, to pur-chase the fabric that Britain's industrial factories were busily churning out at faster and faster rates. As Irene Watson writes, '[p]rior to the colonialists' invasion of our territories there was no reflection of our nakedness . . . The reflection of nakedness came with the other, the clothed colonising peoples.'[182] Hence, as Sir Jospeh Banks, the botanist onboard Captain Cook's Endeavour, commented, 'they seemed no more conscious of their nakedness than if they had not been the children of Parents who eat the fruit of the tree of knowledge'.[183]

Faced with the judgements of European moralists, the female populations of entire continents were declared 'whores': Black women were stereotyped as 'jezebels', Indian women as sly and cunning prostitutes, and East Asian women as exotic temptresses.[184] In order to inflate the virtue of white Western women, women of colour were deemed unvirtuous, in turn magnifying their mistreatment. As Philippa Levine notes '[t]he damning of colonial sites as moral sinks was crucial to the overall picture of their inferiority'.[185] And, where imperialists encountered women dressing more modestly than those at home, then so as to protect the virtue of European women, these more modestly dressed women had to be forced or coerced into unveiling themselves. Veiling, except in Christian forms, was deemed to be the result of an oppressive force, one that required liberation in colonial form. Modesty was defined according to Western standards: the West had, it believed, got it right (not too much, not too little). Everyone else was either over-sexed or oppressed.

The Great Unveiling

By the middle of the twentieth century, head coverings were increasingly seen as a symbol of 'backwardness', and even as 'anti-nationalist'.[186] In central Asia, the Far East, the Middle East and the Balkans, women unveiled – some by choice, others through coercion, and, in the case of Albania, through compulsion.[187]

European colonialists weren't the only ones 'encouraging' unveiling. The Soviets sought to 'modernise' central Asia with a 'revolutionary rejection of tradition', which included unveiling its female population and eliminating the practice of female seclusion.[188] As Adrienne Lynn Edgar notes, 'some of the fiercest battles were fought over the fate of Muslim women'.[189] While the Soviets wanted unveiling to be voluntary, there was widespread use of propaganda and administrative measures, with poorer women in particular encouraged to lead the way. In 1921, at a Comintern meeting in Moscow, a female delegation from Turkestan 'collectively unveiled to applause and tears of joy', and in 1927, on International Women's Day, women marched on the Uzbeki capital and burnt their *paranjis* in a mass bonfire.[190] Resistance to the unveiling was intense and violent, sometimes placing young women at odds with their family patriarchs; during the unveiling campaign of 1927–9, two thousand unveiled women were murdered by opponents of unveiling in Uzbekistan.[191]

In some countries, unveiling was initiated by indigenous women's organisations.[192] In Korea, as Confucian influence weakened, the first women to appear in public without a covered head, and as a form of protest, were those belonging to the country's first women's organisation, established in 1898.[193] In 1906, this and other women's organisation began to push for the repeal of laws surrounding women's head coverings. In 1908, Hansung and Jungshin schools banned the suegaechima, and a backlash against young women showing their faces in public resulted in a compromise: schools began supplying their pupils with black umbrellas to help shield their heads. Once Japan colonised Korea (in 1910), traditional dress was relegated to the dustbin of history.[194]

The unveiling of middle-eastern countries (including Egypt, Iran and Turkey), is, perhaps, better known than the unveiling of women in central Asia and Korea, and debates continue as to the extent to which it was driven by indigenous or colonial forces. In Egypt, in 1899, the Egyptian reformer Qasim Amin attacked the veil, calling for the liberation of women. Unlike in the Soviet world, where poorer women were placed front and centre, it was the unveiling of elite women that went on to capture attention in the region. In Cairo, in 1923, after returning from a feminist conference in Rome, the well-known Egyptian feminist Huda Shaarawi disembarked from a train, whipped off her headscarf and (according to some descriptions) stamped on it. It was said to be a 'seminal moment'.[195] In 1928, Queen Soraya of Afghanistan, the wife of King Amanullah, unveiled while on a six-month public tour that ranged from India to England.

Male dress 'reforms' such as the 1925 Hat Law in Turkey had already been creating widespread resistance in the Middle East.[196] It was only after the male dress reforms, and then a subsequent 'pause for thought' following the overthrow of King Amanullah, that female unveiling became official policy in Turkey (in 1934) and Iran (in 1936). Though the frequency of force and the extent to which such force was backed by the state are still unknown, it is commonly said that, from this point on, 'police tore headscarves off women in the streets'.[197]

Across the previously veiled Middle East, the face veil was likened to a 'muzzled dog'.[198] The fact that reformers such as Amin received the support of prominent European colonisers, including Evelyn Baring (the British Consul General of Egypt), made it 'almost impossible for those opposed to the [British] occupation and to European influence to critique the veil without looking as if they were taking the side of the West'.[199] While most countries stopped short of actually banning the veil, Albania went all the way, banning face coverings altogether in 1937. After the Second World War, unveiling campaigns subsequently spread across the Balkans, including into Yugoslavia and Bulgaria. What was personal was political – across multiple countries and across multiple continents.

The Sixties Prevolution

As Muslim and Korean women unveiled, the Western tide was also turning. According to the front cover of *Time Magazine*, the 'sexual revolution' of the twentieth century took place between 1964 and 1984,[200] but evidence suggests that the seeds were already being sown in the period between the two world wars.[201] Women were increasingly entering the workforce, breaking down the separate spheres of the Victorian age, and Freudian ideas about sexual repression competed with religious conservatism. The United States had entered the roaring twenties and, accompanying the affluence and rebelliousness of the jazz age, premarital sex was on the rise.[202] In the UK, the 1920s was a tale of two halves: the north was marred by poverty and unemployment, while in the south young people were adopting new fashions, dancing to live bands, and staring upwards at new modernist architecture. Perhaps unsurprisingly for a time of transition between Victorian prudery and the swinging sixties, sexual intimacy was filled with hypocrisies and inconsistencies.

To reveal more about this era of 'prevolution', two historians, Simon Szreter and Kate Fisher, spent the turn of the millennium interviewing elderly British couples from across the UK, inviting them to reflect on their youthful courtships over a cup of tea. While naughty seaside postcards and factory girls stealing kisses from male colleagues for the Christmas kitty have at times been spun as 'working-class promiscuity', Szreter and Fisher found that it belies 'intimate relationships prior to marriage which were dominated by fears of illegitimacy and codes of respectability'.[203] Among those who considered themselves working class, 'men and women were clear that men might test women's respectability by pushing at the boundaries of acceptable sexual behaviour . . . Women who chased men or did not resist sexual advances might be rejected, and also risked being labelled "loose".'[204] As Roger (born in 1910) noted in regard to one of his youthful encounters: 'I thought to myself, 'I don't know, I don't know, I don't know. She's so forward, what does it mean?' . . . You see there were no blood tests in those days, you know? And that was the thing that stopped me dead.'[205]

Paternity uncertainty was a worry for young men. They also knew that if their girlfriend became pregnant before marriage 'her father would come after' them;[206] and, if that did happen, they were expected 'to do the right thing'.[207]

According to Diana (also born in 1910): 'You don't cheapen yourself . . . it wasn't even discussed . . . you know it wasn't ladylike . . . it was understood that girls didn't do that sort of thing.'[208] While, to quote June (born in 1914), 'everybody look[ed] down on girls that had to get married in my day. It wasn't the done thing.'[209] Premarital pregnancy neverthe-less happened and it was, at least in northern and western Europe, dealt with through the 'shotgun marriage'. Men were expected to share the responsibility. By contrast, in Ireland and southern Europe, unmarried mothers were sent away from their communities, experiencing the full force of social punishment. There, sexual 'sin' was still squarely placed in the lap of women.

Compared with their working-class peers, middle-class girls appeared to have greater sexual freedoms. The novels of the 1930s and 1940s provided a literary form of sex education for any girl with time on her hands.[210] And while girls' magazines were still shy when it came to sex, fictionalised stories and 'problem pages' showed a degree of sympathy towards women who found themselves pregnant outside marriage.[211] Evidence, including from Szreter and Fisher's interviews, suggests that middle-class girls 'enjoyed significant and prolonged petting sessions while courting, having come to a shared understanding [with their partner] that both were committed to restraining themselves at the last minute, despite the frustrations and anxieties this caused'.[212] For some young women, trying out sexual intimacy before marriage was considered necessary for avoiding a marriage to someone with whom you lacked sexual compatibility.[213] Middle-class girls were becoming informed enough about sex, and happy enough to discuss it, that they were able to set clear and practical limits with their partners.

As middle-class girls 'experimented' and women more generally freed themselves from the home, the Madonna–Whore distinction was threatened. 'It was no longer easy to say that a woman walking through the streets wearing make-up was likely to be a prostitute.'[214] As the lines between 'respectable' and 'unrespectable' women became blurred, sex work ended up back on the agenda. In 1928, the UK's Macmillan Report – the Report of the Street Offences Committee – was published. No stone was left unturned. As Samantha Caslin writes: '[q]uestions were asked about whether girls who had sex on dates in exchange for non-monetary payments such as gifts were in fact engaging in a form of "amateur" prostitution'.[215] And, according to Hugh Macmillan, the Chair of the Committee, a lot was at stake: prostitution was, to his mind, an offence against social stability.[216] Women's wider appearance in public life might have broken down the historic division between 'good girls' and 'whores' but, in the eyes of some, it was a consequence of 'respectable' women becoming unrespectable rather than of 'unrespectable' women becoming respectable.

The Sixties and Beyond

It was the most stolen library book in the United States, labelled 'obscene trash', it sold more than four million copies, and it was translated into 33 different languages: *Our Bodies, Ourselves* was published in 1971 by the Boston Women's Health Club Collective.[217] Women's desire to understand their bodies was insatiable.

Less than twenty years before, in 1953, Alfred Kinsey had shown that women can regularly orgasm, though not necessarily via sexual intercourse. His findings were so controversial that his scientific funding was withdrawn.[218] At that time, women who 'sought out copious amounts of sexual activities' were medically diagnosed with nymphomania and faced prefrontal lobotomies and electric shock treatment. The first edition of the *Diagnostic and Statistical Manual of Mental Disorders*, published in 1952, included both frigidity and nymphomania among its female disorders.[219] Only a handful of years after Kinsey's disgrace, Masters and Johnson also faced resistance. But, by this point times were changing fast.

The proportion of American women estimated to have had sex before marriage rose from a mere 12 per cent of those married in the late nineteenth and early twentieth centuries, to 26 per cent of those married around the time of the First World War, 35 per cent of those interviewed by researchers in 1928, 50 per cent of those interviewed by Kinsey in the 1950s, and 80–90 per cent of those surveyed in the early twenty-first century.[220] Studies of the sexual lives of American college students suggest that the most notable change was for women.[221] Advances in birth control, which helped to break the link between sex, reproduction and STDs, offer an obvious explanation, but women's progress in the workforce also meant that a virginal reputation was becoming less and less important. According to the somewhat blunt words of the social psychologists Roy Baumeister and Jean Twenge, as 'women gained more money, status, power, occupational opportunities, and so forth, they became less needful of using sex to exchange for these resources. In a nutshell, women gained other ways of getting what they wanted, and so they ceased to hold sex hostage.'[222]

But, by the 1970s and 1980s, to match the emphasis on sexual pleasure, sexual danger came increasingly into view.[223] Sexual abuse, pornography, and prostitution moved front and centre within feminism. Questions were being asked about whether women had really gained from the sexual revolution, or whether men were the primary beneficiaries. With the emergence of 'raunch culture' in the 1990s, as epitomised both by Madonna and by the 'Hello Boys' advertising campaign, even more eyebrows were raised. As the power of the World Wide Web was unleashed, the pornographic industry increasingly infiltrated our lives. Pole-dancing classes, Playboy bunny-themed clothing and 'lads' mags' became the order of the day. Feona Attwood has called it the 'mainstreaming of sex', Brian McNair has coined the term 'striptease culture', and feminists speak in terms of the 'sexualisation' and 'objectification' of women.[224] According to Bernadette Barton, in addition to being 'beautiful', women were by now expected to be 'hot and sexy'.[225] Ariel Levy argues that a 'tawdry, tarty, cartoon-like version of female sexuality' has taken hold.[226]

In response to the 'raunch', not only has a widespread anxiety taken hold but a backlash has begun. In the United States, purity culture is on the rise, with a whole host of marketing tools.[227] The abstinence pledge movement, which launched in 1993 as True Love Waits, emphasises 'the importance of giving your spouse the "gift" of virginity'.[228] Purity balls, in which women commit to their fathers to remain sexually abstinent until they are 'given away', have become increasingly popular; the first such ball was held in Colorado in 1998.[229] While this virginity fetish sees the raunch culture offered in our media, film and TV as its enemy, it similarly teaches women that their value revolves around their body but in terms of their virginity rather than their 'sexiness'. As Jessica Valenti notes, '[w]omen are led to believe that our moral compass lies somewhere between our legs'.[230] The gold rose pin handed out in American abstinence-only sex education classes comes with the words: 'You are like a beautiful rose. Each time you engage in premarital sex, a precious petal is stripped away. Don't leave your future husband holding a bare stem. Abstain.'[231]

In the Middle East, the veil has descended once more. Islamist political influence grew from the late 1960s, and even the secular politicians who opposed it adopted their own form of conservatism 'to show that the Muslim Brotherhood does not hold the copyright on piety'.[232] Prominent female figures such as Nawal al-Saadawi and Nimat Sidqi noted their 'disgust' with 'the degradation of women implied in the public display' of their bodies.[233] According to Naila Minai, 'the chador could be a tool for reasserting a woman's human dignity by forcing people to respond to her talents and personality rather than her body alone'.[234] David Patel suggests that as more women adopted the headscarf, women who wanted to signal 'piety', and who once did so with a simple headscarf, have had to go further: from covering their face to covering their voice.[235] To be 'modest' someone else has to be 'immodest'; modesty is a zero-sum competition, and in the process of trying to mark yourself out, bodily coverage becomes ever more extreme.

In Israel, gender segregation, despite its illegality, has been growing since the 1990s, all in an effort to protect women's modesty. Segregated public transport has proven particularly popular, with 'mehadrin' buses competing with non-segregated ones to offer separate seating for men and women.[236] Other forms of services available in a gender segregated setting include post offices, funerals and ice-cream parlours.

As ever, the most immodest women of all bear the brunt of the modesty backlash. In a repeat of the Victorian era, feminist forces have allied with conservative Christian groups in order to oppose pornography and 'prostitution'.[237] Rather than joining strippers and sex workers in their fight for greater rights and recognition, radical feminist groups are now demanding their complete abolition. In 2022, in a partial response to feminist demands, Edinburgh City Council took the decision to close the city's strip clubs. United Sex Workers, a trade union representing strippers, began raising money for a judicial review, insisting that what they want is 'rights not rescue'. Strippers took to the streets armed with protest appendage, some in kilts and others in sexy underwear. The feminist Susan Dalgety responded in her *Edinburgh Evening News* column by stating that 'whether they agree or not, they are being exploited by men'.[238] United Sex Workers replied: 'if sex workers are so incapable of understanding our own working conditions and the potential for exploitation, why are we unionised and fighting for more rights?'[239]

In the twenty-first century, immodest women, from the scantily clad to the stripper, are, once again, presented to us as a threat: a threat to themselves, a threat to other women, and a threat to wider society.

Conclusion

Despite the fact that we each walk around in one every day, humanity has a difficult relationship with the body. While we were once surrounded by nakedness, when the story of a garden, an apple and a serpent started to spread, the nude became rude. Women's bodies came to be seen as the fundamental source of temptation, so much so that the most pious of all women chose to mutilate themselves.[240] Some drew inspiration from Saint Alexandra, locking themselves away, while others followed in the tradition of Saint Jerome, for whom being dirty meant, well, not being 'dirty'.[241] But this cult of female modesty was already festering in the days before the Bible, and it advanced across the world not only through the conquests and missions of Christians but also through the spread of Islam and neo-Confucianism.

While modesty culture is deeply rooted, like the ups and downs in the economy, the modesty cult exhibits its own fluctuations. In the Middle East, North Africa and the eastern Mediterranean, things took a turn for the worse around two thousand years BCE. The veil was to become as much a mark of Ancient Greece as it was of the Arabian desert. By the Roman era, women were not only unveiling, they were mixing publicly. Christianity, Islam and neo-Confucianism were, however, soon stamping on this liberalism. And then, well before the swinging sixties, came medieval immoralities, the bawdy days of Shakespeare, the writer rebels of the eighteenth century and, in between times, the Puritans and the Victorians who happily burst each revolutionary bubble.

These ups and downs in modesty culture are apparent across a number of different dimensions. Perhaps the most striking of these concerns a particularly intimate part of the female body. Indicative of the threat that female sexual desire was assumed to pose, the clitoris was singled out by early adherents to the modesty cult. An 'oversized' clitoris came to be connected with promiscuity and lesbianism. The Greek medic Soranus of Ephesus spelt out a procedure for the removal of the clitoris in the first century CE, while a sixth-century Byzantine physician described prominent clitorises as 'a deformity and a source of shame'.[242] Arab medical texts, translations of which later spread across Europe, identified the clitoris as the source of female sexual pleasure but, rather than embracing this fact, recommended trimming it in the case of sexually deviant behaviour.[243] A silence descended on the matter across medieval Europe, so much so that in what Kate Lister describes as 'the most champion act of mansplaining in the whole of human history' two Italian doctors, Colombo and Falloppio, claimed to have 'discovered' the clitoris in the late sixteenth century.[244] In the seventeenth century, Dutch anatomists made the same claim and argued that when 'overused', the clitoris grew in size, becoming penis like and causing its owner to become a lesbian.[245] Before long, the Victorian moralists were in the driving seat and, by the late nineteenth century, genital cutting was becoming a means of treating women deemed promiscuous and hysterical on both sides of the Atlantic.[246]

The ups and downs of the bathhouse also neatly track the way that female modesty has gone in and out of fashion. In Roman times, the bathhouse was the hub of any community but, as Christianity spread, its popularity dwindled. For St Jerome (c.340–420) 'deliberate squalor' was the route to piety, especially for women.[247] But, as stinking Christians returned from the crusades with perfumes, incense and sweet-smelling oils,[248] bathhouses began to reopen. By the thirteenth century, every small town in Europe appeared to have its own bathhouse. In London there were eighteen, while Paris had thirty-two.[249] But, by the time we reach the sixteenth century, as the Puritans began their march, 'bathhouses went into steep decline'.[250] Then, almost on cue, they made a return in the eighteenth century, this time in the form of the 'spa', giving birth to spa-towns such as Bath. The hygiene movement, a product of the squalor of industrialising cities, may have been the only thing that stood in the way of a further dash towards uncleanliness in the age of Victoria. Cleanliness was by then, as Muslims and Jews knew all along, next to godliness.

Measuring the number of children born outside marriage provides a more quantitative way of capturing the modesty cycle. In Europe, 'illegitimacy' fell in the puritanical seventeenth century, rose again in the late eighteenth century, and fell once more in the second half of the nineteenth century.[251] In comparison with Europe, Japan and Egypt had relatively few cases of births outside marriage.[252] According to Peter Laslett, 'discipline' was 'relatively lax in Europe, east and west, and the Christian Church, even in alliance with the civil power, [was] far less effective [at] controlling sexual behaviour than Islam'.[253] Europe might have had its own periods of modesty revival but, at least according to the data, it was never as successful in its repression as societies in the Middle East or the Far East, where sex and the body still remain more of a taboo.[254]

Whatever measure we choose, it is clear that the cult of female modesty has ebbed and flowed across time. Liberalism can never be taken for granted. History shows that whenever the modesty cult has come under fire, it has eventually risen from the ashes, reasserting itself with claims of being not only 'moral' but in the best interests of women. Having swung in the more liberal direction in the twentieth century, the pendulum is now swinging back towards modesty. As we will see in the next chapter, where we examine the full extent of the damage wreaked by the modesty cult, this return to modesty comes with significant risks. You have been warned.

Chapter 2

The Modesty Cult: The Dangers

When surrounded by advertising, and with our eyes fixed on music videos and our ears tuned to mass media, it might appear that immodesty is still the dish of the day. But, underneath the surface, the modesty cult is rapidly reasserting itself; with the sexual revolution now behind us, the pendulum of history is swinging once again. Wendy Shalit's best-selling American book has called for *A Return to Modesty*.[1] Purity culture, armed with its virginity pledges, is becoming increasingly popular within the growing Christian Evangelical movement. Modest Fashion Week has become all the rage and, across the Middle East, the veil has descended. In Afghanistan, the grip of the Taliban tightens while, in the West, more and more governments are adopting policies that seek to abolish the most immodest women of all – sex workers.

Drawing on experiences from across the world, and armed with a whole host of international data, this chapter reveals the full impact of modesty culture on women and girls: on their education, on their work-based opportunities, on their political participation, on their freedom from harm, and on their physical, mental and sexual health. As we will see, preserving a woman's modesty has long been used as an excuse for depriving women of access to education and to the workplace, and still is today. Moreover, rather than encouraging men to treat women with greater respect, modesty culture encourages them to harass and abuse any woman that they deem to be unsuitably modest, all in the name of providing a public morality service. And worryingly, alongside, it protects abusers, leaving women in too much fear of their reputation to speak out. Not only does modesty culture in these ways enhance the power of the patriarchy, it is also bad for women's sex lives and damaging to their overall health.

As we will see, the modesty cult manifests itself in different ways in different parts of the world. In parts of Africa, women pay the price in terms of their education, while also facing child marriage and genital cutting. In the Middle East and South Asia, the modesty cult has its greatest effect in terms of restricting women's access to paid work, along with their freedom of movement. In Mexico and the Pacific Islands, the modesty cult leaves women subjected to physical harm, by perpetuating intimate partner violence and street harassment. And, in the Western world, modesty momentum fuels lobbies that seek to restrict women's freedom to control their own fertility, including, in the case of the USA, bans on abortion. While the effects of modesty culture are multifaceted, in all cases it inflicts great harm on those it purports to protect. At its most extreme it can cost lives. In 2002, fifteen girls died and another 52 were injured when fire swept through a Saudi Arabian girls school and the 'morality police . . . forced the girls to stay inside the burning building because they were not wearing . . . headscarves'.[2] In June 2013, a 13-year-old girl died in hospital while undergoing FGM; her doctor and her family were acquitted.[3] Across the world, at least 5,000 women each year are murdered for reasons of honour.[4] Modesty culture might seem appealing as an antidote to today's raunch culture but, as we will see, what it offers is a poisoned chalice.

Education, Work and Politics

In 1785, aged only twenty-five, Mary Wollstonecraft, along with her two sisters and her good friend Fanny Blood, opened a school in Newington Green, London. Their aim was to fill the gaping hole in the education of young women, and there seemed no better place to start the roll out. As home to numerous religious radicals and dissenters, Newington Green was a community open to new ideas – one that had already rejected many a status quo. But, despite Wollstonecraft's best efforts, the school soon failed. Rather than giving up, she turned to writing as a means of championing the cause. Her first book, aptly titled *Thoughts on the Education of Daughters*, was published in 1787. By 1792, she had moved to France in search of the Revolution and was publishing what was to become her best-known work: *A Vindication of the Rights of Woman with Strictures on Moral and Political Subjects*.

Contrary to the opinion of the day, Wollstonecraft argued that women were brains, not just bodies: that they were just as capable as men and deserved the same access to education in order to broaden their minds. While this much is, of course, well known, there is a further aspect to Wollstonecraft's work that has been buried in history. It is a golden nugget, and one that allows us to better understand the obstacles girls face. Referencing the popular conduct manuals of the time, which she described as 'specious poisons' that created an 'insipid decency',[5] Wollstonecraft noted that it wasn't only society's warped focus on women's biology that hampered progress towards educational equality but also, more specifically, society's obsession with female 'purity'.[6] Even for a girl whose parents had the means and inclination to support her education, the fear that her virginity could be brought into question made schooling alongside men a virtual impossibility. The answer to this was the governess, but this was expensive and necessarily limited women's ability to acquire a broad education, and to mix and debate with others. Having been a governess herself following the failure of her school, working for the Kingsborough family in Ireland, Wollstonecraft had first-hand experience. In championing girls' schooling, Wollstonecraft might have been the proverbial turkey voting for Christmas, but she knew that much more was at stake than her own job (and, in any case, she didn't much get along with the mother of the Kingsborough brood).

At a time when respectable families placed their daughters' 'morality' ahead of their education, Wollstonecraft stated that '[w]ithout knowledge there can be no morality'.[7] True virtue, she argued, could only ever be achieved by immersing yourself in life and experiencing the world, as men were encouraged to do, including on their grand tours. In her *Vindication*, she writes that 'men have superior judgement' because 'they give a freer scope to the grand passions, and by more frequently going astray enlarge their minds'.[8] Men were allowed to achieve wisdom and virtue because 'the hero is allowed to be mortal'. By contrast, heroines 'are to be born immaculate'. For women, everything was to be lost; for men, everything was there for the taking. What Wollstonecraft ultimately called for was a 'revolution in female manners'.[9]

While the revolution in female manners is still ongoing, progress in regard to women's schooling came in the late nineteenth century, albeit only for the wealthy. In England, Cheltenham Ladies' College opened in 1853, followed by Roedean School in 1885. By the late nineteenth century, young women were able to acquire an education at my own university, Cambridge, in ladies' colleges strategically positioned outside the city centre. The compromise was, of course, gender segregation.

Even if young women could by then acquire a mentally challenging education, the next step, entry to the workforce, also presented a reputational risk. While it was not a viable strategy for the poorest families, families with means expected their daughters to remain at home until marriage, spending their days helping with domestic tasks, preparing themselves to become good wives and mothers. Priscilla Wakefield was, however, no stranger to paid work. Living at the same time as Wollstonecraft, Wakefield managed to carve out a successful career as a writer, publishing a total of seventeen books, while also finding time to establish England's first savings bank for women and children.[10] Informed by her personal experience, Wakefield offered her own solution to the problem of preserving female virtue, one which involved embracing paid work but with strict limitations attached.

According to Wakefield, the central reason why women fell into 'sexual sin', including sex work, was a lack of financial support. Limiting young women's educational development and their ability to earn was, she thought, a recipe for immorality, not morality. Rather than protecting women, their exclusion only succeeded in leaving them vulnerable. The phenomenon of 'fallen women' was, she argued, an economic and not a social problem, one that resulted from a 'dreadful necessity'.[11] By means of a solution, her *Reflection on the Present Condition of the Female Sex; with Suggestions for its Improvement* (published in 1798) proposed an intricate and detailed plan for women's work, tabulated by class, with educational and training recommendations for each 'class'. She attempted to reconcile work and virtue, combining Wollstonecraft-style thinking with social conservatism. With it, Wakefield recommended that poorer women be properly trained as hairdressers, cooks or seamstresses so as to avoid falling into harlotry, and that men should be discouraged from working in such professions, keeping them 'safe' for women. For the handful of women born into families with means, writing and painting were at the top of her list of recommendations, as they could be conducted from the 'safety' of the home, away from men. In addition, Wakefield preached that the noble ladies of the land should shun male hairdressers to create more job opportunities for their less fortunate sisters. Segregation along gender lines was, for Wakefield, the route to liberation.

The cult of female modesty has hampered women's access to education and work for a long time. Sadly, it continues to have the same effect in parts of the world today. While the number of children not in school across the world has fallen over the last two decades, at current rates of progress it will be 2050 before all girls have been educated to at least primary school level.[12] Evidence suggests that girls tend to be withdrawn from school at puberty (between the age of 12 and 14), which equates with lower secondary schooling.[13] In 2020, the countries with the highest out-of-school rate for girls in this age group were: Mali (84% out-of-school), the United Republic of Tanzania (81%), Guinea (78%), Nigeria (78%), Benin (73%), Pakistan (70%), Mauritania (63%), Afghanistan (62%), Senegal (58%) and Côte d'Ivoire (57%).[14] The out-of-school rate jumps further in the 15–17 year age group. Poverty is, of course, a key factor but, as noted by the United Nations, it 'may merge with strict cultural norms to deny girls, in particular, an education'.[15] Children from socially excluded groups are especially at risk, with girls from minority groups twice as likely as boys to be excluded or withdrawn from school, including as a result of what the UN calls a 'mismatch' between their own culture and that of the school.[16]

Figure 2.1 plots the relationship between the lower-secondary-school completion rate for girls and a measure of the degree to which virginity is prized: attitudes to premarital sex.[17] Each point in the scatter plot represents a country and is positioned according to the proportion of the population in that country who think that premarital sex is unacceptable (as measured on the horizontal axis) along with the country's completion rate for girls in lower secondary schools (as measured on the vertical axis). Numerous countries are included, from France and Egypt to Pakistan and the United States.[18] By looking at the positioning of the various countries in the

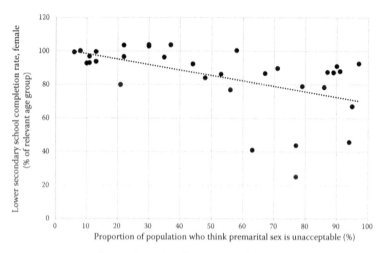

Figure 2.1 Modesty and Education
Sources: UNESCO Institute for Statistics and the World Bank;
Barber, 2018; Diamant, 2020

scatter plot, we can see whether countries with high rates of disapproval of premarital sex (the countries furthest right on the chart) also tend to be those with lower rates of secondary schooling for girls. The dotted line represents the 'line of best fit', a mathematical summation, based on the individual points in the chart, of the relationship between schooling and attitudes to premarital sex. As is shown by the line of best fit, together with the cluster of countries in the bottom right quarter of the chart, the countries where the modesty cult appears strongest (where premarital sex is most frowned upon) are also, on average, the countries where teenage girls are less likely to complete their lower secondary education.[19]

In 2012, the struggle for girls' education in Pakistan came into sharp focus when Malala Yousafzai, then aged fifteen, was shot in the head by masked gunmen on her way home from school. She had become the target of the militant group Tehrik-i-Taliban following her campaign for girls' education. Four years before the attack, in 2008, she and her female friends had been denied schooling when her town, in the Swat Valley, came under Taliban control. Since her recovery, Malala has continued her campaign. So too, sadly, have her enemies.

Following the introduction of the new Taliban regime in Afghanistan in 2021, secondary schools were closed to girls, and young women at university were prevented from attending lectures alongside men, or from being taught by men, unless they were positioned behind a curtain.[20] At the same time, the work of the Women's Affairs Ministry was swallowed up by the Ministry of Vice and Virtue.[21] Under the Taliban, and much as in Wollstonecraft's time, 'morality' comes first and that morality does not include a right to an education. However, even before the latest Taliban victories, many Afghan teenage girls were already being withdrawn from school, with a view that '[k]eeping adolescent girls at home protects them and ensures their purity'; any potential employment benefits of remaining in school were seen as limited in view of the fact that, for the same modesty-based reasons, 'women seldom participate in the labour market'.[22] With the renaissance of the Taliban, the situation has gone from bad to worse.

According to the Global Gender Gap Index (which captures differences between males and females), Afghanistan has the highest gender gap in education. Following closely behind it in the ranking, and alongside Pakistan, Yemen and Iraq, are a number of countries in west and central Africa.[23] Almost half the world's 130 million out-of-school girls can be found in Africa.[24] The continent is also home to nine of the ten countries with the highest child-marriage rates in the world, and six of them are located in west and central Africa.[25] Four in ten young women in this region, a region that also features the largest educational gaps on the continent, were married in childhood.[26] Globally, child marriage and the withdrawal of girls from school are strongly correlated. Using data on numerous countries, Figure 2.2 plots the relationship between the proportion of teenage girls who complete lower secondary

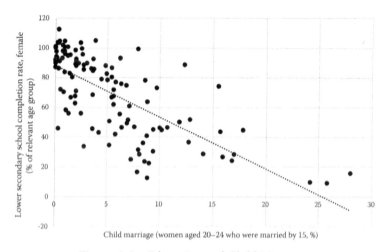

Figure 2.2   Education and Child Marriage
Source: UNESCO Institute for Statistics and the World Bank;
UNICEF

schooling and the child marriage rate (defined as the percent-
age of women aged 20–24 who were married by the age of 15).
As is reasonably apparent, countries with higher rates of child
marriage (those towards the right-hand side of the chart) also
tend to be those with the lowest secondary completion rate for
girls.

Typically, we think that child marriage is what leads to
the cessation of girls' education; that encouraging parents to
'wait' is therefore key to keeping girls in school. Evidence from
Bangladesh suggests that for every year a girl is able to avoid
marriage, her education is boosted by about a quarter of a
year.[27] In other words, a girl who is married at 18 rather than
14 will typically have one more year of education. But another
way of thinking about it is to see both the withdrawal of girls
from school and child marriage as being aspects of modesty
culture. Child marriage is not only an indicator of poverty, it is
also, like the withdrawal of girls from school, a feature of the
modesty cult. The social fear of – and desire to control – the

sexuality of adolescent girls is 'one of the fundamental drivers' of child marriage, but initiatives to tackle child marriage have historically avoided the issue altogether, treating sexuality as taboo.[28] As a recent survey of the social drivers of child marriage noted, '[i]n some contexts, marriage is seen as protecting girls from social stigma, to shield them from being 'tarnished' by rumours of impurity. In particular, marriage may be seen as protection for girls whose sexual or romantic relationships outside marriage are discovered by family members and for those who become pregnant outside marriage'.[29] Breaking the cult of female modesty is, therefore, vital to both tackling child marriage and to keeping girls in school.

Niger has the highest child marriage rate in the world: around three-quarters of today's young women were married by the time they reached the age of eighteen, and just over a quarter were married by the age of fifteen.[30] Alongside, only four per cent of girls in Niger complete lower secondary school.[31] A 'fear of dishonour from pregnancy outside marriage'[32] can be found at the root, with both early marriage and withdrawal from school being seen as a means of avoiding shame. In parts of northern Nigeria, child marriage is – as in Niger – also used as a means of avoiding the dishonour of births outside marriage, with an associated impact on girls' education.[33] Evidence from Sokoto state, Nigeria, suggests that parents worry that attending school will reduce a girl's prospects of marrying early.[34] In Nigeria, at least a third of girls do not complete lower secondary school, and more than four in ten young women are married by the age of eighteen (in the northern regions, it is more than half).[35] With a figure that stands at twenty million, the country is home to more child brides than any other country in the region.[36] In Mali, where only a quarter of girls complete lower secondary school, and more than half of girls are married by the age of eighteen, 'girls stay at home to prevent mixing with boys'.[37] In 2015, Sierra Leone banned pregnant girls from attending school, a decision that was ruled discriminatory in 2019.[38] Nevertheless, pregnancy remains one of the key reasons girls drop out of school;[39] this is not surprising given the fact that four in ten girls are married by eighteen. In Mauritania, unmarried pregnancy is so shameful that it is a crime, which feeds through to child marriage as a means of reducing the risk.[40] The child marriage rate in the country has barely budged since 1990; then and now, around four in ten young women were married in childhood.[41]

According to the United Nations, 'we do not yet fully understand the interplay between decisions around child marriage, the withdrawal of girls from school and perceptions of the value of girls' education'.[42] The cult of female modesty offers what should be an obvious explanation. But, in the recent 2021 UNICEF report 'Towards ending child marriage: Global trends and profiles of progress', the words virginity, purity or modesty do not make a single appearance. Recent policy recommendations aimed at limiting the withdrawal of girls from school focus on what could, however, be thought of as attempts to placate parental concerns about modesty. These recommendations include increasing the number of female teachers, as is backed up by evidence from Nigeria that suggests that expanding the number of female teachers helps to reduce the drop-out rate of girls.[43] In addition to a general lack of female teachers, particularly at secondary school level, a lack of female-only toilet facilities has also been identified as an area of concern in many of the countries discussed, with policy recommendations also therefore focusing on separate washing facilities for girls.[44] A third factor is the lack of safe transport to and from school, a particular problem in rural areas where schools are located some distance away.[45] All three factors can be thought of as posing potential risks for female modesty.[46] Within modesty culture, reducing the risk of premarital sex (and therefore pregnancy) is a necessary requirement for parents both to keep girls in school and to keep them from being married young. Until parents are placated, or modesty culture is broken, girls will continue to lose out educationally, something which will, sadly, affect them for the rest of their lives.

After education, the next step along the typical life-path is paid work. The countries with the lowest female labour force participation rates at present are as follows: Yemen (6%), Iraq (11.5%), Jordan (14.6%), Syria (14.7%), Algeria (17%), Iran (17.6%), Palestine (18.2%), Egypt (18.5%), India (20.8%) and Morocco (21.6%).[47] Table 2.1 ranks regions of the world from those with the lowest to those with the highest female employment levels, and places educational data alongside.[48] The female labour force participation rate for sub-Saharan Africa is the highest of all world regions, standing at 61.2 per cent (as can be seen at the foot of Table 2.1), despite a relatively low secondary school completion rate for girls. We can also look at a more granular level than Table 2.1 allows. When doing so, it is notable that while many of the western and central African economies considered so far exhibit low levels of education for girls, along with high levels of child marriage, female labour force participation is nevertheless relatively high at 54 per cent. This is also the case in eastern and southern Africa (where female labour force participation is 66%). By contrast, and as can be seen in the top rows of Table 2.1, while both the MENA region (Middle East and North Africa) and South Asia (including India) have recently made great strides in terms of girls' schooling (with, as shown, more than three-quarters of girls completing lower secondary school), when it comes to women's employment (in the first column), progress has been slow. India is in fact moving backwards. In terms of the modesty cult, and as Table 2.1 helps to reveal, it is therefore at this second life stage – at the stage of paid work as opposed to education – that MENA and South Asia most falter.

Using countries from across the world, Figure 2.3 plots the relationship between women's labour force participation and the proportion of the population who think that premarital sex is unacceptable.[49] As the line of best fit helps to make clear,

Table 2.1   Women's Labour Force Participation and Education by World Region

	Female labour force participation, 2019 (%)	Lower secondary school completion rate, girls, 2019 (%)
Middle East and North Africa	19.8	77.5
South Asia	23.6	80.4
Central Europe and the Baltics	49.2	90.0
European Union	50.9	95.8
Latin America and Caribbean	52.5	82.2
North America	57.2	95.1
East Asia and Pacific	58.8	91.0
Sub-Saharan Africa	61.2	41.3

Sources: World Bank and International Labour Organization (modelled estimates); UNESCO Institute for Statistics and the World Bank

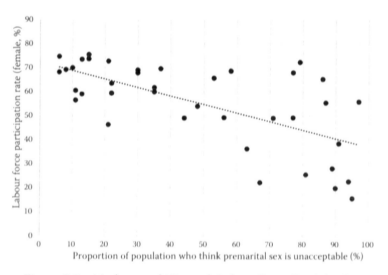

Figure 2.3   Modesty and Women's Labour Force Participation
Sources: World Bank and International Labour Organization
(modelled estimates); Barber, 2018; Diamant, 2020

in countries where people are less opposed to premarital sex (where bodily modesty appears less of a concern), a higher proportion of women engage in paid work; by contrast, in countries with stronger opposition to premarital sex (those on the right as opposed to left-hand side of the chart), women are, on average, less likely to be in paid employment. As with education, this suggests that expanding women's involvement in paid work either requires policies and practices that placate concerns about modesty – or, even better, that break the modesty cult.

Across the world, one in two women engage in paid work. In MENA, by contrast, the figure stands at only one in five. For the minority of young women who are in the labour force in the region, the unemployment rate is an astonishing 50 per cent, compared with 10–20 per cent for young men.[50] According to the World Bank, 't]he academic consensus on what explains MENA's low female labour force participation has yet to emerge'.[51] Discussions have tended to focus on three factors: oil, Islam and patriarchal norms. It is, however, clear that not all oil-rich countries, which also include Norway, the USA and Russia, experience low female participation in the workplace.[52] According to Ronald Inglehart and Pippa Norris, Islam is instead to blame. They write that 'an Islamic religious heritage is one of the most powerful barriers to the rising tide of gender equality'.[53] But while, on average, Muslim countries might have lower female labour market participation rates, there is a great deal of variation between them.[54] At one end of the spectrum is Yemen, where only six per cent of women go out to work. By contrast, in the United Arab Emirates (UAE), 48 per cent of women engage in paid work, which is close to the world average.[55] Moreover, in some of the predominantly Muslim countries in the sub-Saharan African region, women's employment rates are even higher.

What matters much more specifically than religion is, of course, attitudes to gender: individual-level studies of women's employment in Cairo (Egypt), Amman (Jordan), and Sana'a (Yemen) find that conservative attitudes to women adversely affect women's employment.[56] Across the MENA region, only 24 per cent of men (and 36% of women) think that women should be able to travel independently, and these percentages have been falling rather than rising since 2010.[57] In Iran, Oman, Saudi Arabia and Yemen, women are required to have permission from a male relative in order to apply for a passport.[58] Limitations on women's ability to travel freely are not only a sign of conservative social views, they directly limit women's work opportunities.[59] In some MENA countries, 'Guardianship Laws' continue to require a woman to have permission from her father or husband in order for her to work.[60]

The strength of the modesty cult and the degree to which measures have been put in place to placate it would therefore appear to present itself as an even more specific explanation for the differences in women's employment within and across regions.[61] Evidence from focus groups held in Yemen and the Palestinian territories reveal what is at stake where the modesty cult is strong. As one teenage boy noted, '[w]e are afraid for our sister . . . Our sister is our honor.' As one young woman added, 'a boy's reputation can be fixed; a girl's can't'.[62] What matters in terms of the modesty cult is not simply a family's own gender-based attitudes to work, but how they think other people will judge women. Where women's social value depends on purity, a woman's involvement in the workforce has reputational effects: affecting the degree to which others will treat her and her family with respect. Evidence from Saudi Arabia suggests that these reputational effects, as opposed to a family's own beliefs about women, are what is important in determining women's labour force participation. In other words, even where men are themselves in favour of female relatives working, they nevertheless fear that the rest of society will look down on them, which in turn leads them to limit the choices of wives and daughters.[63] Where concerns about reputational effects are eased, male relatives are, however, happier for female relatives to go out to work.[64]

In the UAE, where a much greater proportion of women go out to work than in many other parts of the Middle East, careers are carefully chosen so as to ensure that women can preserve 'modesty in dress and behaviour when interacting with male colleagues', which 'is necessary for Arab families to maintain their honour and reputation in their communities and avoid being shamed or disrespected'.[65] Women are guided into careers which are female-dominated and sedentary in nature. Construction, IT and engineering are generally avoided. Healthcare roles that involve working with other women, along with jobs in the public sector, where gender segregation is better catered for than in the private sector, and working for a family business, are the main options open to young women.[66] In addition to focusing job searches on female-dominated sectors, donning modest dress has also become a tool to placate worried parents across the Middle East more generally, contributing to a widespread re-veiling as more and more women have entered the workforce.[67]

Like women in MENA, women in South Asia are also less likely to engage in formal employment compared with those elsewhere in the world. Seema Jayachandran has linked the lack of female employment in both regions to a culture of purity, noting that the seclusion of women is not only a practice traditionally used by many Islamic families in the form of *purdah*, but also one employed by Hindu families, especially wealthier ones: 'One of the tenets of the Hindu caste system is that women should be protected from 'pollution', which includes men outside their families. Disallowing women from working outside the home is one way of maintaining their purity.'[68]

India is the largest of all the southern Asian countries. Not only is women's labour force participation low on average in India, but women have been 'dropping out of the labour force at an alarming rate' in recent years, despite falling fertility and increased education, both of which tend to boost rather than reduce women's employment in Western countries.[69] Evidence suggests that as income and wealth rises at the family level, women are less likely to enter – and more likely to exit – the workforce in India.[70] At present, only 20 per cent of Indian women are in the paid workforce (down from one in three in 2000), which compares with 70 per cent of men.[71] In striking contrast, women's labour force participation in Bangladesh has increased in recent decades, from 27 per cent in 1990 to 35 per cent in 2021, with many women being drawn into the garment sector.[72] In between the two extremes is Pakistan, where women's labour force participation has been increasing from 11 per cent in 1990 to 21 per cent by 2021 but nevertheless remains low, something which has long been explained in terms of the practice of *purdah* (i.e. secluding women).[73] Much as in India, women from wealthier families in Pakistan are less likely to work than those from poorer families, and the decision of whether or not to work is commonly made by a woman's father or husband.[74] In one extensive survey, around half of non-working Pakistani women said that their male relatives forbade them from working.[75]

In East Asia, women were once as secluded as those in South Asia, but economic growth has served to draw women into the workforce, rather than, as in India, causing them to exit. According to some commentators, this is due to the nature of economic growth: whether sectors in the economy emerge and expand that are labour intensive and so lend themselves to high levels of demand for female workers. In both East Asia and also in Bangladesh, labour intensive factory production, including in the garment industry, has played an important role in economic growth.[76] The resultant high demand for female labour interacts with cultures of modesty, with women drawn into the labour force where modesty culture is less strong, or where it can happen in tandem such that, in relative terms, one woman's reputation is unchanged relative to all others. Alice Evans suggests that the policing of women's sexuality was historically stronger in South Asia, as indicated by higher historic rates of child marriage, meaning that the honour–income trade-off was such that families in South Asia preferred to forego any female income earning opportunities arising from economic growth, rather than risk a loss of honour. In East Asia, by contrast, not only was it already common for women to engage in paid work from within the home (particularly in textile manufacture), but when factories quickly spread, they could draw the extensive pool of young but unmarried women into the formal labour force en masse.[77] Rising *demand* for women could be met with a response in terms of the *supply* of women, as the speed of change and opportunities on offer meant that, in relative terms, women's reputation was not damaged: 'When all families wanted to do it, there could be no social condemnation.'[78]

Women's labour force participation is also high in both sub-Saharan Africa and in Western countries. Nevertheless, there are significant differences within the population. Many studies have explored the role of religion.[79] Evidence from Nigeria, for example, suggests that Muslim women are less likely to engage in work outside the home than Christian women.[80] In European countries, according to one study, 'Muslim women seem to be those with the lowest average employment probability', which stands at 32.3 per cent, while for Hindu women, the probability of employment is a little higher (40%), followed by Jewish women (54%), Catholic and Buddhist women (65%), and Protestant women (80%).[81] Globally, and after adjusting for differences in average age and family responsibilities, the probability that a Muslim woman is employed is 31 per cent compared with 56 per cent for Christian women.[82] In the USA, Arab immigrant women have a particularly low rate of labour market participation,[83] while in the UK, Bangladeshi and Pakistani women have the lowest labour force participation rate (which stands at 39% compared with 72% for women as a whole).[84] In contrast with women, the labour force participation rate for men of Bangladeshi and Pakistani ethnicity living in the UK is much closer to that for men as a whole (73% and 80% respectively).[85]

Focus groups held with women in West Yorkshire have helped to identify some of the social reasons behind low female labour force participation. One 60-year-old working woman noted the way in which non-working women in her community would, in her youth, ostracise her and describe her as 'loose': 'you see they didn't know about work, they had never worked, they assumed that I was going to a place that was full of men. Actually all the workers on the production line were women.'[86] A 21-year-old wife and mother noted: 'I want to work when my youngest child goes to school but my husband won't like it . . . he wouldn't like me working with men.'[87] Nazim Akthar of the Muslim Women's Network UK has similarly spotlighted the type of family concern that can limit women's engagement with the workforce: female relatives being seen with other men. She invites families to question cultural norms, asking:

> [W]hy can a man and a woman not be seen together? Why does there have to be something sordid about it? It could be for professional reasons, they could be friends, or it could be for any reason whatsoever. That must obviously be challenged by us and by everybody involved, and we must address these issues.[88]

Despite multiple studies which identify the impact of religion, there is wide variation in terms of how supportive families are of women's employment, suggesting that Islam is, once again, too superficial an explanation.[89] Gender traditionalism – and more specifically the cult of female modesty – rather than Islam provides greater explanatory power.[90] Islamophobia and discrimination, whether at work or on the journey to and from work, provide another part of the explanation for relatively low labour force participation,[91] especially given that 'Islamophobic hate crime disproportionately affects Muslim women, as those who wear headscarves or other religious dress are more identifiably Muslim when compared with Muslim men.'[92] This is consistent with the fact that the unemployment rate among Pakistani and Bangladeshi women in the UK is three times higher than among white women.[93] Sadly, and contrary to what was once believed, evidence now suggests that the labour market inequalities faced by Muslim women are not decreasing generation-on-generation.[94]

Limited access to educational and work opportunities aren't the only costs of modesty culture; so too is access to politics. Across the world, and based on 2020 figures, 26 per cent of parliamentary seats are held by women.[95] In MENA, recent years have seen the opening up of political space to women in Kuwait, Bahrain, Oman, UAE, Iraq, Jordan and Saudi Arabia (among others).[96] But, nevertheless, only 17 per cent of parliamentary seats in the region are held by women,[97] and two-thirds of people still think that men make better leaders.[98] In Yemen, women engaging in political protest are accused of 'mingling with men', making political activism a risk to a woman's reputation.[99] In Egypt, in 2011, the military began virginity testing female protesters.[100] And, according to Ruhollah Khomeini, the former leader of Iran, '[i]t is permissible to give women the right to vote in the elections, but giving women the right to be elected will lead to prostitution'.[101]

When it comes to those responsible for legal restrictions on women, their declarations reveal the whorephobia that is so central to the cult of female modesty. In the 1950 manifesto published by Navvab Safavi, the leader of the Fedayeen Islam, it was claimed that: 'Flames of passion rise from the naked bodies of immoral women and burn humanity into ashes.'[102] The architect of the Iranian revolution, Khomeini, felt not only that women's election to political posts would 'lead to prostitution',[103] but that, more generally, '[t]he unveiling of women has caused the ruin of female honor, the destruction of the family, and untold corruption and prostitution'.[104] In July 2019, three Iranian women were sentenced to a total of fifty-five years in prison for removing their hijab and handing out flowers of peace on public transport. By not covering their hair, the state claimed that they were 'inciting prostitution'.[105] In Saudi Arabia, the case against women being permitted to drive was also that it risked 'prostitution', along with (apparently) pornography, divorce, adultery and homosexuality.[106] Whorephobia has proved a powerful tool for those who harness the modesty cult.

So far, we have seen that the modesty cult plays out in different ways in different countries. In some, child marriage and/or the withdrawal of teenage girls from school is used as a means of guaranteeing a woman's reputation, limiting the possibility of births outside marriage and of a girl's reputational damage in her teenage years. This is particularly common in parts of Africa, but also in some parts of central and southern Asia. The sacrifice comes in terms of a girl's education and her future earning potential, limiting her to badly paid unskilled work. In other places, the problem erupts most clearly later in life, with modesty culture restricting access to paid work (instead of education). India may have lower rates of child marriage than west and central Africa (27% versus 41%), and its progress has been relatively impressive in educational terms, but women are much less likely to engage in paid work. In some countries, gender segregation, at school and in the workplace, has been used to satisfy economic needs, while maintaining modesty. This compromise is not, however, without a cost, both in the form of limited opportunities for women and in terms of the lower levels of pay that are associated with gender segregated workplaces.[107]

The irony is that the measures taken to 'protect' women – measures to preserve their reputation and keep them safe from 'whoredom' – hurt rather than help them. By limiting their educational and work-based opportunities, the modesty cult hampers women's financial independence, leaving them poor and dependent on men. Their limited involvement in politics in turn limits their ability to push for change. And it doesn't end there. Rather than encouraging men to treat women with greater respect, the modesty cult, as we will see next, allows them to harass and abuse without guilt any woman who they deem to be unsuitably modest, which, rather conveniently, is left for them to judge.

Abuse and Harassment

Are women safer where a culture of female modesty prevails? Table 2.2 ranks a wide variety of countries according to the proportion of the population who believe that premarital sex is unacceptable, allowing us to see where virginity is most – and least – prized.[108] The countries are divided into three groups: the first column lists those parts of the world in which at least two-thirds of people view premarital sex as unacceptable; the middle column lists those where between a third and two-thirds of people find premarital sex unacceptable; and, the final column lists those where under a third of people object to premarital sex. While these data are only available for a hand-ful of countries, this nevertheless helps us to examine whether women are safer in those countries with a greater or lesser cul-ture of modesty. Ultimately, what we wish to gauge is whether women in the first column are subjected to less or more abuse and harassment than those in the middle or final column.

  Some might argue that a culture of modesty helps to protect women and girls from prying eyes, keeping them safe from harm. Until recently, this was difficult to judge. Neither inci-dents of street-based harassment nor incidents of intimate partner violence were well recorded. But, in 2017, the United Nations Inter-Agency Working Group on Violence Against

Table 2.2   Countries Ranked by Modesty Culture

High Modesty Cult (%)	Medium Modesty Cult (%)	Low Modesty Cult (%)
(More than 2/3 of people think premarital sex is unacceptable)	(Between 1/3 and 2/3 of people think premarital sex is unacceptable)	(Less than 1/3 of people think premarital sex is unacceptable)
Indonesia (97)	Senegal (63)	Russia (30)
Jordan (95)	China (58)	USA (30)
Pakistan (94)	El Salvador (56)	Argentina (22)
Palestine (94)	Bolivia (53)	Poland (22)
Turkey (91)	USA Evangelicals (52)	Venezuela (21)
Egypt (90)	South Africa (48)	Japan (21)
Tunisia (89)	Mexico (44)	Canada (15)
Malaysia (87)	Israel (37)	Australia (15)
Ghana (86)	South Korea (35)	Chile (13)
Lebanon (81)	Brazil (35)	Britain (13)
Kenya (79)	USA Catholics (35)	Greece (11)
Nigeria (77)		Italy (11)
Uganda (77)		Czech (10)
Philippines (71)		Spain (8)
India (67)		Germany (6)
		France (6)

Sources: Barber, 2018; Diamant, 2020

Women Estimation and Data (VAW-IAWGED) was established, which has provided us with one of the best pictures to date of intimate partner violence.[109] In addition, the Thomson Reuters Foundation and YouGov have polled women living in sixteen of the largest global cities to gauge women's experiences when 'out and about' in public.[110] While the results must necessarily be treated with caution, especially since they are unlikely to properly capture abuse and harassment where concerns about reputational damage affect how a woman answers questions about her experiences, such evidence nevertheless deserves to be considered. As we will see, doing so suggests that countries in which the modesty cult is strong (those in the first of our three columns) also tend to be those in which both gender-based violence and 'rape culture' run deep, exposing women to danger, and limiting their ability to speak out. The notion that modesty culture protects women is therefore not borne out by the data.

Across the world, one in three people rank sexual harassment as the biggest issue facing women in their country.[111] But, in Turkey, Malaysia, Mexico and India, it is seen as a particular problem, with around half of people ranking sexual harassment as the most pressing issue women face.[112] In all four countries, and according to Table 2.2, modesty culture is either strong or very strong: in Turkey, Malaysia and India, more than two-thirds of people think that premarital sex is unacceptable; in Mexico, it is more than four in ten, exceeding North America and Europe. The recent survey of women living in the world's largest capital cities gives us further evidence on three of these four countries: across all sixteen of the cities surveyed, Mexico City ranks second for its lack of safety, New Delhi ranks fourth, and Kuala Lumpur ranks seventh.[113] As we are already therefore starting to see, the countries in the world where women feel least safe are not countries where women are scantily clad, but countries where the modesty cult is strong. Modesty culture does not protect women.

According to Table 2.2, modesty culture is also strong in many parts of South Asia, Africa and the Middle East. While we lack comparable data on the safety of capital cities for women in these regions, we do know that around 60 per cent of women surveyed in Egypt, Morocco and Lebanon have experienced street-based harassment.[114] In addition, evidence on intimate partner violence suggests that women in all three regions are subjected to relatively high levels of physical and sexual violence compared with parts of the world where the modesty cult is less strong. Table 2.3 ranks world regions according to lifetime intimate partner violence, while also providing data on experiences over the last twelve months, along with – where data are available – the rank of any associated major cities in

Table 2.3 Physical and Sexual Violence by World Region

	Lifetime prevalence of physical/sexual intimate partner violence (% of women)	Experience of physical/sexual intimate partner violence in the past 12 months (% of women)	Unsafe public transport (ranking of 16 major cities, from worst to best)
Melanesia	51	30	
Southern Asia	35	19	4 (New Delhi)
Sub-Saharan Africa	33	20	
Northern Africa	30	15	
Western Asia (incl. Middle East)	29	13	
Latin America and the Caribbean	25	8	1 (Bogotá); 2 (Mexico City); 3 (Lima); 6 (Buenos Aires)
Northern America	25	6	16 (New York)
Northern Europe	23	5	
Australia and New Zealand	23	3	
South-Eastern Asia	21	9	5 (Jakarta); 7 (Kuala Lumpur); 8 (Bangkok); 10 (Manila)
Western Europe	21	5	11 (Paris); 13 (London)
East Asia	20	7	12 (Seoul); 14 (Beijing); 15 (Tokyo)

Note: Moscow's public transport ranks ninth for lack of safety, but it is omitted as Russia spans multiple regions.
Sources: WHO, 2021, p. VI; Thomson Reuters Foundation with YouGov (reproduced in Bruce-Lockhart, 2016).

terms of women's lack of safety.[115] While the first two numeri-
cal columns capture violence perpetrated by partners, the final
column captures experiences with strangers.

In addition to South Asia, Africa and the Middle East, the
Pacific Islands of Melanesia also feature highly in Table 2.3; in
fact, this region is at the very top of the table, ahead of the other
regions so far discussed. While comparable data is lacking on
attitudes to premarital sex in this part of the world (as a result
of which they do not feature in Table 2.2), qualitative evidence
suggests that this is also a region where virginity is highly
prized. Although the Pacific Islands do not commonly feature
female genital mutilation/cutting, purdah, and compulsory
head coverings, they do feature other signs of modesty culture,
including an emphasis on virginity. The payment of a bride
price is a common practice in the region. According to some,
it is a demeaning practice that 'is akin to selling a daughter',
while for others it is a celebration of 'the social value and the
virtue of women'.[116] But, while that much is debated, what is
abundantly clear is that the 'price' a young woman's family can
command for her marriage depends on her bodily modesty.
A young woman whose reputation can be questioned in this
sense typically commands only half the bride price of one who
is known to be a virgin, while marriage to a divorcee is referred
to as a 'bargain [i.e. cheap] marriage'.[117] Alongside virginity,
widow chastity is also a feature in Pacific Island countries. In
Tonga, a widow who 'fornicates . . . loses her right to live in the
home that she lived in before her husband's death. For the rest
of her life, she must be sexually faithful to her dead husband or
risk losing her home.'[118]

Taken together, it seems that the Pacific Islands, South Asia,
Africa, the Middle East, and Latin America and the Caribbean
are some of the most dangerous places in the world for women,
whereas women in North America, Europe, Australia, New
Zealand and East Asia are relatively safer. In the former, unsafe,
group, and as a quick look back at Table 2.2 makes apparent,

the modesty cult is strong. In the latter, relatively safe, group, the modesty cult is relatively weak. Altogether, therefore, the evidence suggests that in countries with a culture of modesty, where virginity is highly prized, women are certainly not safer. And, to make matters worse, and as we will see next, these modesty-valorising countries are also those in which victim-blaming is endemic, limiting women's ability to seek justice.

Victim Blaming

In recent years, stories of the rape and the murder of women in Pakistan and India have proliferated. On 1 December 2019 a female law student in Pakistan was kidnapped from a public place by a group of five men. Here were just some of the responses from members of the public:[119]

Jab mithayi ko khula chorro ge to makhyan zaroor ayen gi. (If you leave the sweet box open, it will inevitably attract flies.)

Ye to hona hi tha, kapre to dekho. (This was inevitable, look at what she is wearing.)

Well done kidnappers . . . Jo log apni bachio ko be lagaam chor dete hain. (Those who leave their daughters unconstrained deserve this.)

A survey of attitudes in Egypt, Morocco, Lebanon and Palestine reveals that between one-third and two-thirds of men admit to engaging in street-based sexual harassment, and the vast majority (two-thirds to three-quarters) blame women for dressing 'provocatively'.[120] In Latin America and the Caribbean, a region which is home to fourteen of the top twenty-five countries for femicides, 70 per cent of people think that a woman who is groped or cornered is herself responsible, including because of the way she dresses.[121] In Mozambique, Ghana and Kenya, girls are encouraged to behave modestly so as, in the words of one Kenyan schoolgirl, not to 'entice the boys'.[122] Girls are positioned as 'innocent and chaste, and lacking in sexual agency' and so, if they find themselves pregnant or are the subject of sexual abuse, they are 'blamed and shamed for going against norms around femininities'.[123] Women and girls in Sierra Leone are also subjected to high rates of sexual abuse and violence, made all the worse by 'a climate of impunity in which survivors are often blamed ... with perpetrators portrayed as victims'.[124] The sexual abuse of girls by male teachers is all too common, and 'the blame is often put on survivors, with perpetrators portrayed as victims who could not control themselves'.[125]

Three features are common to all of the above country-specific or regional examples: victim-blaming; the notion that males are incapable of resisting; and a belief that women are 'asking for it'. Taken together, it equates to what has been called a 'culture of rape'.

The United States is not immune to this rape culture, and a closer look suggests that this is concentrated in the parts of American society where the modesty cult is strongest. Within the general US population, only three in ten people disapprove of premarital sex. However, among the church-going Evangelical population, the modesty cult is strong – even stronger than it is among American Catholics. More than a half of Evangelical Americans disapprove of premarital sex, and it is within this same population that evidence has recently come to light not only of a growing 'purity culture' but also of a culture that leaves women vulnerable. A recent study of Evangelical Christian dating advice books found that '[f]requently, many authors advise their readers that it was the woman's fault if the date progressed further sexually than intended ... Women are blamed for inciting others' behavior in nearly all of the books'.[126] Lookadoo and DiMarco's book *Dateable* suggests

that '[y]ou get treated the way you dress. Hey, if guys are treating you like you are EZ, you are probably dressed like you are
EZ.'[127] As a result, 'sexual violence loses its impact as a violent
act and instead becomes a mere "giving in" to temptation'.[128]
Rape is deemed 'boys being boys', with young women – rather
than young men – being left to feel guilt and shame. Immodest
women are presented as the problem, and modesty as the solution. The extent to which women are judged on the basis of
their bodily modesty could not be more clear; young women
are taught that premarital sex 'makes them like a screwed up
piece of paper, a chewed piece of gum, or a jar that loads of
people have spat into'.[129]

As Klement and Sagarin write, this culture 'can lead to
stigmatisation of other women who have sexual experience,
as well as confusion and internalised victim-blaming for
women who are sexually assaulted or abused. This may result
in self-blame for harassment or violence women experience,
as they believe their behavior or clothing choices caused their
abuse.'[130] Consent becomes poorly understood, leaving women
in a more vulnerable situation than if boys were encouraged
to take responsibility for their own sexual behaviour. As
Dianna Anderson concluded, '[b]y failing to equip women to
understand their own agency and bodily autonomy, the evangelical purity movement creates an environment that is ripe
for rape'.[131]

In Israel, where modesty culture is also growing, including in the form of gender segregated buses, women can face
insult if they cross the societally imposed gender divide. As Zvi
Trigger recounts:

> Women who do not go to the back of the bus or are not dressed
> modestly according to ultra-Orthodox standards, whether
> because they did not notice they were boarding a 'mehadrin'
> [gender-segregated] bus or because they refuse to adhere to its
> rules, are often verbally and physically abused . . . The violence

has escalated to such an extent that in December 2011 the Jerusalem District Attorney indicted an ultra-Orthodox man who shouted 'whore' at a female soldier who refused to walk to the end of the bus pursuant to his demand.[132]

As Triger notes, '[w]hile its motivation is to "clean" the public sphere from any manifestation, real or perceived, of female sexuality, by being so preoccupied with women's "modesty" it in fact puts their sexuality at the center of attention'.[133]

Peter Sutcliffe, who murdered numerous sex workers in the north of England in the 1970s and early 1980s, also claimed to be 'cleaning up the streets'.[134] As researchers have since shown, 'whore stigma' and the 'discourse of disposal' feeds the violent treatment and murder of sex workers.[135] Sex workers are commonly portrayed as 'social pollutants' and equated with rubbish.[136] The fact that they are seen as worthless means that they are treated as worthless, both by those who, as a result, abuse them, and by those with the power to bring the abusers to account. As Marleen Laverte, a sex worker, writes: 'There is a lack of understanding that first and foremost, it is social prejudices about prostitution that render it difficult for us to protect ourselves. That is because they lower the threshold to use violence against us – among clients, among the police, among everyone.'[137]

Not only does the cult of female modesty fuel mistreatment and abuse by marking immodest women out as unworthy and as deserving of harassment, humiliation and punishment, it also makes it more difficult for victims to seek redress. A recent survey of attitudes among the Egyptian population revealed that more than three-fifths of men believe that the victim of an honour killing 'usually deserves such punishment' and, perhaps astonishingly, almost a half of women agreed. Egyptian courts have 'discretion to dispense reduced sentencing' for perpetrators, and a third of men and women believe that 'perpetrators should go unpunished'.[138] Authorities that internalise the modesty cult pay scant attention to crimes committed against women, seeing the women themselves as to blame. In the West, this is most apparent when it comes to sex workers. The fear of not being taken seriously, along with the fear of being 'outed', means that sex workers are reluctant to report abuse, which allows abuse to continue, and gives power to abusers, who are fully aware that they are unlikely to be prosecuted. As Belinda Brooks-Gordon writes, 'exploiters can only be held to account with an increased chance of being caught. Currently, the likelihood of being caught is low because sex workers are so stigmatised they are reluctant to report offences.'[139]

This situation mirrors that faced by women more generally in countries where the modesty cult is strong. Where a woman's value rests on her bodily modesty, speaking out about harassment and abuse is tantamount to an admission of guilt. It is itself a declaration of immodesty, one which therefore comes at a cost of respectability. As Anam Zakaria, Jalaluddin Mughal and Maria Abi-Habib note '[s]exual violence often goes unreported in Pakistan, as victims risk being cast out by their parents, are forced to marry their rapists or are killed over the perceived injury to their family's "honor"'.[140] Similarly, in Morocco, the loss of virginity, even in the case of rape, is 'a social stigma that dishonours the entire family'.[141] A survey of attitudes in Egypt and Morocco reveals that around 60 per cent of men think that a woman who is raped should marry her rapist.[142] Marrying your rapist is, apparently, often the only way to 'restore the family honour'. According to a recent UN report, twenty countries across the world allow rapists to go free if their victim marries them.[143]

In 1998, during a period of repeated conflict between India and Pakistan over the Kashmiri region, Nasreen and her five children spent days, on and off, sheltering in a local bunker. The eldest daughter, Ayesha, began begging her mother not to return to the shelter, telling her that a man was touching her.

Weeks later, it became clear that she was pregnant. She was thirteen and the perpetrator was at least twice her age. One newspaper reported on what happened subsequently:

> A jirga, or community gathering, judged that Ayesha should be married to her rapist to save what remained of her honor. Nasreen said they accepted the decision as the will of God. A few months later, Ayesha died during labour, her body unable to handle the birth and doctors unable to stop her from haemorrhaging to death. Her son, born premature, died a few months later.[144]

The modesty cult has long served to provide cover for rape as a weapon of war. The bloody partition of India by the British in 1947, which created the two separate states of India and Pakistan,[145] resulted in twelve-million refugees, numerous riots and massacres with deaths that ran into six figures, and extensive violence towards women. This violence included stripping women, raping them, parading them naked, branding their naked bodies with enemy slogans, mutilating and disfiguring their bodies, amputating breasts, cutting open their wombs, and killing foetuses.[146] The subsequent 1971 war, when Pakistan was split in two, with East Pakistan becoming Bangladesh, similarly left its mark on women's bodies. Yasmin Saikia refers to what she calls the 'Untold Stories' of rape during this time, noting that while cases have since been documented, 'the victims themselves are invisible, in order to hide their "shame", and maintain family honor and men's pride'.[147] Rape has continued to be used as a weapon in more recent conflicts in the region, including in the 2002 pogroms, where 'men were recorded by human rights groups as deliberately raping or sexually mutilating women with the aim to destroy their honour'.[148]

Sunny Hundal explains how modesty culture fuels such attacks:

Traditional, conservative South Asian culture fetishises women to such an extent that, while the official line says they are held in high esteem and regard, in actual fact, they are treated simply as vessels of that honour, and their lives are forced to be structured around preserving that. They are not allowed to do anything that compromises those ideals ... Partition exposed this deeply ingrained misogyny in the most brutal fashion. When Muslim, Hindu and Sikh men wanted to take revenge for their peers being killed by the other, they deliberately went out searching for women of other religions to rape and kidnap. When villages were confronted with angry baying mobs, the women were told to commit suicide by jumping in the well for their own benefit rather than fall in the clutches of the other.[149]

In the words of Antonia Navarro-Tejero, '[t]here is no doubt that the sexual crimes committed against girls and women at times of conflict are a direct consequence of the appropriation of women's bodies for symbolic uses within the dialectics of patriarchal communalism'.[150] What is striking is not only the enemy outside, but the enemy within. In a small town near Rawalpindi, more than twenty Sikh women were killed by their own family elders to avoid the dishonour that would come from the anticipated Muslim attack; around the same time, more than eighty women and children committed suicide to avoid the same fate.[151] The fact that death was considered a better option than living with the 'dishonour' of rape is particularly striking.

In the Pacific Islands, rape has also been used as a weapon of war or a form of punishment designed to bring shame. As Imrana Jalal notes, '[e]ven after the cessation of tensions in the Solomon Islands, women married to men from the opposite side were still being raped, as punishment'.[152] Like South Asia, the Pacific Islands also exhibits high levels of violence against women and girls. In fact, it is the only part of the world to exceed southern Asia in terms of the extent of physical and sexual intimate partner violence in particular (Figure 2.3).[153] The fact that a woman robbed of her virginity is seen as less valuable than one who is not feeds into a culture of rape in the form of punishment, payback and forced marriage:

> In such cases a group of men or youths rape a girl to punish her father or brothers. In some cases, to 'payback' the rape of a complainant, the men of the complainant's clan will rape a woman of the perpetrator's clan. Sexual assault on a girl, to rupture her hymen, may also be perpetrated to force her into marriage; the rape being seen to culturally 'devalue' the girl by taking her virginity.[154]

We cannot end our discussion of abuse, harassment and victim-blaming without acknowledging the significant levels of harassment faced by Muslim women in Western societies, particularly those adopting head coverings. As we have already seen, modest women cannot escape the abuse and harassment that the cult of female modesty breeds. And, when it comes to explaining the high level of street-based harassment that many Muslim women experience from non-Muslims, the indirect impact of modesty culture should not be discounted. Where non-Muslim women fear being bumped down the modesty ranking, they may lash out at those who adopt more modest dress. This is because modesty is a zero-sum game: for someone to be modest, someone else must be immodest. Non-Muslim women who internalise the cult of female modesty, who are liable to labelling other women 'whores', may in turn fear women who are more modest than themselves. In relative terms, more modest women leave them feeling 'naked' and must therefore be forced to uncover. Breaking modesty culture is, therefore, key not only to reducing the harassment faced by immodest women, but also to reducing that faced by women who, in clothing terms, appear the most modest of all.

Physical and Mental Health

Sparkling urine that whistles, upright breasts, an inability to smell burning coal, bloodied bedsheets and the two-finger test: virginity testing has a long and checkered history. Despite calls from the World Health Organization for it to be banned, testing women in order 'to assess their virtue, honour or social value'[155] is still considered the norm in at least twenty countries across the world today.[156] As a human rights activist based in Morocco notes, 'a woman is a human being with her faculties and her capacities, not just a hymen [but] . . . [w]e are still living with old-fashioned and useless traditions that we pass from generation to generation'.[157]

Even though a virginity test is painful and humiliating, in some countries, a woman's ability to access education or jobs is dependent upon it.[158] In Indonesia, women have until recently had to submit to a virginity test to work in the armed forces or the police. In Sweden in 2015, an undercover investigation brought to light doctors who were performing virginity tests on teenage girls, at the request of their parents.[159] In 2016, one South African municipality established a scholarship for young women who passed a virginity test. At times, virginity testing is also used as a form of punishment, including for women protesters who took part in the Arab Spring.[160]

While on a different scale, recent investigations have also revealed that 'virginity testing' is practised in the UK and the USA.[161] A survey of American gynecologists found that around 10 per cent have received requests for virginity testing, and a third of them went on to perform the test. In the UK, investigations have shown that tests cost between £150 and £300 and involve an intimate examination to confirm whether the hymen is intact. If a 'problem' is found, hymen repair is offered at a mere £1500–£3000. It begs the question: Why would any woman pay a stranger to intimately examine her vulva region, and then undergo an expensive and painful process?

The answer is, of course, that a woman whose body has been 'seen' or 'used' is perceived as 'damaged goods', as someone who no 'respectable' man would want to marry, and whose reputation within her community would be in tatters. Because, in other words, she faces a society in which her value, worth and respect rest on her bodily modesty.

'Honour killings' represent a related scourge, but are under-researched and commonly seen as one-offs.[162] Estimates suggest that at least 5,000 women each year are murdered for reasons of honour, with most such killings taking place in South Asia and the Middle East.[163] In Nangarhar, Afghanistan, one in sixteen women interviewed by researchers have experienced an honour killing within their own family.[164] In their 2021 Report, 'My body is my own', the United Nations note that '[a]lthough both men and women can commit or be victims of honour killings, the "code of honour" has different standards for men and women, including stricter standards of chastity for women and a perceived duty for men to commit violent acts to secure their honour or that of their family'.[165] In Egypt, Morocco, Lebanon and Palestine, between 68 and 95 per cent of men think that their honour depends on the dress and behaviour of their female relatives.[166] Where social networks, as opposed to anonymous market relations, are central to community relations, a woman's behaviour matters to the entire family. Only where a family is seen as 'respectable' are they able to access jobs and credit. Where a woman is deemed to have transgressed her respectability, it leaves her family exposed to being cut off from social networks, endangering their livelihoods as well as the future marriages of other female members of the family. This can be particularly problematic for poorer families.[167] By resorting to an honour killing, relatives are attempting to 'prove' to their community that, despite their daughter's transgression, they still believe that immodest behaviour is unacceptable. A signal is sent far and wide that the family do not approve of such behaviour, in the hope of protecting the reputation, and so livelihood, of the wider family. As Rula Quawas poignantly writes in response in her testimonial poem:

I have had enough
My duty is to honour myself
Owning and honouring it,
I am not an appendage[168]

In China, historically, mothers broke their daughter's feet, limiting their ability to freely roam, thereby acting as a guarantee of purity.[169] While this practice has been discontinued, an equivalent practice remains alive and well in parts of Africa.[170] Female genital mutilation or cutting (FGM/C), which can include everything from cutting the clitoris to sewing up a woman's vaginal opening, can make sex painful and orgasm more difficult, thereby constraining a woman's libido.[171] Over 200 million women and girls worldwide have been subjected to these acts, which are common in at least forty countries, and another three million girls a year are estimated to be currently at risk.[172] The practice is common in Djibouti, Mauritania, Somalia, Sudan, Egypt and Yemen, but also affects an estimated 38 per cent of Kuwaiti women, 34 per cent of women in UAE, along with many in Indonesia, Malaysia, Pakistan, India and northern Iraq.[173] While there are numerous explanations for this practice, the way it acts as a guarantee of a young woman's chastity and honour features highly among them.[174] According to the WHO, 'FGM is in many communities believed to reduce a woman's libido and therefore believed to help her resist extra-marital sexual acts.' Needless to say, it is a painful practice and comes with the risk of sepsis, haemorrhage and future complications with childbirth.[175] But those involved typically feel that they have no choice in the matter. Female matriarchs, in the form of female elders, are often central to making arrangements, leaving girls and even their mothers with little option, especially since those 'who choose to abandon FGM/C can face high social costs, including exclusion from social support, events, and opportunities'.[176] As a result, some researchers point to the fact that an individual family, even where it disagrees with the practice, will find it difficult to stand up to it until there is a 'broader social acceptance of uncut daughters' with fewer social sanctions.[177] The result is that a critical mass of noncompliance is required in order for society to switch away from the practice. This might require society-wide pledges that families sign up to en masse, such as the United Nation's 'Dear Daughter' campaign, currently underway in Somalia, where nine in ten women and girls are cut.

Feminist thinkers suggest that the persistence of genital cutting is also linked to the degree to which women have alternatives to marriage. Where it is difficult for a woman to support herself outside marriage, and so where marriage is seen as necessary to survival, non-compliance with the practice of genital cutting could result in a serious long-term cost. However, where women have opportunities to work and support themselves independently, marriage is less important, and so too therefore is the 'purity' guarantee that genital cutting purports to offer.

Other researchers have pointed to the importance of community heterogeneity: 'If ethnically diverse communities have weaker social ties and weaker enforcement of norms, they also may have lower levels of FGM[/]C, net of community norms and opportunity structures.'[178] In other words, where women can survive without being dependent on connections within their own community, their families are likely to feel under less pressure to comply with community norms.[179] Sadly, continued regional conflict in parts of the MENA region, along with parts of sub-Saharan Africa, limit wider social connections.

In 2015, the United Nations committed to eliminating FGM/C worldwide by 2030. While evidence suggests that it is on the decline in countries where fewer girls were historically cut, the decline is proving to be much slower in countries where it has historically been highly prevalent.[180] A recent survey of attitudes towards FGM/C in Egypt, where it is practised in Christian as well as Muslim communities, found that 'a large proportion of the participants supported the continuation of FGM/C in spite of adverse effect and sexual dysfunction'.[181] Where a woman's respectability, and that of her family, depends on her bodily modesty, no amount of pointing to the adverse effects of practices such as FGM/C seems to impact attitudes. Survival literally depends on being cut.

Aside from virginity testing, honour killings, footbinding, and FGM/C, communities have developed other ways of limiting immodesty, with more subtle health consequences. Coco Khan notes the way that modesty culture can stand in the way of women's participation in sports: 'Women are either fully prevented or discouraged from playing because it's immodest. It's either too manly and ungainly, or too tempting for men.' She notes how her own mother didn't think that sport was an option for her, referring to such an attitude as 'toxic modesty'.[182] The rejection of sex education has also been employed as a modesty-enhancing tool. While there are many things that make birth control and abortion taboo, prominent among them is the notion that they produce a society of harlots, rather than one of chaste wives and mothers. In Saudi Arabia, sexual and reproductive 'ignorance' signifies 'modesty and purity'.[183] Many parents and communities worry that sex education will encourage premarital sex and promiscuity.[184] In the United States, sex education has been cast as 'pornographic' and has become increasingly oriented around abstinence.[185] By 2003, close to one in three sex educators taught abstinence-only until marriage (AOUM), without mentioning contraceptives.[186] Across the period from 1982 to 2003, funding for abstinence-only education increased from $10.9 million to $120 million.[187]

It was more than a quarter of a century ago that the Beijing Declaration recognised that 'the right of all women to control all aspects of their health, in particular their own fertility, is basic to their empowerment'.[188] Women's sexual and reproductive health services are now considered a basic human right. But, almost three decades on, in more than a third of countries, sex education is not mandatory in schools.[189] Across the world, only one in two women and teenage girls are free to make their own informed decisions about sex, contraception and reproduction.[190] Lack of knowledge of sexual and reproductive health feeds through to unplanned pregnancy, unsafe abortions and sexually transmitted diseases.[191] But many women and girls are locked out of accessing knowledge about their bodies as a result of the modesty cult.

According to Deborah Tolman, author of *Dilemmas of Desire*, 'it is not only unfair to deny female adolescent sexual desire but ultimately unsafe and unhealthy'.[192] We live in 'a world where "good", nice, and normal girls do not have sexual feelings of their own'.[193] She warns of 'our consistent refusal to offer girls any guidance for acknowledging, negotiating, and integrating their own sexual desire and the consequences of our refusal: sexual intercourse, most often unprotected, that "just happens" to girls'.[194] Studies of teenage girls in the United States suggest that those who take virginity pledges are a third less likely to use contraception during sexual encounters than those who have not taken a pledge, and, when they do, it is often poorly used; in other words, 'they are less likely to be prepared for an experience they have promised to avoid'.[195] Additional evidence also suggests greater sexual risk-taking among members of chastity clubs, in part explained by the fact that '[w]hen only the most literal and ritualised definition of sex is promoted, that is, penile penetration of a vagina, those who pledge chastity also report a sharp increase in unprotected fellatio and anal sex'.[196] Sadly, as Michelle Fine sums it up, '[w]hile too few safe spaces exist for adolescent women's exploration of sexual subjectivities, there are all too many dangerous spots for their exploitation'.[197]

Even where young women know and understand safe sex, the fear of a sullied reputation can put sand in the wheels of taking the necessary steps, as the 'purchasing or seeking of prescription contraception could constitute an admission or anticipation of sexual activity'.[198] For those whose reputation depends on sexual abstinence, seeking contraception risks friends and family finding out and causes concern that medical staff will tell parents. Even among their peers, a teenage girl who takes the pill, or who asks boys to use condoms, is seen as fair game for the label of 'whore'.[199] As Tolman notes based on her interviews with teenage girls from the United States, the Whore–Madonna distinction is alive and well and, while some girls actively reject it, many still live in fear of their reputation being ruined.[200] More generally, as Holland et al.'s interviews with young women have revealed, '[t]o be conventionally feminine is to appear sexually unknowing, to aspire to a relationship, to let sex "happen", to trust to love, and to make men happy. Safer sex is not just a question of using protection, avoiding penetration, or being chaste, it brings questions of power, trust and female agency into sexual relationships.'[201]

Monique Mulholland's more recent interviews with Australian adolescents reveals that, despite the increasing 'sexualisation' of society, 'young people made a vitally important distinction between Slutty and Hot'. While being 'hot' certainly can now be seen as respectable, being 'slutty' is not.[202] Despite our supposed culture of raunch, 'sleeping around too randomly', being 'fake' and adopting 'hooker style' are still seen as lacking in respect. This distinction between 'hot' and 'slutty' is one that is commonly missed by those critiquing modern-day 'raunch culture', with the cult of female modesty and its associated risks, including for women's health, continuing to go under the radar as a result.

In addition to reputational fear, the guilt associated with sexual encounters in the context of modesty culture also adversely impacts women's health: women who feel guilty about sex find it more difficult to seek help, advice and support, even when those who can offer it present no risk to a woman's reputation.[203] Shame and embarrassment are powerful emotions. In the mid nineteenth century, in the heights of Victorian Britain, a woman died of septicaemia after the handle of a hairbrush became lodged in her vagina. She had not sought help, presumably because she was embarrassed to admit what she had been doing with the hairbrush.[204] While not many women die from hairbrush related incidents, they do live shorter and less healthy lives as a result of failing to seek help with bodily matters, whether of a sexual or non-sexual variety.

Regular smear checks and breast examinations, despite their health benefits, are not always easy within the context of the modesty cult. Evidence relating to South Asian immigrant women in the UK, USA and Canada suggests that a culture of modesty adversely affects cervical screening uptake.[205] As a group, South Asian immigrants are less likely to take up screening opportunities for breast and cervical cancer. For some, '[r]especting and honouring family were maintained by not discussing sensitive female health-related issues such as cervical or breast cancers within the family . . . or with others in the community'.[206] The shame associated with simply talking about screening serves to limit the spread of information that otherwise aids take-up. It is in part explained by the fact that female cancer is, in some communities, assumed to be associated with 'negative lifestyle behaviours such as promiscuity' as well as being seen as 'retribution for past sins; and a form of punishment'.[207] The very idea of being screened can therefore itself be seen as an admission of immodesty. Alongside the reputational fear is, of course, the fear of a male doctor.[208]

Looking more globally, in India, only 22 per cent of women have undergone cervical screening, and 'embarrassment or anxiety related to the screening procedure, fear of being judged for lack of modesty, and stigma' have been identified as 'common barriers'.[209] Recently, scientists have begun to explore more fully the reasons for the low uptake, interviewing and conducting focus groups with women in Himachal Pradesh, Meghalaya and Karnataka. However, they found that '(m)ost young women were too shy to discuss the topic'.[210] Those who did revealed a degree of resistance from family, noting that 'discussing the topic of screening [at home] raised questions about their modesty or trust in their partner, which made them feel uncomfortable to even mention the matter'.[211] As the authors summed it up, '[t]he women explained that there was a stigma related to cervical cancer and that their character and modesty would be questioned if they went for an examination of their cervix'.[212] The more commonly discussed explanations for the lack of take-up (poverty and a lack of education) are, as with child marriage and FGM/C, certainly not the only things that stand in the way. Tackling women's heath issues requires us to admit to and confront the cult of female modesty.

Sexual Pleasure

Even if a woman is 'succeeding' within the bounds of the modesty cult, managing to hold on to her all-important reputation, and avoiding rape in a world where men treat women as 'fair game', she nevertheless faces an intimate problem of her own. The cult of female modesty can leave women feeling that their body is not their own and, in doing so, it disempowers them in the bedroom. A woman dissociating from her body is not only a means through which she can deal with physical trauma and sexual abuse, it is also a means of straitjacketing ourselves into what society expects of us, denying our natural selves.[213]

In the resultant self-repression, pain replaces pleasure, passivity replaces action, and embarrassment replaces humour. Sex becomes a minefield.

Vaginismus, where the vaginal muscles tighten, which can cause pain during sex, affects one in ten women in the UK.[214] Many women simply live with it, unable to discuss the matter with their doctors. Those who do seek help are often pointed in the direction of training their pelvic muscles through the insertion of increasingly sized dilators into the vagina, or even of botox injections to deaden the pelvic muscles altogether. But, according to Peggy Kleinplatz, 'rather than training women to relax their muscles . . . we might want to pay closer attention to the feelings and cognitions that underlie their pain and constriction'.[215] While 'the causes of vaginismus are complex . . . they tend to include a history of trauma in the genital area including childhood sexual abuse or sexual assault in combination with being raised in sex-negative environments with little or no sex education'. The NHS 'Health A to Z' currently lists 'believing sex is shameful or wrong' among the top five causes.[216] In their book *Understanding Human Sexuality*, Janet Hyde and John Delamater examine the physical and psychological causes of sexual disorders, relating them either to low sexual excitation or high sexual inhibition.[217] They note the way in which prior learning 'inhibits the enjoyment of a full sexual response'.[218] In particular, '[m]any women whose sexual response is inhibited in adulthood were taught as children that no nice lady is interested in sex or enjoys it'.[219] Disgust with sex or with the body 'is the enemy of arousal'.[220]

In the early twentieth century, French writers saw women's experiences on the all-important marriage night as the cause of a whole wealth of sexual problems:

> The husband needs to keep in mind – although all of our doctors of sexuality seemed convinced that he won't – that the imprint of this first night on the woman is likely to be indelible:

'From that first night, her senses and her mind may bear a memory that will never be erased. According to what happens, that memory will be good or bad.' The 'moral' imprint of this event, to use a favored expression of the time, is such that, for better or for worse, the woman's sexual life is likely to be forever governed by the memory of her wedding night. It is the moment of greatest danger, the occasion par excellence for psychosexual trauma.[221]

[T]he cause of vaginismus is to be found in the man who, in most cases, did not show the delicacy of touch and the awareness of preliminary caresses that are owed each time he approaches the woman. He begins with a kind of rape, causing sharp pain, giving rise to insurmountable repulsion, and thus provoking vaginismus through moral impression.[222]

In some ways the French were forward thinking. According to a Dr Eynon, author of *Manuel de l'Amour Conjugal*, published in 1909, a husband 'must never forget under any circumstances that his spouse has as much right to the delightful sensations of love as he has'.[223] But, the fact that a woman was, and in many cases still is, expected to, in the space of one evening, cast aside 'all conventional prudish constraint' to make the most of sexual pleasure is no mean feat.

In addition to this, women were, and in some cases still are, walking on proverbial eggshells. As Katherine Angel notes, in the early twentieth century '[t]oo much – or too little – desire' was an indicator of developmental psychopathology as far as psychiatrists were concerned, one that 'involved the failure to adhere to norms of gender and femininity'.[224] Once married, women were expected to 'meet' their husband on the same sexual plane; anything else was 'understood as pathological frigidity or pathological nymphomania and the etiology of those disorders traced to traumatic events – very often a bad wedding night'.[225] In the 1950s and 1960s, Masters and Johnson's infamous studies of American couples, which used various measuring devices to monitor their sexual activity, estimated that only around ten per cent of the aetiology of sexual dysfunction was organic, meaning that 90 per cent was psychogenic, 'originating in sex-negative psychosocial expectations'.[226]

From a feminist perspective, sexual problems should be seen and treated not simply as individual problems, but as social problems resulting from patriarchal conditioning: the social expectation that women are passive rather than active creatures, that they are lacking in sexual desire, and that 'taking charge' of their sexual feelings is 'unfeminine'. One can ask is it any wonder that women sometimes struggle to become comfortable with their own sexual feelings, or to play an active as opposed to passive role in sexual relations, both of which act to facilitate orgasm and to limit pain, when they have been raised within the cult of female modesty?

The problem starts from a young age. Deborah Tolman's already mentioned interviews with teenagers provide a detailed look at adolescent desire and the double standards that exist in regard to boys and girls. Her book includes a powerful and poignant question from a teenage girl:

Is it right? Is it right that I should have yielded so soon, that I am so ardent, just as ardent and eager as Peter himself? May I, a girl, let myself go to this extent?[227]

The girl in question is Anne Frank.[228] While her words were written eighty years ago, they could well have been written more recently. The notion that women should not be sexually desirous, that desire is a threat rather than something to be embraced, is taught to us from a young age. What accompanies it is guilt and fear. As Tolman notes:

To act upon one's own sexual feelings and desire is still, for girls, to invite the risk of being known as a 'bad' girl, a girl who deserves any consequences she suffers, a girl who loses her eligibility for social and legal protections against sexual harm … The enduring split between 'good', chaste, feminine girls and 'bad', sexual, aberrant girls is a crucial aspect of societal denial of female adolescent sexual desire.[229]

We are as a society used to assuming that boys are dictated by their 'raging hormones'. We think it normal that they should feel intense sexual desire and to want to act on those desires. But, 'we have effectively de-sexualised girls' sexuality, substituting the desire for relationship and emotional connection for sexual feelings in their bodies'.[230] We define 'female adolescent sexuality only in terms of disease, victimisation, and morality and our avoidance of girls' own feelings of sexual desire and pleasure'.[231] With it, 'the possibility that girls might be interested in sexuality in their own right rather than as objects of boys' desire is met with resistance and discomfort'.[232]

We have already highlighted the pain and discomfort that can, as a result, accompany sexual intercourse. Related is the problem of 'sex guilt', which occurs where individual behaviour and taught values diverge.[233] When women acknowledge and 'give in' to their sexual desire, the feelings of guilt can be difficult to avoid. As summarised by Tara Emmers-Sommer and her co-researchers, '[s]ex guilt constitutes a feeling of shame or negative feeling as a result of failure to enact a set of standards that a person believes that should be enacted. The failure to live up to the standard indicates an internal set of psychological turmoil that causes some angst.'[234] Sex guilt can lead to 'the inhibition of sexual behaviors, struggle and discomfort with sexual temptation, and feelings of remorse regarding sexual activity'.[235] Among young American women, those who consider themselves to be more religious experience higher levels of guilt following sexual activity outside marriage, whether that involves contact with another person or solo masturbation.[236] Indeed, guilt has been shown to be the

most common emotional response to the first sexual encounter of Canadian teenagers,[237] and this guilt is felt to a greater
degree among females.[238] Within Christian communities, sex
guilt exists in regard to premarital sex whether or not that sex
occurred within a committed relationship and whether or not
the experience was positive or negative and, notably, the effect
lingers through to marriage: Christian women whose first
sexual encounter was outside marriage experience lower levels
of sexual satisfaction within marriage.[239] Furthermore, these
experiences of guilt are not restricted to a small minority; an
extensive study of young American couples found that while
those with more religious tendencies are less likely to engage
in premarital sex, the majority nevertheless do.

While around 97 per cent of non-religiously affiliated
Americans engage in sex before marriage, so too do 91 per cent
of Catholics and 84 per cent of conservative Protestants. The
most abstinent group of all are Mormons, where 'only' 57 per
cent have had sex before marriage. Overall, only 11 per cent
of all young couples actually abstain until marriage.[240] This
means that a lot of sex happens, but that that sex is burdened
with feelings of guilt, with women carrying the weight of this
guilt. Sex guilt can have implications not only for individual
enjoyment, but for romantic relationships: 'A sexless marriage,
for example, or a relationship that experiences curtailed sexual
behavior due to sex guilt could have negative implications for
the satisfaction or longevity of the relationship considering
that communicating about sexual desire tends [to] impact a
relationship positively.'[241]

Sex guilt isn't only an issue within Christian communities.
Women in any society that places value and emphasis on
virginity encounter the same feelings.[242] Sadly, women who
experience sex guilt have been shown to have noticeably lower
levels of life satisfaction.[243] You don't have to be a psychologist
to realise that 'developing a strong sense of self and engaging in authentic, meaningful, and joyful intimate relationships

requires an acknowledgement and acceptance of one's own bodily feelings'.[244]

At its worst, the modesty cult can destroy the capacity for sexual pleasure altogether. As anti-FGM/C activists make clear, the practice is a 'means of controlling' when, how and with whom 'a woman has sex'.[245] Rethinking and eradicating FGM/C requires us to stop seeing women's sexuality as dangerous and to value women's sexual health and pleasure.[246]

Sex is a normal part of human life, but the fear, guilt and shame that accompanies it, particularly in the modern world where pregnancy and STIs are not the risks they once were, should not be seen as natural; the fear, guilt and shame is a social construction.[247] If we want to 'protect' women from the 'bad' side of sexuality, such as preventing unintended pregnancies, STIs, and eliminating rape and violence, that is fully understandable. But, as Tolman notes, achieving these goals requires something other than 'purity culture':

> If these risks [really] were our deepest concerns, we would be pouring funds into effective, accessible forms of birth control and protection against diseases, providing comprehensive sexuality education, widely disseminating information on masturbation and mutual masturbation as the safest forms of sexual exploration, declaring 'zero tolerance' for sexual violence or the threat of it and for homophobia.[248]

The virginity pledge agenda achieves none of these things. It is perfectly possible to tackle the risks associated with sex without also forcing on women the notion that virginity is the ideal and that women who have sex are 'sluts'. For too long, women's sexual desire has been depicted as dangerous, either for themselves or for their community. It is time to scrutinise and dismantle the man-made obstacles that stand in the way of women feeling and acting on their own sexual desire. Women are not sexual objects who exist to please others; they have their own sexual desires that deserve to be recognised and set free from guilt and shame.[249]

Conclusion

Throughout numerous societies, rich and poor, there exists a seemingly universal and inbuilt belief that modest women are both more worthy than other women and deserving of greater respect. Immodest women by contrast, are seen as 'used cars', 'fair game' and social pollutants. Armed with the Madonna–Whore distinction, parents and communities often wish to raise girls in a way that protects their worth, a worth that can so easily be dissolved in a momentary lapse. But, as we have seen throughout this chapter, rather than protecting women and girls, the modesty cult leaves them in a more, not less, vulnerable position.

The modesty cult manifests itself in different ways in different parts of the world. In some, including in parts of west and central Africa, it leads to the withdrawal of girls from school, and early marriage. In others, including in the Middle East and North Africa, it leads to women being restricted in terms of their ability to leave the home to engage in paid work. In Evangelical America, it leads to victim-blaming and unnecessary sexual risk-taking. And in all societies where the modesty cult is strong, women are exposed to greater violence, whether in the form of FGM/C, street-based harassment, intimate partner violence or honour killings.

Rather than covering women up, isolating them from men, shaming them for seeking medical help, and encouraging them to sign 'virginity pledges', we should instead be questioning the cult of female modesty. Despite what its proponents claim, rather than helping women, the cult of female modesty leaves every woman in a vulnerable and precarious position. As Catherine MacKinnon notes, '[v]irtuous girls' are 'up on those pedestals from which they must be brought down' while 'unvirtuous girls . . . deserve whatever they get'.[250] As R. Eberle sums it up, 'female modesty when "enclosed" by masculine mockery and violence seems dangerously fragile'.[251] Each day is a constant battle to maintain an unsullied reputation; and, once that reputation is sullied, it is often irredeemable. A woman risks a shift from respect to worthlessness with every single gust of wind and with every single encounter with a man. Rather than living a life filled with study, exploration and enjoyment, the focus of life instead becomes fending off the forces of nature and avoiding those who get kicks from embarrassing and demeaning a woman, whether by forcibly removing her headscarf, peeping and photographing under her skirt, or circulating photographs without consent. By challenging the idea that a woman's worth, value and respect depend on her bodily modesty, we place women in a much stronger, as opposed to a weaker, position.

None of this means that every woman should be running around scantily clad, and having sex at every possible opportunity. What it means is that women should be able to take charge and make decisions for themselves, rather than being pushed in one direction or another. There is nothing wrong with a woman covering up, just as there is nothing wrong with a woman not doing so, as long as she is choosing either action for herself. There is equally nothing wrong with a woman abstaining from sex, just as there is nothing wrong with a woman enjoying numerous sexual encounters, as long as this happens of her own choosing. We should be capable of respecting women whether or not they are 'virgins' and whether or not they cover up. If it is possible to respect men who have enjoyed lots of sex, as well as men who enjoy the sunshine topless, why can't we equally respect women who do the same?

The evidence we have uncovered in this chapter speaks for itself: countries and communities where virginity is most highly prized are not paragons of gender equality. Women pay a price for their modesty, whether in terms of education, work, safety, health or sexual pleasure. In contrast, those countries that do lead in gender equality terms have a more liberal attitude to the body, valuing women on the basis of things other than their bodily modesty. Questioning the idea that a woman's value and respect rest on her bodily modesty is vital to challenging the policies and practices that harm women's lives across the world and to improving women's sexual and physical health.

Chapter 3

The Modesty Cult: The Causes

Almost 2,500 years ago, Phryne walked naked into the sea at a public festival. While it earned her the role of life model for one of Greece's most famous artists, it also landed her in court on the charge of 'impiety', for which the penalty was death.[1] More than two millennia on, in 1931 New York, another nude model, Audrey Munson, was also locked away, but this time in a mental asylum. Munson had modelled for many of the statues that grace the buildings and landmarks of New York City to this day. She was also the first woman to appear fully naked on film. The confidence with which she used her body meant that her life veered from celebrity to scandal and, ultimately, the asylum.[2] Fast forward to the 1960s and, in Indonesia, in response to the entry of women into the workforce, virginity testing was introduced for women applying for the military and the police.[3] Then, in 2011, in the middle of the Arab Spring, the Egyptian military began virginity testing female protesters as a form of intimidation.[4] A year later, in 2012, in Morocco, a 15-year-old girl, Amina Filali, was raped by a 23-year-old man. She was subsequently forced to marry him to preserve her respectability. She committed suicide, drinking rat poison and falling dead in the street.[5] Around this same time, a Kuwaiti woman was denied custody of her children after photographs came to light of her wearing a bikini.[6] In July 2019, three Iranian women were sentenced to more than thirty years in prison for removing their hijabs.[7] In that same year, an American high-school swimmer was initially disqualified from winning a swimming competition because her school-issued swimsuit was judged indecent.[8] In 2022, having already limited the educational opportunities of girls and the working opportunities of women, the Taliban compelled all women in Afghanistan to cover their heads.

In this chapter, we ask a simple question: Why is modesty culture common to so many countries and time periods, each with its own particular modesty standards and practices? Why should women's bodily modesty matter? And why are some countries and eras more steeped in modesty culture than others? While practicality might have some role to play – the need to keep warm, to protect ourselves from the sun, or to avoid STDs – it cannot explain the gendered nature of the modesty cult. To find answers, we therefore need to hunt far and wide, drawing on religion, biology, geography, economics, warfare, politics and sociology. As we will see, many early societies placed few constraints on women's sexuality, but, as agriculture developed, as economies grew, as wealth inequality emerged, as population blossomed, and as human beings took up arms, women's virginity became a valuable asset, both in terms of the marriage market and as a means of controlling who could or could not reproduce, and with whom. Immodest women became a threat to fatherhood, a threat to inheritance, a threat to population control and a threat to group identity. The state and religious authorities conspired to further the level of repression, while competition between women led to modesty practices snowballing. But, just as societies can tip in one direction, they can also tip in the other. The modesty cult may be common, and it may, at present, be on the rise, but it is not immovable.

It's Not All About Religion

From the Bible's story of Adam and Eve to the Quran's command that the wives of Muhammad engage with the world
from behind their hijab, it would be easy to blame religion
for modesty culture. According to Elizabeth Cady Stanton
(1815–1902), the early American feminist, organised religion
of all kinds is the major agent of women's sexual subordination.[9] Farha Ternikar has noted the many similarities between
modesty culture in Islam, Christianity and Judaism.[10] And, if
anything, the 'modesty' strands within these religions are on
the rise rather than decline today. Despite the predictions of
Galileo and Mark Twain,[11] religion is here to stay and provides
one possible explanation for society's continued obsession
with female modesty.

More than 80 per cent of people globally consider themselves religious, 32 per cent declaring themselves Christian,
23 per cent Muslim, 15 per cent Hindu, 7 per cent Buddhist
and 0.2 per cent Jewish.[12] Islam is the world's fastest growing
religion, and is predicted to surpass Christianity by the year
2070.[13] While Christianity is on the decline in the West, it is on
the rise in Africa. According to research from the Pew Research
Center, 'Africa is set to be the global centre of Christianity.'[14]
Evangelical Christianity is the 'fastest-growing segment of the
global Christian Church',[15] growing at a rate of 2.6 per cent a
year – more than double that of Christianity more broadly, and
faster than Islam.

In the West, Islam in particular is often in the spotlight
in regard to women's rights, and some have identified a correlation between Islam and gender inequality and, even more
specifically, between Islam and sexual repression.[16] But,
as one Muslim women's activist notes: 'There are so many
rights given to women in the Quran that are not found in
the books of any other religion. But the religious authorities
mislead people, they misuse their position.'[17] Feminist writers

such as Fatema Mernissi and Leila Ahmed have challenged some of the more patriarchal interpretations of Islam, such as Wahhabism and Salafism, including by questioning compulsory head coverings.[18]

Within Judaism, Zvi Triger notes that 'the enforcement of gender segregation is relatively new, both in Jewish history and in the history of the State of Israel. Even less controversial forms of segregation (at least in Israel), such as in synagogues, are only about 900 years old ... The representation of the modesty requirement by current advocates of gender segregation as an essential part of Jewish law and culture is therefore an ideological repositioning.'[19]

In Christian circles, the saintly sex-negative trio, Paul, Tertullian and Augustine, promoted modesty culture for women, while blaming womankind for the sins of men, but the Bible provides mixed messaging that can serve interpretations spanning from extreme sexism to feminist liberation. While male misogynists focused in on aspects of scripture that supported women's subordination, early Christian women reinterpreted religious scriptures as a means of challenging patriarchal thought, forming their own Christian feminist consciousness.[20] Infinite variety can still be found within Christianity today. Modern-day American Evangelical Christianity champions 'purity culture', offering virginity pledges and purity balls, and equating women's worth with their sexual behaviour.[21] According to Shaunti Feldhahn and Lisa Rice's guide, *For Young Women Only: What You Need to Know About How Guys Think*, '[y]our virginity is the one thing that you can give only once to your spouse. Spend it wisely.'[22] By contrast, Christians for Biblical Equality (CBE), founded in 1988, offer a new interpretation of the Bible in which 'Adam was no less culpable than Eve'. They argue that the 'rulership of Adam over Eve [was] ... not a part of the original created order', and they are not afraid to critique 'purity culture'. According to one of their writers, '[t]he irony is that purity culture is anything but pure. It is woven with oppression and lies. It is yet another weapon of patriarchy to control and marginalise women . . . the church will continue to breed shame, sexual dysfunction, and pain until purity culture is rejected and replaced with a new ideology.'[23]

Even nakedness has a much less straightforward history within the Judeo-Christian tradition than might at first be apparent. Jewish baptism traditionally involved the immersion of a naked body in water, as did early Christian baptism. Nakedness was also a way of life for a handful of saints (including St Mary of Egypt, St Onuphrius, St Vassily and St Francis of Assisi). And, in the Quaker tradition, the nude body came to be associated with prophecy.[24] In fact, Christian theologians of the medieval era categorised nakedness into four kinds: the state of humanity before the Fall; poverty or voluntary rejection of earthly goods; innocence and truth before God; and lust and vanity (with only the latter being known as *nuditus criminalis*).[25]

Not only can religion be channelled in numerous different directions, but many modesty-based rules existed long before today's major religions, while some of the practices that have come to be associated with religion, such as FGM/C and honour killings, are altogether absent from religious texts.[26] In advance of Christianity and Islam, virginity and chastity were already central to male honour throughout the eastern Mediterranean and Middle East,[27] and head coverings were as common in Ancient Greece as they were in early Christianity and Islam.

While, as we will see, religion has certainly been a powerful tool to preach and propagate modesty culture, the variation within and between religions and the prior existence of the modesty cult suggests that we need to go much deeper if we are to explain it. So too does the presence of modesty culture outside religious circles. In their interviews with young American men at the start of the twenty-first century, Shaunti

Feldhahn and Lisa Ann Rice found that while nine in ten Christians wanted to marry a virgin, so too did six out of ten men who described themselves as being unreligious.[28] And it is, of course, not only within religious circles that the words 'whore', 'slut' and 'slag' represent an insult. So, what else might explain the cult of female modesty?

The Biological Curse

Is female modesty a natural tendency, biologically inbuilt? Is it a natural defence mechanism that women adopt in a world in which sex is not always consensual and comes with the possibility of unwanted pregnancy? Are women who behave or dress in an immodest way in an impossible battle with biology? And, is there a natural preference among heterosexual men for a modest partner, with a view to ensuring that their offspring truly are their own? In other words, when immodest women are treated as worthless and unrespectable, is it a result of societal attitudes that are open to change, or is it a result of biologically inbuilt behaviour from which it is difficult to escape?

While biology is reasonably constant over time and so cannot by itself explain why some societies and some time periods have placed more emphasis on modesty than others, it could nevertheless act as an anchor, creating a pendulum effect, meaning that as we swing away from female modesty, we will at some point swing back, resulting in periods of modesty revival, such as the one that is underway today. So, does biology have anything to offer in terms of explaining the modesty cult?

Paternity uncertainty is at the heart of scientific explanations for patriarchy. While the mother of a child can always be known, the father cannot. According to socio-biologists, this uncertainty created an evolutionary advantage for men who sought to monitor and restrict the freedom of their female partners. In the words of Roy Baumeister and Jean Twenge, 'men want to pass on their genes, and because a woman can have only about one child per year, men jealously guard their female mates to prevent other men from possibly impregnating them'.[29]

One way of gauging the difference that paternity uncertainty makes to the cult of female modesty is to consider societies in which belief systems create a disconnect between pregnancy and sex. The sexual permissiveness of Trobriand Islanders in Melanesia was commented upon at length by Bronislaw Malinowski (1932), including women's freedom to engage in premarital sex, and to divorce a partner after marriage. For the Islanders, sexual intercourse and pregnancy have historically been considered two separate things, breaking concerns about paternity uncertainty. Pregnancy was traditionally believed to arise because of spiritual forces and, as a consequence, was not believed to require male assistance. In some indigenous American populations, including the lowland south Amerindians and the Bari of Venezuela, intercourse with multiple men is considered necessary 'to "build" the offspring', which also leads to limited policing of women's sexuality, as men are not in competition when it comes to paternity.[30] Children are thought of as having multiple fathers, known as partible paternity. This system has the advantage that it allows women to draw on the resources of a whole community of men, 'resulting in an increased likelihood of carrying pregnancies to term, and higher infant survival'.[31] Rather than virginity being the route to female success, women with multiple partners have the upper hand.

Where, however, the link between sex and reproduction is known, paternity uncertainty can weigh heavily on the minds of men. Alongside the problem of paternity uncertainty is the possibility of rape. Men may, as a result, prefer women who do everything possible to avoid attracting the attention of other males. After all, not only is consensual sex a risk to paternity, so too is nonconsensual sex. According to the controversial evolutionary-psychologist Donald Symons, because males can 'potentially sire offspring at almost no cost . . . selection favors male attempts to copulate with fertile females whenever this potential can be realised'.[32] Rape, he argues, is a side-effect of evolutionarily selected adaptations which maximise men's mating success, and with it the reproduction of the human species. So too, accordingly, is what some see as male sexual obsession: 'the human male's greater visual sexual arousal, greater autonomous sex drive, reduced ability to abstain from sexual activity, much greater desire for sexual variety per se, greater willingness to engage in impersonal sex, and less dis-criminating criteria for sexual partners'.[33] Randy Thornhill and Craig Palmer's *A Natural History of Rape* agrees. While this type of evolutionary explanation for rape has been controver-sial, with some interpreting explanation as justification, the threat of rape also has a central place within feminist writ-ing. While many feminists argue that sexual violence is the result of socialisation rather than biology, not everyone agrees. According to Susan Brownmiller, author of *Against Our Will*: 'Men's structural capacity to rape and woman's corresponding structural vulnerability are as basic to the physiology of both our sexes as the primal act of sex itself.'[34] Ironically, the female anti-suffragists of the late nineteenth century also agreed, arguing that men had a physical superiority and ability to rape that left women inherently vulnerable. Separate spheres, with women restricted to the home, were, they argued, the best form of protection. By entering the world of work and politics, women were, they thought, embracing a poisoned chalice. Today, Louise Perry advises young women to avoid being alone with unfamiliar men and argues that liberal feminism has 'done a terrible thing in advising inexperienced young women to seek out situations in which they are alone and drunk with horny men who are . . . bigger and stronger than they are'.[35]

The fear of rape remains central to the minds of many parents and partners today. On a Saturday evening in July 1991, at St Kizito Mixed Secondary School in Kenya, a gang of male students attacked female classmates in the girls' dormitory. Seventy-one were raped and nineteen were killed.[36] Sexual harassment and abuse has recently been identified as a major factor contributing to the withdrawal of girls from school:[37] for example, evidence from Tajikistan finds that 15 per cent of girls who are out of school 'reported that parents or other relatives had prevented them from going to school because of concerns for their safety'.[38] In sub-Saharan Africa, there is mounting evidence of male teachers demanding 'sexual favours in exchange for good grades, preferential treatment in class, money and gifts', and in Ghana, Kenya and Mozambique, girls have reported a fear of retaliation if they refuse the sexual advances of male teachers. In Mozambique, where less than a quarter of girls complete education to the lower secondary level, four out of five schoolgirls report experiencing violence in school 'including instances of male teachers asking girls for sexual favours in exchange for passing grades'.[39] In Malawi, 22 per cent of girls have reported that they have missed school due to 'unwanted sexual experiences' while, in Honduras, more than one in two girls say that they have not attended school at some point as a result of the violence they have faced from teachers.[40] In northern Nigerian states, such as Borno, Adamawa and Yobe, continued conflict has served to magnify fears of sexual violence. In 2014, Boko Haram abducted 279 girls from a Chibok school, and the kidnapping of girls has continued since, meaning that 'taking girls out of school or entering girls into marriage can seem like protective safety measures amid targeted attacks on girls' schools, abductions and violence'.[41]

Taken together, the twin biological forces that are paternity uncertainty and rape could combine to create what may be thought of as an incentive for men to police female partners and kin. At the same time, women may be encouraged to embrace modesty as a means of protection in a world in which rape is, we are told, hardwired into mankind.[42] But, by itself, biology makes it very difficult to explain differences across countries, such as why modern-day Iran, Pakistan and Afghanistan are more within the grip of modesty culture than, say, Britain, Germany or New Zealand. And biology changes too slowly to explain the sometimes rapid swings in modesty culture. To help explain the cross-country and cross-time differences in modesty culture, we therefore need to look at the way biology interacts with other factors, including kinship, geography, property rights, inequality, population pressure and armed conflict, producing a whole range of different outcomes – from sexual permissiveness to the complete seclusion of women.

Kinship

For paternity uncertainty to produce modesty culture, men need to stay put. Desertion after mating is, of course, common in the animal kingdom, and, in so far as we can tell, few animals seem to value female modesty. In a world of 'cads' rather than 'dads', paternity becomes moot and so too therefore does modesty: guarding women's sexual behaviour would not only be pointless, it would be counterproductive. Only where conditions favour long-term relationships is the door open to the cult of female modesty.

Evolutionary biologists Hanna Kokko and Michael Jennions suggest that whether 'dads' or 'cads' proliferate in the biological race depends on whether the mortality rate is higher when men are competing or when they are caring.[43] If men find it easier to survive and pass on their genes when they form families, rather than when they mate and desert, 'dad' genes proliferate.

Environmental change is one factor that had a powerful effect on the survival chances of 'dads' versus 'cads'. Between

five and eight million years ago, Africa began to experience
drought. The land dried out and food was harder to source.
The most successful communities were those where people
cooperated rather than abandoned one another. Where that
occurred, infants were healthier and, as a result, 'dad' genes
proliferated.[44] While on one level, women benefited as they
were no longer left literally 'holding the baby', on another level
it gave men all the more reason to worry about paternity – and,
with it, to impose modesty requirements, whether in the form
of veiling, seclusion or through more physical means.

There was, however, another solution: matrilineality. While
the father of a child cannot be known for sure, the mother certainly can be, and so it might have historically made sense for
lineage to be traced through the female rather than the male
line. Within a matrilineal system, rather than favouring sons,
'grandparents bias their investment in favour of daughters/
daughters' offspring rather than sons/sons' offspring, and men
bias their investment in favour of sisters' offspring rather than
wife's/partner's offspring'.[45] This is because it is the children of
women who are guaranteed to be their own. Of course, when
human beings were few and far between and land was abundant, greater value was attributed to people rather than land.
Additional people presented minimal cost in terms of land
and resources, and may even have brought benefits in terms of
providing extra hands for the community. Women were also
therefore highly valued by their families and communities as
the creators of new life, and repressing their sexuality made
little sense.

Matrilineal societies in the present day include the Mosuo
of China, the Akan of Ghana, the Bribri of Costa Rica and the
Jarai of south-east Asia,[46] but Victorian anthropologists proposed that all societies were, in their early days, matrilineal.[47]
Though this is now considered something of an exaggeration,
evidence certainly does suggest that many more societies were
matrilineal in the past than today. While numerous societies

have shifted from matrilineal to patrilineal kinship over the course of human history, it is very rare for a transition to take place in the opposite direction.[48] With time, more and more human societies have therefore moved in the patrilineal direction, with descent, rank and property passed down the male, as opposed to female, line.

While in matrilineal societies there is less reason to police women's bodies and behaviour, in patrilineal societies paternity uncertainty poses much more of a threat, which makes female modesty much more important. Alice Evans summarises the consequences for women:

> In patrilineal societies, the function of women is to produce sons who would perpetuate their husbands' lineage. This generates profound anxiety about women's sexuality. Since the paternity of sons must never be in doubt, the slightest hint of sexual activity by a woman outside the confines of marriage constitute[s] a threat to the social order. The entire sense of honour and shame in a patrilineal society is bound up in the sexual propriety of women. Therefore, the whole society is organised around removing any and all doubt about the virginity of unmarried women and the fidelity of wives.[49]

Where patrilineal kinship structures favour marriages within the same family, such as cousin marriage, modesty norms are even stronger. Evidence from Kurdish communities in Iraq suggests that women who marry cousins are more likely to be the victim of an honour killing.[50] In these strong kinship networks, women's sexuality is tightly policed to ensure that reproduction takes place within the limits of the kinship group, preventing 'outsiders' from polluting the clan or getting their hands on the family's assets. Biological studies of the gene pool confirm that such restrictions have been very successful; there are few 'leaks' into or out of the gene pool where kinship ties are especially strong.[51] By contrast, where kinship struc-

tures are weaker, as has long been the case in Europe, where
the Catholic Church clamped down on cousin marriage and
encouraged nuclear as opposed to extended families,[52] women
have experienced relatively less policing.

If we want to explain the modesty cult, it therefore helps to
understand how and why patrilineal kinship emerged, usurping the types of societal structures that cared less for policing
women's bodies. It also helps, more generally, to understand
why kinship came to be of more (or lesser) importance in some
parts of the world than others. As we will see, developments in
agriculture and the establishment of private property, along
with widening inequality, expanding populations and conflict,
all had a role to play.

Agriculture

When human beings moved around, foraged the land and
practised slash-and-burn horticulture, secluding women was
as impractical as it was costly. In extreme and uncertain environments, sexual freedom may even have had something to
offer. Committing to, and relying on, a single partner may have
been risky; if your partner died, you and your children could
be in an impossible fight for survival. In Maasai and Inuit culture, infidelity has traditionally been not only permitted but
encouraged, and involves not only the 'sharing of spouses as
sexual partners, but as domestic and productive partners'.[53]
In the Himba population of north-west Namibia, 'there is an
informal rule that a man should not return home after dark
if he is kept away late, as arriving at night could cause him to
find his wife with her lover'.[54] While arranged marriages are
not uncommon for first marriages among the Himba, women
frequently divorce, extra-marital births are not stigmatised,
and it is 'common and normative for both men and women to
have non-marital partners'.[55] In fact, the Himba can lay claim

to having the highest ever recorded rate of extra-paternity: 48 per cent of children are fathered by 'someone other than the husband'.[56] They also possess a fosterage system, one in which grandmothers play a key role. The Himba practise bilateral descent, which means that every person belongs to two tribes, maximising their chances of survival.

Where the fruits of the land were, or became, more certain, in part thanks to developments in farming, it opened the door to the modesty cult. Where human beings began to shift away from a hunter-gatherer existence, to farm the land, to breed livestock and to build homes, it also became physically possible to box women into a corner (or, more accurately, a hut).[57] While the so-called Neolithic Revolution might have been a technological revolution for mankind, it was a retrograde step as far as women's freedoms were concerned. This was particularly the case where farming the land required brute strength: little required more muscle power than the plough. In parts of the world where the land was best suited to plough production, women today are still less likely to work outside the home and are more likely to veil themselves in public.[58] Men have become accustomed to mixing beyond the home while women's contribution has been sidelined into sex and babies, with modesty practices to guarantee paternity.

The plough wasn't the only enemy of womankind; so too was pastoral farming, particularly where it required a nomadic existence.[59] While early farmers often combined arable and pastoral farming, with time they came to specialise. Livestock and those who looked after them were increasingly on the move, pushed to terrain that was unsuited to growing crops, and heading off in search of additional grassland to feed their expanding herds. Expanding herds along with marginal terrain required the seasonal movement of livestock, often by quite some distance. It was, in other words, easier to take animals to water (and fodder) than it was to bring water (and fodder) to animals. The domestication of the horse, which enabled humans to move with greater ease, made this even more of a reality. The resultant pastoralism generated spousal separation: men were away from their female partner(s) for protracted lengths of time. This increased the perception of men's (relative to women's) contribution to production, and also raised fears of paternity uncertainty, in response to which men sought to guard their mates from competing males.[60] While there are exceptions, such as the Himba of Namibia (where the harsh environment worked in the opposing direction), nomadic pastoralism has often come hand-in-hand with a shift from matrilineal to patrilineal family structures, thereby making paternity uncertainty more of a concern in terms of guaranteeing the male lineage and avoiding valuable inheritable livestock being placed in the wrong hands.[61]

Nomadic pastoralism initially took off in the Eurasian Steppes, which stretch all the way from eastern Europe to Manchuria, and by 2000 BCE it was diffusing in all directions, eventually reaching central Asia, north-western India, the Mediterranean and eastern Africa. From eastern Africa, around two thousand years ago, it subsequently spread across the African continent into the south-west, usurping hunter-gatherer matrilineal societies along the way.[62] This historic dispersal has been linked to everything from the seclusion and veiling of women to female genital mutilation, all of which can be thought of as limiting women's ability to engage in non-marital sex.[63] In her extensive study, Anke Becker found that women from ethnic groups that were traditionally pastoralist have less freedom of movement, are more accepting of intimate partner violence, adhere to stricter and more restrictive sexual norms, and are more likely to have experienced FGM/C.[64]

Thankfully the horse-backed pastoralists did not take over the world. In some cases, geography acted to limit their spread: where natural barriers existed, whether in the form of the oceans or the tsetse fly, women's lives were on average less encumbered by the modesty cult. Women in western

Europe, in America and in south-east Asia escaped the worst of
nomadic pastoral culture – all parts of the world where there is
(relatively) less of a history of modesty culture. In the parts of
China where rice farming was historically more common than
either plough-based or pastoralist farming, foot-binding and
other modesty practices also became less widespread than they
did in the surrounding areas.[65] America, the land of the bean,
historically escaped both the plough and nomadic pastoralism (at least until Europeans arrived). In the South American
Andes, the textile-based contributions of women, including
in the form of gigantic fishing nets, rivalled the contributions
of men.[66] In western Europe, which in terms of the Neolithic
Revolution was late to the party, the hunter-gatherer way of
life lived on for longer and modesty norms had less time to
take root.

Property

Newly ploughed fields and expanding herds were of great
value, providing men with an incentive to assert ownership,
and to seek an heir. According to Friedrich Engels, the famous
compatriot of Karl Marx, it was this arrival of private property, hot on the heels of agricultural development, that first
gave rise to patriarchy. In the same way that Marx saw private
property as being at the root of wealth inequality, Engels saw
private property as being at the root of gender inequality. He
argued that the hunter-gatherer state was one of primitive
communism in which men and women worked cooperatively
to achieve the common goal of subsistence.[67] But, once livestock farming developed and became private property, with
the rights held by male herders, sexist practices set in, with
propertyless women becoming dependent on men. Unable to
support themselves and their offspring without being under
the thumb of a man, women were left with little choice but

to bow down to the male insistence on purity as a means of guaranteeing paternity.

For the anthropologist G.P. Murdock, movable wealth (such as livestock) was of particular importance to the shift in power between men and women, as it allowed men to free themselves from matrilineal family life and to build a life beyond their wife's family or their sisters' kin, offering them the opportunity to pass on an inheritance 'to their own sons rather than to their sororal nephews'.[68] In a matrilineal system, while men can acquire wealth, that wealth tends to be destined for their sisters' children (who are guaranteed to be close in bloodline) rather than their own children (over which the threat of paternity uncertainty hangs). When people lived communally off the land, this matrilineal system may not have been all that frustrating to men. But, where they could become individually wealthy, they may have had a preference to pass on their wealth to their own children, rather than to their sisters' children. Of course, to ensure that they really were their own children, this came hand in hand with a preference for 'pure' wives. And so once movable wealth entered the picture, patrilineal families increasingly usurped matrilineal ones, and modesty requirements for prospective wives became all the more important.

Andrey Korotayev, Alexander Kazankov and Alice Schlegel have studied multiple traditional societies, finding that where property changes hands upon marriage, whether through brideprice, dowry or other means, virginity is held in high regard.[69] Furthermore, where private property exists, women can themselves be seen as property and, according to the somewhat blunt Lawrence Stone, men prefer 'purchasing new and not second-hand goods'.[70]

For Engels, and for socialist feminists, a return to communal ownership, with communal care for the next generation, allows women to be liberated from the need to repress their sexuality, as they would no longer be dependent on men.[71] In the Soviet Union, women were not only free to exit the sphere of domesticity, they were also free to control their own fertility. Soviet campaigns in central Asia sold themselves as 'liberating' women by eradicating seclusion and veiling.[72] In a communal world where, in theory, everyone is taken care of, no woman is dependent on a man, and no child is born 'illegitimate'. And, as we have already noted, hunter-gatherer societies which share food and resources tend to be sexually permissive. By contrast, where markets have introduced opportunities for the individual acquisition of wealth, such as in mining or in tourism, as has been the case in south-west China and in parts of Africa, kinship systems have begun to shift away from matrilineal to patrilineal structures.[73]

But the extent to which private property really does hurt women's freedom, including their sexual freedom, ultimately depends on the degree to which markets offer opportunities for women and, in particular, opportunities that take them beyond the home. Historically, where women were able to engage in paid work outside the home, such as working as dairy-maids, or spinning and weaving in factories, modesty norms carried high financial costs; families faced a trade-off between honour and income, and the financial temptations, particularly when faced with meeting basic needs, made a culture of modesty rather expensive. Opportunities for paid work enabled women to escape the clutches of family; young women could credibly stand up to seclusion and arranged marriages, as they could support themselves financially through their work. This was for example the case in Europe after the Black Death in the fourteenth century, when European farms faced shortages of male labour, leading farmers to turn to women. In the north-western edge of Europe, including in Britain and the Netherlands, where low-lying geography had already contributed to the early emergence of markets, allowing people to survive without strong kinship ties, women were particularly responsive to labour market opportunities. In the twentieth century, economic transformation in East Asia also opened up job opportunities for women. Young women left their villages behind to move to the expanding cities. They earned their own income, sent money home to their parents, and escaped the social constraints of their home communities. Perhaps unsurprisingly therefore, East Asia began its own escape from the modesty cult as opportunities for women to earn outside the home expanded, which made it 'costly' for women to stay at home; there were, in other words, financial benefits to reneging on footbinding, seclusion and veiling.[74] And the more other families 'reneged', the more likely your own family was to do likewise. The metaphorical snowball was set in motion.

What is important here is whether work-based opportunities exist beyond the home. Economists have long argued that where production has historically depended on male as opposed to female labour, women are in a weaker position.[75] But there are also cases in which women's economic contribution has been high and it has had the opposite effect. In a sense, the more valuable women are, whether as producers or reproducers, the more others may wish to dominate and exploit them. Foot-binding was, for example, more common in the regions of China where women's textile work was substantial. Melissa Brown and Damian Satterthwaite-Phillips argue that foot-binding was a means for families to capture the economic value of their daughters, by restricting them to the home, where they were tasked with producing handicraft items that could be taken to market and sold for a high price.[76] More generally, even where women have not been busy either in the fields or taking livestock to water, they have nevertheless made significant contributions to human survival in the form of reproductive, caring and domestic labour, but this has not guaranteed their freedom. It is, therefore, when women have economic opportunities that take them beyond the home and beyond their family that these opportunities are best able to support women's freedoms, sexual and otherwise.

There are, however, two potential problems along the way. The first is the proverbial chicken and egg: women taking advantage of economic opportunity beyond the home risk their reputation. And, where this is the case, policies and social practices may actively dissuade women's economic participation. Economic opportunities require abandonment of the modesty cult, but abandonment of the modesty cult requires economic opportunities. This creates a modesty trap, one that may only be overcome if a critical mass of women going out to work is reached quickly enough. The second problem is a reputational asymmetry. Markets, unencumbered by policies and practices that forcibly limit the employment of women, care far less about reputation than do families and communities. Where women's lives go beyond their family, where they can support themselves independently, family honour becomes less important to individual women. But, ties being cut in one direction do not mean that they are also cut in the other. A woman's family may still be dependent on her reputation for modesty, even if her own life has become less restricted by it. Where a family's survival depends on social networks, and participation in those networks depends on the family's reputation, transgressions by female members of kin can have serious ramifications: your father's job could be at stake; customers may no longer wish to buy from your family's market stall; richer members of your clan or caste may no longer wish to lend to you; and the sons of promising families may no longer wish to marry your sisters. Honour killings are commonly used to punish women to maintain the broader family's reputation. And this serves to make every woman think twice before taking a leap into the unknown. Only, therefore, when the survival of the wider family no longer depends on female 'honour' can this backlash be escaped. And that in turn depends on family honour being disconnected from female modesty: through market connections (or the communist state) replacing family based connections.

These two obstacles help to explain why economic opportunity has not lured women out of the home across the globe.
In South Asia, even in regions that have witnessed substantial
economic growth, the modesty cult has held on tight and
many women have remained house-bound. As Alice Evans
notes, 'even as commerce flourished in the early 1900s, many
castes in Uttar Pradesh restricted female mobility because they
prioritised honour over earnings. Ahir men prevented women
from selling milk. Urban Dalits put their wives in seclusion.
When mills opened in Calcutta, Bengali women worked from
home at a third of the factory wage.'[77] In many Indian communities, women have remained in the home, despite their
increasingly high levels of education, and falling fertility rates.
Economic opportunities have been sacrificed to maintain
family honour.

In sum, therefore, economic growth appears to be most
liberating for women where family ties, especially those of a
patrilineal nature, are less strong and where economic opportunities are evenly distributed both between the sexes and, as
we will see next, between the social classes.

Growth and Inequality

Is the modesty cult at its heart a symptom of 'underdevelop-
ment', something that has the potential to correct itself over
time as economies grow and human survival becomes easier?
Looking at economies across the world today, it certainly seems
to be the case that women appear to be more free in richer, as
opposed to poorer, regions. But looking across the longer span
of history suggests that the relationship between the economy
and the modesty cult is much more complicated. In the earliest
days of humanity, when we lived as hunter-gatherers, locking
women up and keeping watch on their every move was simply
not practical. And, as we have noted, including with reference

to some of today's remaining hunter-gatherer tribes, immodesty, not modesty, paid.

Subsequent economic growth was associated with modesty crackdowns as much as it was associated with lifting the modesty cult. Just as the Neolithic Revolution failed to bring benefits to women, the British Industrial Revolution of the nineteenth century also let women down. As heavy industry expanded, such as in mining and iron and steel, jobs increasingly depended on muscle power. At the same time, agriculture mechanised, creating a further marriage between muscle and machinery. The best women could hope for was being born into a comfortable family, having a lucrative and dependable marital match, and, as the twentieth century emerged, being able to draw on a national welfare system that took account of reproduction, offering some form of 'child benefit' to mothers. As women retreated from the workforce, not only did the cult of domesticity set in, so too did the cult of female modesty.

Where economic growth has brought increasing wealth at the top of the ladder, it has provided wealthy families in particular with reason to police their daughters. By secluding their daughters, a family can protect them from seducers – from men who might be interested in a young woman more for her family's status and property than for herself. Alice Schlegel thereby argues that:

> [V]irginity is valued in those societies in which young men may seek to better their chances in life by allying themselves through marriage to a wealthy or powerful family. In preserving a daughter's virginity, a family is protecting her from seduction, impregnation, and paternity claims on her child . . . In societies in which dowry is given (or daughters inherit), it would be attractive to seduce a dowered daughter (or heiress), demanding her as wife along with her property. Her parents would be reluctant to refuse, since the wellbeing of their grandchildren

would depend upon their inheritance from both of their parents, and another man would be unlikely to marry the mother
if it meant that he had not only to support her children but also
to make them his heirs.[78]

Indeed, as Michel Foucault noted in his *History of Sexuality*,
sexually repressive practices often have roots within the practices of the elites: 'the most rigorous techniques [of sexual
repression] were formed and, more particularly, applied first,
with the greatest intensity, in the economically privileged and
politically dominant classes'.[79] While Marxist writers tend to
see sexual repression as a disciplining tool used by capital-
ists to 'shift the energy available for useless pleasure toward
compulsory labour' within the working class, Foucault suggested that sexual repression was instead propagated by elites
for elites.[80] In Korea, Confucian modesty culture spread first
among the upper classes, and then filtered down from there.[81]
In the pre-modern Muslim world, the face veil was a feature of
wealthier rather than poorer families.[82] And, as Evans writes
of north-western India, 'Muslim rulers practised purdah, and
upwardly mobile families followed suit to gain prestige.'[83]

Social copying from the top-down has long meant that female
modesty has carried with it a prestige that social climbers wish
to acquire. As the wealth of the middle classes grew, such as
in nineteenth-century Britain and also in post-independence
India, the modesty cult became more affordable; families could
bear the loss of earnings of female members of the household
in order to cultivate a reputation for purity. When it comes to
the fortunes of the modesty cult, what matters is not simply
a woman's ability to survive financially independently of her
menfolk, but whether the family can survive financially without her contribution. If they can, then familial pressure may
still lead to her seclusion, rather than her release, particularly
where elite and religious practices place a value on women's
purity.

Competition in the marriage market pushes further in this direction: modesty practices provide a stick with which to beat down the competition faced by middle-class daughters from working-class girls, giving their offspring something supposedly 'special' to offer to well-to-do men. The success of this strategy is rooted in the fact that preserving a young woman's bodily modesty comes at a price: her family must, for example, ensure that she is chaperoned at all times, is taught separately to boys, and does not have to work alongside men to support herself financially. It is a cost that better-off families are able to bear, but one that working-class families, by design, find unaffordable. By trumpeting the virtues of modesty, the middle classes are thereby able to ensure that working-class girls, despite their freedom to earn, cannot compete with their own daughters when it comes to the all-important market for a husband. Working-class girls are sneered at and gossiped about; middle-class girls are deemed 'respectable', and the middle classes retain their societal advantages from one generation to the next.

This marriage market competition is particularly intense where economic growth offers greater opportunities for men than for women, together with when it brings increased inequality between men, in turn increasing the importance to a woman of a good marital match. A woman's virginity becomes a valuable asset that she and her family can use in an attempt to 'marry up' – to climb the social ladder. The value of her virginity can, in a sense, be measured by the uplift in standard of living she is able to obtain through a good match in the marriage market.[84] This is particularly the case where class structure is fluid, allowing women to marry beyond their own social class or rank.

Xinyu Fan and Lingwei Wu argue that the Civil Examination System in China (587–1905) offered opportunities for upward social mobility for men, creating a strata of eligible bachelors. In response, they argue, families competed for marital matches by binding their daughters' feet in order to guarantee their purity and increase their value as wives.[85] This was particularly so in regions in which women could continue to contribute to their household while being sedentary (such as producing textile products from the safety of the home). In rice growing regions, where women were active in agriculture, foot-binding was less common.

Ironically, the more women's bargaining power within marriage improves, the greater are the benefits to marriage, and the more intense the 'rat race' in the marriage market becomes. In Britain and America in the nineteenth century, just as women were losing opportunities in the workplace, their rights within marriage were expanding. Divorce rights, inheritance rights, and women's rights over their own children all moved in a more positive direction, in part thanks to feminist activism. This, however, gave women even more to gain from marriage and, in turn, even more to gain from the perception of purity.[86] Modesty momentum gathered steam.

As economies grow, there is no guarantee that the modesty cult will be cast aside; the inequalities economic growth brings, along with the human desire to climb the social ladder, can lead to the spread of modesty culture. This is particularly so where women's opportunities for upward mobility depend on a suitable marriage match. By contrast, for women who are instead part of a propertyless class, with no potential to 'marry up', virginity is both less valuable and less policed.[87] When it comes to the modesty cult, not only does gender matter, so too does class.

Population Pressure and Pregnancy

Many early human societies celebrated women for their reproductive powers; for their ability to produce new life, on which the future of a whole community could depend. Repeated and regular occurrences of pregnancy, childbirth and breastfeeding would have been a feature of many women's lives and would have marked women out compared with men. According to one calculation, 60 per cent of women's prime age years were spent either in pregnancy or breastfeeding.[88] In what was then a much more sparsely populated planet, the survival of the species depended on reproduction. Parallels were drawn between women's fertility and the fertility of the natural world. From Romania to Nepal, young women danced, worked and performed naked rituals in the belief that it would improve the fertility of the soil. Goddesses were common and were praised and celebrated. Women were the gatekeepers of the human race and, by controlling the gates, you could control humanity. While on one level, the value placed on women had its advantages, on another level it left them vulnerable to capture and control, including by their own family, who could charge a 'bride price' for a young woman's hand in marriage, or 'gift' them to another family.

How society has responded to women's immense reproductive powers has depended on one thing above all: population pressure. Where population was low, and had not yet reached the limits of the land, every new birth was a celebration rather than something to be feared. Where food was abundant, pregnancies did not result in smaller slices of the pie for everyone else. In this sense, there was little reason to shun sex and little reason to celebrate virginity. In historically land-abundant parts of Africa, women today still experience few restrictions on their mobility. And, rather than obsessing about paternity uncertainty, what matters is the total number of children: where land is abundant and people are scarce, who the biological father is matters far less than the creation of new life. Land that is abundant is also of course cheap, meaning that there is also less to worry about in terms of inheritance. However, where land was scarce and people, relatively, too plentiful, there was more reason to guard women's chastity.

Where population growth has exceeded the ability of society to feed the extra mouths, society's response has been cruel
if unsurprising: sex has been portrayed as sinful, particularly
where women (as the child bearers) were concerned. Bringing
up your daughter with a constant emphasis on her virginity,
labelling women who transgressed 'whores', and even chopping off your daughter's genitals or breaking her feet, may
have seemed like a form of society-wide 'protection' in a world
that struggled to feed a growing population. And, if all of this
nevertheless failed to keep population in line with resources,
there was an even more extreme option, female infanticide:
killing the very thing destined to give life. Where land was
scarce, women's sexuality was therefore policed not just to
ensure paternity, but also to limit the extra pressure placed on
resources.

The clergyman and economist Thomas Malthus is, perhaps,
the historical figure who most feared the 'passion between the
sexes'. In his *Essay on the Principle of Population*, first published in 1798, he argued that population expanded in a rapid
'geometric' fashion, outstripping the earth's ability to provide
food and raw materials, which he argued increased at a slower
– 'arithmetic' – pace. At that time, Britain was on the verge
of the Industrial Revolution, and the economy was expanding faster than ever before. Rather than relishing it, Malthus
feared that economic growth would bring forth too many extra
mouths. In some ways, he was right. British society witnessed
a baby boom and the price of food began to soar, with wages
barely keeping up with the higher cost of living. Despite the
fact that the economy was growing, people's earnings were
stretched over an expanding number of mouths, and food was
increasingly scarce and expensive.

Despite being a religious man, Malthus objected to attempts
by government and revolutionaries to support the poor. He
believed that the redistribution of income, an aim of the
French Revolutionaries, would simply lead to a larger number

of people, rather than improving the lot of each one. He also argued that welfare in the form of 'poor relief' acted to subsidise family formation, worsening competition for food, and so pulling more families into poverty. His thinking proved to be highly influential: by the 1830s, Britain's welfare state was toughening up. Those in need of support now had to commit themselves to the horrors of the workhouse. Law and order was also tightened, punishing those who stole bread to feed their hungry families. Colonisation was seen as a release valve for the hungry masses; the criminal poor were shipped to Australia, and the non-criminal poor were encouraged to go in search of their fortunes in America.

At the same time that Malthusianism was all the rage, the cult of female modesty grew: moral reform and chastity pledges became the order of the day. The earlier age of Puritanism, as we saw in Chapter 1, similarly followed an era of economic and population expansion, and also saw the punishment of single mothers and the demonisation of sex work. The fight for human survival has, therefore, periodically encouraged societies to embrace the cult of female modesty. While society might not have a mind of its own, it is composed of individuals, all of whom feel the effects in their daily lives of a world in which population is expanding beyond limits: increasingly expensive food and shortages of resources. As population pressures lifted in the twentieth century (as they similarly did in the early eighteenth century), there was less to fear from female sexuality, and so modesty norms relaxed.

While some have argued that birth control drove the sexual revolution of the twentieth century, releasing young women from sexual repression by reducing the risks of pregnancy,[89] it is far from the only factor. Indeed, as we saw earlier in the book, sexual permissiveness in the West was already on the rise years before the roll-out of the contraceptive pill. The swinging sixties were not simply a product of the pill, they were also the product of an era in which it was easier for mothers and their children to 'get by': the combination of a booming economy, women's paid work, and the welfare state. Malthusian pressures, in other words, were being lifted. But, even so, whenever state finances have swung into the red, child benefits and welfare support for mothers have become common targets.

In the last three decades, popular culture within Britain has witnessed 'the fetishisation' of the teenage mother, with the fictional Vicky Pollard being presented to us as the 'chav mum *par excellence*': depicted as 'loud, white, excessive, drunk, fat, vulgar, disgusting . . . she embodies all the moral obsessions historically associated with young white working-class mothers in one iconic comic body', writes Imogen Tyler, who also notes that 'the disgust for and fascinated obsession with the chav mum's 'easy fertility' is bound up with a set of social angst about infertility among middle-class women, a group continually chastised for 'putting career over motherhood' and 'leaving it too late' to have children'.[90]

Today, two opposing forces are at work. On the one hand, women's ability to control their own fertility has tipped us in the direction of what is considered to be too few births. Economists argue that our economy's potential is being harmed by falling fertility. We can already see the effects at work on the political front, from the maternal nationalism enveloping eastern Europe to the racist nationalism of America, where women's reproductive freedoms are being trampled. Women's wombs are the 'origin of the world', which makes the mantra of 'my body, my choice' the enemy of nationalists and racists alike.[91] On the other hand, we also face the forces of climate change. The environmental toll of humanity suggests that Malthusian concerns are not entirely dead and buried. As a result, Western countries face two conflicting narratives; one in which the domestic population is felt to be expanding too slowly, and a more global narrative that points to our increasing human presence damaging the planet. How this will be resolved – whether it will take us in a direction of relinquishing or revisiting the modesty cult – is yet to be determined.

Conflict

Competition for land and resources can fuel another common ingredient of the modesty cult – warfare. Bringing together our Chapter 1 modesty history with the history of warfare suggests a correlation between crackdowns on women's sexual freedoms and political ruptures: Egypt in the 'dark period' (c.2181–2055 BCE), and similarly across the wider Middle East, as the nomads on horseback made their presence known and pioneered a new weapon, the chariot; in India around 1500 BCE, where nomads similarly brought the destruction of the Indus civilisation; in Song China in the era of Mongol invasions (in the 13th century); and in north-western India during the Ghurid invasions and onwards through to Mughal rule. In all of these cases, homes and farms were raided, women were raped, and daughters were kidnapped and sold as sex slaves. At the same time, modesty practices increased, and so too did society's concern with lineage – in China to the point of ancestor worship.[92]

According to Murdock, warfare 'enhances men's influence';[93] and, 'if fighting occurs between neighboring communities, families would want to keep their fighters at home for protection'.[94] In other words, in war-torn societies, families might reject matrilineal practices in which sons leave home, to be absorbed into their wives' communities.[95] Families might instead want to keep their sons at home, to act as protectors. Families also have an incentive to band together in order to provide for their defensive needs, forming their own 'clubs' with their own bands of warriors. While in early history, there were many notable female warriors who led troops and defended their communities, men nevertheless dominated, whether as a result of physical strength or fewer caring responsibilities. As warriors became highly prized, so too did their lineage. So as not to let outsiders into the 'club', and to maintain the 'club's' identity, it was important that paternity was guaranteed. As a result, women's chastity became increasingly important. Modest dress became not only a form of protection, but also a means of communicating identity and so of reaping the benefits of club membership.[96]

The increased risk of rape in the context of warfare has also served to deepen modesty norms. Ongoing hostilities between Hindu and Muslim communities in India have created a constant fear of rape on both sides, leading some communities to respond with increased seclusion, curfews, stricter dress codes, and limits on travel.[97] As Susan Brownmiller writes, rape is 'a conscious process of intimidation by which *all men* keep *all women* in a state of fear'.[98] It is also a conscious process by which one community can keep another community in a state of perpetual uncertainty, forcing motherhood on women while depriving their partners of fatherhood. As Amnesty International's Gita Sahgal notes, 'if one group wants to control another they often do it by impregnating women of the other community because they see it as a way of destroying the opposing community'.[99] Sadly, the fear of rape has long been harnessed by nationalists and racists alike in an attempt to fan the flames of hatred and division, as well as by the patriarchy as a justification for limiting the freedoms of women under the veil of 'protection'.[100]

Not only can conflict serve to push societies in a patrilineal direction, in so doing it can in turn inflate the chance of conflict, as matrilineal societies have a natural resistance mechanism to local warfare. As Melvin Ember and Carol Ember (1971: 582) explain, '[t]his is because if warfare between intermarrying communities were to occur, the men who are living in other than their natal communities would have to participate in the initiation of warfare against the very communities in which they and their wives and children reside'. The result is that when war breeds patriliny, it in turn breeds more war or, at the very least, less natural resistance to it. Patriliny and war are mutually reinforcing.

The Patriarchy

Paternity uncertainty, rape and childbearing all place women's (as opposed to men's) sexual behaviour in view. Time and time again, the result has been seclusion, veiling, genital mutilation and the demonisation of women's bodies. But, one might nevertheless ask: are there not alternative means of ensuring paternity, of limiting rape, and of limiting population growth? Why haven't we seen a long history of curfews for men, of male castration and of the demonisation of men's bodies, in place of the seclusion of women, female genital mutilation and the demonisation of women's bodies? Helena Swanwick, editor of the newspaper of the National Union of Women's Suffrage Societies, summed up how many women feel about the double standards: '[w]hen it was explained to me that a young girl by herself was liable to be insulted [harassed] by men, I become incoherent with rage at a society which, as a consequence, shut up the girls instead of the men'.[101] Barbara Smuts notes the way in which female rhesus monkeys cooperate, by building strong long-term bonds with one another, which enables them to fend off male attacks successfully, despite their biological disadvantage.[102] In the baboon kingdom, women also form strong bonds and are able to protect themselves from male sexual aggression. But, rather revealingly, studies have shown how quickly a confident and 'liberated' female baboon, when 'deprived of her network of relatives and friends, will learn to submit to a male who punishes her for independence'.[103]

The cult of female modesty is, therefore, not only consistent with biology, it is also consistent with a history in which

men have held the reins of power, including through state
structures and religious authority, and have used those powers
to limit women's ability to act as a collective force. Smuts notes
that, in comparison with rhesus monkeys, female orangutans
disperse from a young age, leading to a lack of female bonding, leaving them much more vulnerable to male coercion.[104]
Indeed, rape is the rule rather than the exception within the
orangutan community. Hence, where men are able to act collectively, and to limit women's ability to do likewise, women
are left vulnerable. Female modesty is, therefore, not only a
tool to guarantee paternity, it is also a more general means for
men to assert power over women.

The 'magic' that is a woman's ability to bring new life into
the world, along with the lust and fear that they can inspire,
seems to have been too much for some men to handle. Rather
than feel beholden to this power, and rather than celebrate
women's life-giving abilities, powerful men have sought to take
back control by demonising women and their bodies. As Ruth
Mazo Karras, author of *Common Women*, notes, '[t]he arena
of sexuality was the only one in which women could compete
with men in importance . . . and it was the one in which men
most feared they would not be able to control them'.[105] From
natural disasters to man-made destruction, women's sexuality
became a convenient scapegoat – one that let men off the hook
while giving further impetus to keep women 'in their place'.

By appealing to religion, men were able to consolidate their
patrilineal gains. According to Mernissi, a patriarchal version
of Islam sold itself on its ability to ensure paternity certainty
by placing women's sexuality under wraps. The offer may have
proved all too tempting for men who were used to matrilineal
control, where inheritance and lineage passed down through
the female line.[106] As this version of Islam spread, so too, therefore, did patriliny. With it, women were stripped of power. As
Confucianism spread it also rendered women subservient. So
too with Christianity, where women's apparent need to dress

and behave modestly was justified by appealing to the notion that men are biologically incapable of resisting temptation and that women must therefore dress and behave modestly so as to protect themselves and avoid bringing out the 'worst' in men. Common to all of these belief systems was the idea that, unless it is brought under control, women's sexuality drives social instability and leads to economic ruin.

Patrilineal gains were also enhanced by the development of state structures. Fields of wheat, the same fields that brought the plough along with property rights, offered surpluses that could be taxed, thereby enabling a well-funded state. As family practices shifted towards patriliny, the state modelled itself on the same basis.[107] Parts of the world where state structures first came into existence are also the parts of the world with the highest levels of gender inequality today.[108] Women were placed on the back foot, not only as a result of social pressure – a soft form of power – but also in response to growing state power, backed up by the force of law and by the state's monopoly on violence. Political structures also served to reinforce inequalities between men, generating powerful and privileged male–male alliances that acted to limit resistance from other men. As Smuts writes:

> In any gregarious species, male attempts to dominate and control females are likely to be successful only to the extent that males can also dominate and control other males. If no male is capable of dominating any other male . . . then coercing females into mating will not work because other males will always have the power to intervene, and they will do so because intervention will simultaneously reduce a rival's reproductive success and increase the intervener's own chances of gaining sexual access to the female. Thus, the coercive strategy will be unstable, and the most reproductively successful males will be those who compete by providing females with benefits that lead the females to voluntarily choose them as mates. In contrast, to the

extent that some males in an animal society dominate others, the more dominant males can adopt a coercive mating strategy with less interference from other, less powerful males.[109]

Not only have religion and the state independently contributed to patriarchal control, but, where they have provided support and legitimacy for one another, religion and the state have proven to be a near invincible force. In the Middle East, where Islam proved to be a powerful force for state-building, the state and religion have developed hand-in-hand.[110] In Europe, however, the Roman state existed prior to Christianity, resulting in a relatively weaker link between state and religious authorities. As the Romans retreated, Christianity stepped into the power vacuum and modesty culture expanded: by 1100, the Church had its own permanent courts, which punished fornication and illicit sex with public beatings.[111] But, when the Puritans decided that even more action was needed to stamp out the medieval immoralities, that parliament itself should crack down on sexual sin, people's patience soon ran out. In the UK, while there were initial successes for Oliver Cromwell and his 'party-poopers' from 1648 through to the 1650s, by 1660 the monarchy had been restored and the 1650 'Adultery Act', which carried the death penalty, was abolished. Charles II had little patience for purity and, though the 1688 Glorious Revolution brought monarchs with more of an appetite for 'reforming manners', their supporters failed to get their puritanical bills through parliament. Ironically, in reaching for the stars, the Puritans had undermined the prior (Church Court based) system of sexual regulation, which ultimately left them with very little. As religious freedom increasingly became seen as a means of avoiding future religious strife, the liberty-based arguments that were used to support it were also eventually applied to sexual freedom.[112] Compared with the Middle East, where Islam and the state were in cahoots, European women therefore faced (relatively) fewer hurdles as they fought to break modesty culture, including in regard to battles such as birth control, divorce and sex education. Sadly, however, none of this stopped the grip of Christianity taking hold when it came to colonisation. Puritans took their Godly utopias to the American east coast, while Catholic Iberia stamped sexual repression on the populations of southern America. In African matrilineal societies, the colonial state combined forces with Christian missionaries to undermine women's prior freedoms,[113] and when they protested women's power was eviscerated with the force of the gun.[114]

While some male authorities – state and religious – have tried to sell the modesty cult as a much-needed form of protection for women, the reality, as we saw in Chapter 2, is otherwise. Rather than leaving women in a less vulnerable position, the cult of female modesty renders women more vulnerable; it deprives them of educational and labour market opportunities, along with political representation, and makes them less healthy and less happy. And, somewhat conveniently for men, the modesty cult also limits women's ability to compare and contrast the sexual prowess of individual men.

The Matriarchy

Patriarchy, backed up by the state and by religious authorities, helps to complete our explanation for the cult of female modesty. But it does not entirely finish our story. The fly in the ointment is that many modern-day feminists claim that patriarchy produces the opposite of modesty culture – a culture of 'raunch'. As Andrea Castillo writes:

> [T]empering female sexuality would be, at best, a Pyrrhic victory for the patriarchy. Restricting the supply of 'sluts', after all, significantly limits the potential for misogynistic indulgence in female sexual objectification . . . We would expect a patriarchy

to weigh the trade-offs of maintaining power by repressing female sexuality against the option to easily satisfy a considerable carnal appetite. Given the high value ostensibly placed on both, any patriarchy's optimal allocation of sexual repression and sexual objectification would not likely be as one-sided as observed in history and today. A society ruled entirely by misogynists would probably not discourage, or might even actively encourage, female promiscuity.[115]

In the Middle East, re-veiling has been championed not only by patriarchal authorities but also by women themselves, first becoming noticeable among university students. Young, educated, middle-class, urban women have actively adopted modest dress, without legal compulsion and without family pressure.[116] According to Arlene Elowe Macleod, '[v]oluntary support of the new veiling, by educated, working women, part of the modernising middle classes, presents a paradox'.[117] In the United States, a 'return to modesty' is similarly being championed by women, including by writers such as Wendy Shalit. And, when it comes to present-day crackdowns on strippers and sex workers – the most immodest women of all – feminists are leading the way.

When surveying various explanations for the suppression of female sexuality, the social psychologists Roy Baumeister and Jean Twenge concluded that '[t]he view that men suppress female sexuality received hardly any support and is flatly contradicted'.[118] While it might appear heretical to even consider it, we will need to confront the possibility that women themselves have contributed to the modesty cult – and to understand why. That will be the topic of our final chapter.

Conclusion

Why might you encourage your sister or your daughter to cover up? And why do some people squirm at the suggestion that a friend or family member has a reputation for promiscuity? There is probably no single answer to these questions, and there is also no single reason why people abide by and propagate the cult of female modesty. But, biology – concerns about rape, unwanted pregnancy and paternity uncertainty – together with religion might appear the most obvious explanations. The problem, however, is that biology – which differs little across countries and changes very slowly – cannot explain why some countries and periods have been steeped in modesty culture but not others. And where religion does embody modesty culture, it in turn leaves us needing to explain why.

In many early societies there were few constraints on women's sexuality. Matrilineality, a communal way of life, a dearth of people, and relative peace are all factors that tend to be associated with limited restrictions on women's sexuality, including in early history. The various explanations for the subsequent emergence of the modesty cult, as put forward in this chapter, can help us to understand where and when the cult of female modesty subsequently took hold, and why the pendulum has swung across time. They include changes in agriculture: the onset of the plough and the spread of horse-backed pastoralism, together with growing inequality, increasing population pressure and, of course, warfare. Immodest women came to be seen as a threat to fatherhood, a threat to inheritance, a threat to group identity and a threat to their society's survival.[119] A woman's virginity became a valuable asset and something that is valuable is also inevitably policed.

As we saw in Chapter 1, modesty culture appears to have taken hold in the Middle East around four thousand years ago. The explanations put forward in this chapter can help to explain why. Agricultural developments, inequality, population pressure and warfare, including the clashes brought by the movement of the nomadic pastoralists from the Eurasian Steppe, all likely made a contribution. And, once modesty culture was set in motion, state structures and religious authorities developed in a way that added fuel to the fire. To make matters worse, religion and the state came to conspire with one another, making an escape from the modesty cult all the more difficult.

Further West, including in Britain and the Americas, the hunter-gatherer way of life lived on, making modesty culture impractical, while the nomadic pastoralists that descended from the Eurasian Steppe, bringing patriliny to the Middle East, parts of Asia and south-eastern Europe, remained relatively distant. Unlike in the Islamic Middle East, Christianity also had a more difficult relationship with the state, creating less of an unassailable force for those who transgressed modesty rules. At the same time, the Church actively weakened kinship bonds, meaning women could more freely mix with men and select their own mates. By contrast, in Islam, women's right to inheritance gave families greater reason to police marriage matches, and even to favour cousin marriage. As the modesty cult spread across China and the Far East – which could in turn be argued to be the result of factors such as warfare and population pressure – medieval Europe, by comparison, looked like a world of immoralities.

As history shows, modesty practices can, once they are set in motion, quickly become widespread. Even aside from religious doctrine and the laws imposed by the state, social pressure can lead a society to converge on almost universal compliance.[120] From veiling to genital cutting, by adopting a particular behaviour in an effort to enhance your own reputation and in turn achieve a suitable marriage match, others are encouraged to do likewise, reinforcing and even magnifying your own behaviour. Social interdependence – the degree to which our survival and our respect depends on what others think of us – along with social competition (including in the marriage market) can lead people to adopt or abide by practices even if they have little intrinsic value, or don't even approve of them.[121] But, these social interdependencies and snowball effects also mean that if something changes, things can start to tip in the opposite direction, one of sexual liberalism. The pendulum can swing, and it can swing quickly, particularly where, as was the case in Europe, the state and religious authorities lacked coherence. The repeated sexual revolutions in European history provide a particularly extensive testing ground for the various modesty cult explanations set out in this chapter.

In medieval Europe, modesty culture waned. At the same time, the Black Death reduced population pressure, and also served to temper inequality. Land became less valuable and wages rose. Women worked and they married late, without relying on family support. Strong kinship ties were undermined both by active labour markets and by the Church, which shunned cousin marriage and encouraged nuclear as opposed to extended families. But, over time, population pressure began to build and, as it did, inequality increased once more. Women's sexuality was demonised as the source of the resultant instabilities, and puritans increased their grip.

By the eighteenth century, the size of the population stabilised, reducing Malthusian pressures, and religious forces were challenged by Enlightenment thinking. Yet, once again, the pendulum swung. As the nineteenth century steered a course of industrialisation, population growth exploded, women retreated into the home, and inequality grew. As women joined together to fight for greater marital rights, the marital rat-race deepened. While male interests had historically been busy constructing modesty culture, intra-female competition helped to maintain it. But the tides were to turn once more.

In the twentieth century, women achieved equal access in terms of education, work and politics, and society became more tolerant of premarital sex.[122] Building a life outside the home meant that a woman's survival and worth did not rest on marriage or on reproductive functions, such as the ability to guarantee an heir. The race between women for the 'best' husbands was reduced, and so too was the desire of families to signal future fidelity by restraining their daughters. Competition between men to seduce rich virgins was also tempered by the fact that 'in modern societies the disposal of assets is up to the individual with legal ownership of them', which reduced the potential family losses from the seduction of their daughters, and so reduced the need to police their daughters.[123] Falling inequality also served to reduce the extent of intra-female competition in the marriage market,[124] as did the expansion of the welfare state. Technological change had a supportive role to play: paternity testing helped to reduce men's concerns about paternity uncertainty and the contraceptive pill cut the connection between sex and reproduction, reducing the fear of unwanted pregnancy, and enabling women to plan careers alongside motherhood.[125] And, as fertility fell, the society-wide fear of over-population receded, and so too did the associated demonisation of sex that served to limit births. Altogether, women were able to chip away at the altar of virginity and, once a critical mass was reached, that chipping quickly turned into full-scale demolition. Within less than a century, the cult of female modesty was replaced by a culture of raunch.

But, despite the numerous sexual revolutions, and despite our present-day raunch culture, modesty culture was never completely dislodged, and we are now witnessing its return. In part this is not surprising: inequality has been rising,[126] food and resources are under pressure, and the welfare state is faltering. After decades of decline, religion is also once again on the march and, in some parts of the world, the state and religious authorities are again providing support and legitimacy for one another, making the modesty cult more difficult to break. But the reality is that modesty momentum is building not only among religious conservatives, but also among feminists.

Whether, and for how long, this marriage of conservatism and feminism will last will depend on whether the feminist case for modesty can stand up to scrutiny. That will be the topic of our next chapter.

Chapter 4

Beware Puritanical Feminism

In the spring of 2018, I donned my necklace and my shoes, picked up my handbag, and walked into the Royal Economic Society's gala drinks reception wearing nothing but a smile. It was a protest that will be familiar to any reader of *The Sex Factor*.[1] What will be less familiar, however, was the reaction I received from some of the most senior female economists present. According to one, I was an embarrassment to women in the economics profession. Another questioned whether an economics conference was an appropriate place to protest about economists' neglect of women. Where precisely would be a better place I wondered? But, of course, her objection was less about my choice of location, and more about my choice – or rather lack of – attire.

While it is easy to blame the patriarchy for the modesty cult, evidence suggests that women are themselves active participants.[2] Whether in the form of footbinding in pre-modern China or female genital cutting in modern-day Egypt, the cult of female modesty has been passed on from generation to generation with active female participation. In pre-modern England, the Church Courts were riddled with defamation suits in which women had publicly called other women 'harlots' and 'whores'.[3] In 1965, a survey of American college students revealed that women engaging in premarital sex were seen as immoral by 91 per cent of women and only 42 per cent of men.[4] Today, around a half of comments classified as misogynistic on Twitter come from women, with the words 'slut' and 'whore' dominating the language of abuse.[5] In-depth interviews reveal that young women today, just as in the past, continue to fear slut-shaming at the hands of their female peers.[6] And this slut-shaming is not restricted to the heterosexual population; research from the United States shows that it also exists within the lesbian community, where 'sluts' are seen as harming 'others and themselves'.[7]

Feminists can also be found lambasting immodest women. While what has been called 'the first consciously separatist women's liberation movement in history',[8] the Saint-Simoniennes, identified sexual repression as being key to women's subordination, they were soon outnumbered by feminists of a more puritanical persuasion.[9] Victorian feminists promoted purity of body and spirit and, as we will see, they bear a striking resemblance to today's radical feminists. Armed with their distaste for immodest women, those women who have used their bodies in art or protest, from Hannah Wilke to Femen, have been ostracised for, apparently, submitting to the 'male gaze', while working-class women adopting hyper-feminine dress and beauty regimes have been dismissed as 'living dolls'. In the 1970s, feminists were heckling the contestants of Miss World, and today they heckle exotic dancers. Having already ended the employment opportunities of Formula One 'grid girls',[10] their aim is now to abolish the most immodest women of all: sex workers.

In this chapter we consider why women themselves might throw their weight behind modesty culture, not only adopting modesty at a personal level but also judging immodest women to be a danger to themselves and to other women. Three possible reasons are considered: firstly, that women partake in modesty culture because they feel they have little choice but to abide by its dictates; secondly, that patriarchy 'socialises' women to unwittingly adopt and perpetuate modesty culture; and, thirdly, that modesty culture is, they believe, in women's collective best interest. As we will see, unpicking this third possibility, the notion that modesty culture can be 'feminist', will bring us to the secret battle that has long raged *within* feminism: the battle between naked feminists and those of a puritanical variety. By immersing ourselves in this battlefield, we consider the justifications used by feminists who embrace modesty culture before making the case for feminism to challenge, rather than be complicit in, the notion that a woman's value and respect rest on her bodily modesty.

Modesty and Matriarchy

Almost a century ago, Simone de Beauvoir asked: 'Why do women not contest male sovereignty?'[11] As she herself noted, women are not the only group in history who have witnessed oppression but, unlike many other groups, they are certainly not in the minority; women constitute a half, and sometimes more, of the global population. If the modesty cult really is antithetical to women's best interests, the fact that there are so many women who could in theory rise up against it makes the persistence of modesty culture all the more difficult to explain. So, why, despite millennia of sexual repression, have more women not organised and resisted?

The first possibility is that of reluctant acceptance; of women being fully aware of the dangers of modesty culture, but feeling unable to take action and so grudgingly abiding by its practices. If correct, it would suggest that women who slut-shame, who instruct one another to cover-up, and who engage in practices such as FGM/C, are doing so with gritted teeth, feeling that they have no other option. This can be summed up with the phrase, 'resistance is futile'. Faced with little choice and with tough punishment for transgression, women may descend into a rat-race with one another, adopting modesty practices to protect or enhance their reputation, and to signal that they will be faithful wives, allowing them to attract the 'best' matches in the marriage market. The outcome, as modelled by economists and sociologists, is one of self-reinforcing but zero-sum self-repression.[12]

The reluctant adoption of modesty measures may also serve as a means of buying women freedom in other areas, making it a second-best response when the first-best option, that of disposing of modesty culture altogether, is not achievable. Some have explained the 'dramatic and widespread' re-veiling across the Middle East in such terms, and, in particular, why young, educated, middle-class, urban women have chosen to adopt the veil. According to Asef Bayat, such women are already seen as 'sinning' by going to university and entering the workforce, where some mixing with men is inevitable, creating a guilt or reputation loss that is compensated for by a show of piety in the form of the veil.[13] In the words of Jean-Paul Carvalho, veiling is 'a strategy for taking advantage of outside economic opportunities while maintaining esteem within the community'.[14] According to Pat Mule and Diane Barthel, it is 'a coping strategy'.[15]

In this first possibility, women effectively face a 'collective action problem': each individual woman feels that she has too little power to resist the modesty cult by acting alone and so, fearing punishment for transgressions, and to consolidate her precarious position, abides by and even preaches aspects of modesty culture. Accordingly, the extent to which women can pull together and 'plot' will determine when, where and how the modesty cult is challenged. Cooperation needs to replace competition, but it is, of course, difficult to achieve in a situation where the incentive of each individual woman is to abide by the modesty norms. And, where there is little realistic chance of success, cooperation might instead lead to the second-best solution, such as trumpeting the veil for university students and career women, giving the appearance of women themselves propagating modesty culture.

This first possibility implies centuries worth of unhappy women; women who have felt trapped within modesty culture but unable to bring about change. Sociologists also offer a second mechanism for the persistence of social norms, one that could in turn help us to explain why the modesty cult persists: that women are socialised into accepting their position. This alternative explanation suggests that women can be happily (as opposed to reluctantly) abiding by, and passionately preaching, modesty culture without realising the consequences.

Simone de Beauvoir is the mother of socialisation theory, and wrote extensively about how the relationship between the sexes is one in which '[h]umanity is male, and man defines woman, not in herself, but in relation to himself; she is not considered an autonomous being . . . the male sees her essentially as a sexed being; for him she is sex'.[16] In other words, 'the man sees, the woman is seen; man is subject, woman is object', and, as a result, women come to see themselves through the eyes of men, with men's perceived thoughts and feelings dictating their dress and behaviour, rather than their own comfort and life goals.[17] The cult of female modesty could therefore be seen as an internalisation of what Laura Mulvey later termed the 'male gaze', or what Holland et al. have called the 'male-in-the-head,'[18] with women being socialised to see themselves through the eyes of men, and to adjust their behaviour in response. In her book *The Creation of Feminist Consciousness*, Gerda Lerner outlines how this subtle but powerful form of social control has been reinforced by the family, by religion and by the state. In her book *Girlfriends*, Alison Winch considers the way in which adolescent female friendship also acts as a 'school of correction', with women 'bonding through the bodies of other women', which are mocked and humiliated, with the associated cruelty bringing some girls closer together while making others objects of disgust and shame.[19] According to Jessica Ringrose, slut-shaming expresses 'a dynamic where jealousy gets sublimated into a socially acceptable form of social critique'.[20] The result is that 'women collude in creating and generationally recreating the system which oppress[es] them'.[21]

In our first explanation, women are wise to this socialisation, and have to make an unenviable choice between a life of submission or one of precarious independence, lacking the support of the society they transgress. But, as far as socialisation theory is concerned, women exhibit a form of 'false consciousness', involving an 'unconscious, routine, and voluntary adherence', unaware of their complicity in a system that actively works against them.[22] It is what Adrienne Rich termed 'semiconsciousness'.[23] According to Lerner, overcoming this state of mind involves four steps: becoming aware of oppression; acknowledging that it has brought suffering; realising that it is not natural; and then working together with other women to overcome it.[24]

In practice, however, feminists have tended to employ the idea of socialisation to explain the opposite of the modesty cult: a culture of beauty and raunch. For example, Simone de Beauvoir problematises women's quest to appear attractive, writing that a 'flamboyantly dressed woman is lying when she ingenuously claims she is simply dressing to suit herself, and that is all'.[25] Mary Evans argues that 'a new responsibility for women' emerged in the early twentieth century: maintaining herself as a desirable object.[26] Cosmetics were no longer the reserve of 'fallen women' but became part of the daily routine of almost every woman.[27] In 1930, Elizabeth Arden wrote in *Tatler* magazine that 'there are no ugly women, there are only lazy women'. Women were not only to care for others, but to care for themselves; and, if they did not, they were 'letting themselves go'.[28] While free to earn money, the income women earned was bolstering a growing beauty industry: 'The pursuit of the perfect body and the perfect self were made possible by that very engagement into paid work which is often regarded as emancipatory.'[29] According to Evans, these new cosmetic aspirations lumbered women with additional burdens on their time in order to achieve 'respectability'.[30] For Naomi Wolf, the 'beauty myth' is not only an economic manipulation of women, but also a political one, 'a political weapon against women's advancement'.[31] The more women have achieved in other areas of life, 'the more strictly and heavily and cruelly images of female beauty have come to weigh upon us'.[32] Beauty is, she argues, a backlash against feminism;[33] a means of depriving women of self-esteem through the creation of unachievable standards,[34] not only in terms of gender but also in terms of race.[35] A recently edited feminist collection therefore insists that '[t]he force of neoliberalism in shaping experiences and practices related to beauty needs urgently to be understood'.[36]

After Iranian women unveiled in the twentieth century, criticism of the beauty and fashion industry also began to build there, with women being denounced by critics as 'painted dolls', and even accused of being 'conduits for a corrupting luxury and waste'.[37] According to Katherine Bullock, 'hijab acts as an empowering tool of resistance to the consumer capitalist culture's beauty game'.[38] But, despite the widespread re-veiling, women are still criticised for being too interested in fashion and beauty. 'Pious fashion' has become a growing trend, as typified by popular websites such as HauteHijab and muslimgirl.com, along with Modest Fashion Weeks. As Farha Ternikar points out, 'modest fashion is much more than hair covering', embracing clothing, accessories, jewellery and makeup. Despite the modesty label, the modest fashion movement has, like all other fashion, been problematised as being overly consumerist and beauty-obsessed. In countries such as Indonesia, where the market now offers head coverings in a wide abundance of colours and designs, those who have chosen to inject personality into their headscarf have been called 'superficial'.[39] As Ternikar notes, based on her interviews with Muslim American women, wearing makeup is a further 'point of negotiation':[40]

> Some women considered wearing heavy or bright makeup to be immodest. One woman spoke at length about how she wore more makeup when she wore hijab because she felt the focus was on her face. Their different opinions and choices reflect autonomy and agency in negotiating norms around modesty to fit their modern and active lifestyles.

In addition to critiquing beauty, feminists have also critiqued raunch. According to Evans, while 'the demand to appear as a sexual subject was once seen as not respectable, [it] has now acquired the actual meaning of respectability'.[41] Feona Attwood summarises the way in which 'sex is becoming more visible in contemporary Western cultures . . . Porn stars are entering the world of mainstream celebrity, writing bestselling books, [and] acting as sex advisors in lifestyle magazines . . . [and] sex appears to become more and more important'.[42] Bernadette Barton argues that from a young age women are socialised to appear 'hot and sexy' for men. She points to the way in which pornographic assemblage has penetrated mainstream fashion, music and advertising, surrounding us all with a hyper-sexualised culture, one that we abide by, rather than challenging. In response, she aims to 'deprogram' raunch culture's 'conditioning in your subconscious'.[43]

This application of false consciousness and socialisation to feminist critiques of beauty and raunch brings us to a third explanation for women's involvement in the modesty cult. This third possibility – one that runs directly counter to Chapter 2 – suggests that modesty culture is in women's own collective best interests.

As we will see, there is a long history of the women's movement embracing modesty culture for the perceived collective
interest of womankind. In the Victorian age, feminists were
busily promoting modesty culture while men were left com-
plaining to doctors that their wives were cold and indifferent in
the bedroom.[44] When this moralism was abandoned between
the wars, the feminist movement split. Then, in the last quarter of the twentieth century, as sex workers campaigned for
equal rights, radical feminists campaigned to abolish sex work
altogether, a campaign that is continued today. When, in 1986,
sex workers took to the international stage to speak, feminists
threw coins at them and refused to recognise their agency.
Not only have sex workers been the target of feminist critique,
so too have immodest women in general, written off, as we
will see, as 'living dolls' or 'female chauvinist pigs'. Whether
stripping for money or in the form of protest, women who
transgress modesty norms are still today derided and portrayed
as the enemies of the women's movement. When it comes to
the persistence of the modesty cult, feminism needs to take its
fair share of the blame.

The Suffragettes

The suffragettes knew a thing or two about marketing.
Admittedly, facing a constant stream of cartoons that depicted
them as monster-like, vicious and 'unwomanly', it was a necessary part of their arsenal. Harnessing the power of clothing was
central to their campaign, allowing women to show allegiance,
to recognise comrades, and to take charge of their image. Rather
than insisting upon a uniform, Emmeline Pethick-Lawrence
(1867–1954) designed their famous tricolour branding: purple,
white and green. And she didn't just have an eye for colour; as
co-editor of the *Votes for Women* magazine, she had the means
of ensuring that supporters of the cause could coordinate. In

the June 1908 issue, she included a message for those attending
the 'Women's Sunday' march later that month:

> [W]e have seven hundred banners in purple, white and green.
> The effect will be very much lost unless the colours are car-
> ried out in the dress of every woman in the ranks. White or
> cream tussore ... should if possible be the dominant colour,
> the purple or green should be introduced where other colour
> is necessary ... You may think that this is a small and trivial
> matter but ... I wish I could impress upon every mind as deeply
> as I feel myself the importance of popularising the colours in
> every way open to us.[45]

This set of three colours is recognisable to this day, embraced
by countless women at contemporary women's marches, just
as was the case in 1908. Purple represents dignity, green stands
for hope and white, the colour most encouraged above, represents purity.

The tricolour branding was the culmination of a purity
movement that had been gathering steam in the previous
half-century. This movement for moral reform, one that we
spotlighted in Chapter 1, was not only close to the hearts of
many feminists, it was driven by feminist figures. They 'understood that sexual difference had been used to sustain weakness
but could equally be harnessed to exploit strength'.[46] Facing
deep gender inequalities in their everyday lives, feminists
had little armoury, and so used what was, perhaps, their only
weapon: the moral superiority granted to them by society.

In nineteenth-century Britain and America, a wall had been
erected between men and women, dividing them into twin
spheres. Men had been granted sole ownership of the public
domain, the world of politics and paid work, while women had
been pushed out of the workplace and relegated to domesticity, made fully responsible for the care of their husbands and
children. While the lives of men were felt to be burdened by

the brutality, grit and greed of the world beyond the home, women were seen as pure and innocent: as the angels of the home.[47] The ideal wife was expected to provide the moral backbone for her family, and it came with the approval of the Bible itself, which instructs wives to:

> [A]ccept the authority of your husbands, so that, even if some of them do not obey the word, they may be won over without a word by their wives' conduct, when they see the purity and reverence of your lives. (1 Peter 3:1–3:9)

Central to the demarcation of these separate spheres was a new view of sexuality: that men were dominant and active, and women were passive and pure. This was in stark contrast to the centuries-old view of women as temptresses and men as passive responders, unable to control themselves when under the powerful influence of women.[48] While much medical literature still recognised female sexual passion, the medic William Acton popularised the view that women were bereft of sexual desire and men were naturally desirous with a rapacious appetite.[49] The American doctor Theophilus Parvin taught his 1883 medical class that he did 'not believe one bride in a hundred, of delicate, educated, sensitive women, accepts matrimony from any desire for sexual gratification; when she thinks of this at all, it is with shrinking, or even with horror, rather than with desire'.[50] And as far as the authorities were concerned, the gaping chasm between male and female sexual desire was bridged by prostitution, with prostitutes being seen as 'martyrs of purity' whose sexual availability served to uphold the respectability and virtue of all other women.[51] As Susan Kingsley Kent writes: 'The image of the respectable, passionless middle-class lady, in fact, depended upon a contrast with the other image of the "fallen" woman.'[52]

While feminists harnessed the idea that as women they were sexually pure, they did not necessarily buy into the Madonna/

Whore dichotomy, instead pointing to the similarities, as opposed to contrasts, in the lives of sex workers and of women more generally. They argued that all women were victims of the sexual appetites of men, married women as much as sex workers. What they called for was a complete overhaul of male sexual morality, an end to male promiscuity, an end to marital infidelity, an end to sexual violence, and, as we will see, an almost complete end to sexual intercourse.

The double standards within marriage became the first major battleground: the fact that men could divorce women for sexual transgressions, but that women could not do the same, something which the UK's 1857 Divorce Act had further enshrined.[53] Feminists questioned the notion that marriage offered protection to women, in return for which they surrendered rights to their property and person, by pointing to cases of domestic violence and cases where marital infidelity had exposed wives to venereal disease. Rape within marriage also came to the fore. Elizabeth Wolstenholme Elmy (1833–1918), a writer who co-founded the 1889 Women's Franchise League, suggested that all women were, in one way or another, sexual slaves to men.[54] The fact that women had limited ability to divorce, and no legal rights to their own earnings or to resist marital sex, meant that there was little escape for a woman trapped in a poverty-ridden and brutal marriage. While the 1882 Married Women's Property Act, the result of intense campaigning over three decades, was a cause for celebration, the struggles along the way 'brought home the point that the very structure of sexual and marital relations presupposed a double standard'.[55]

Alongside marriage, prostitution was also high on the feminist agenda. Expanding cities and an increasing realisation of the prevalence of venereal disease among the armed forces, with three in ten soldiers admitted to hospital in 1862 receiving treatment,[56] led the British state to introduce the 1860s Contagious Diseases Acts (CDAs). By 1869, the 'Ladies National

Association for the Repeal of the Contagious Diseases Acts' had formed, condemning what they saw as the state-sanctioned provision of 'healthy women for profligate men'.[57] According to Wolstenholme Elmy, the Acts 'tend to intensify in the minds of men the horrible notion that woman is merely an appendage to man for the purpose of the gratification of his basest sensuality'.[58] Rather than protecting women's virtue, she argued that prostitution contributed to women's sexual subjection, which in turn she saw as being at the root of women's oppression.

While the state's intervention in the 'private' sphere in the form of the CDAs was condemned by feminists, the state's willingness to break the public/private divide offered an opportunity: an opportunity for discussions of morality to enter onto the 'public' stage. With the CDAs, the personal had, in a sense, already become political, and the conspiracy of silence surrounding sex was now broken.[59] Having won the moral high ground in regard to the CDAs, with their campaign for repeal resulting in a suspension of the Acts in 1883 followed by full repeal in 1886, many feminists were now inspired to channel their energies into wider moral reform, including through the formation of the Social Purity League and the Moral Reform Union. They campaigned for a 'female defined and alternative morality'[60] that set women free 'from the hell' of male tyrannies 'to redeem the world',[61] with those male tyrannies being deemed social as opposed to biological, and so open to reform.[62] This campaign for moral reform meant challenging powerful groups such as the state, the police, medics, brewers and even the Church but women's presumed moral superiority meant that the various authorities had little choice but to stand up and listen.

To maintain their moral high ground, feminists worked hard to maintain their 'respectability'. As the historian Philippa Levine notes, '[t]he unimpeachable personal respectability of many of the most vocal campaigners – Josephine Butler, Millicent Fawcett, Frances Power Cobbe – lent their campaigns a strength which often bewildered their opponents'.[63] Women who broke the rules of the modesty cult were ostracised. When Wolstenholme Elmy began cohabiting with her partner and became pregnant, 'she was forced by fellow suffragists to marry lest she harm the suffrage cause with scandal'.[64] According to Millicent Garrett Fawcett, who urged her to resign from her role as secretary of the Married Women's Property Commission, she had done 'a great injury to the cause of women'.[65]

Central to Wolstenholme Elmy's writing, which included children's books that introduced them to human reproduction, was a theme of women being in charge of their own bodies. In particular, she drew attention to women's experience of rape within marriage, agitating in 1880 against the attempt in the Criminal Code Bill to embody in law a definition of rape that excluded that between married women and their husbands.[66] But even her notion of women's bodily integrity did not include support for birth control. Rather than relishing it as a means through which women could take charge of their own bodies, feminists shied away from efforts to legalise it.[67] They worried that by supporting it, they would be 'sanctioning and licensing the male sexuality which they felt to be responsible for their [inequitable] position'.[68] Instead, in *Phases of Love*, Wolstenholme Elmy preached 'psychic love', a form of love that usurped sexual relations and that freed every woman of the 'degradation of her temple to solely animal uses'.[69] Sexual intercourse should, she thought, take place solely for the purpose of reproduction, which, according to Lucy Re-Bartlett (1876–1922), had the advantage that '[w]omen would no longer need to feel the indignity or humiliation if in the act of union they knew they had never given themselves to their husbands only, but always to God and the race'.[70] By 1891, even Annie Besant (1847–1933), the birth-control campaigner who found herself in court, had been won over by the philosophy of celibacy.[71] As far as Victorian feminists were concerned, sex degraded true love.

This purity feminism was not unique to Britain. Across the
Western world, feminist demands for equal rights to property, education and employment culminated in campaigns for
moral reform.[72] When American feminists gathered together
at the Seneca Falls Convention in 1848, they demanded an
equal morality for men and women but in the direction of
greater chastity for men as opposed to sexual liberation for
women.[73] One traveller to the United States reported that the
most respectable of ladies refused even to say the word leg,
preferring the term limb and that, in one girls' school, the limbs
of the piano had been covered in frills as a show of modesty.[74]
Through colonisation, this purity feminism spread beyond the
West, with the respectability of white middle-class women
resting on the demonisation of women of colour. Against a
backdrop of racism and a colonial heritage that labelled Black
women promiscuous,[75] Maria Stewart (1803–79), a Christian
feminist and the first Black American woman to speak publicly
on women's rights, saw 'moral regeneration' as key both to
improving women's position and to Black Americans obtain-
ing equal rights.

This moral judgement had consequences for immodest
women, which included sex workers and entertainers, with
women such as Josephine Baker condemned by feminists and
anti-racists alike. Harnessing her sexuality on stage, including
with her famous banana dance, Baker was seen by many as
self-interestedly profiting from 'European sexual desires and
fantasies of savage primitivism', to the disservice of the Black
community.[76] Some, however, felt that Baker was simply doing
the best she could with the hand she had been dealt. To quote
one historian, her stage career and performances 'can be made
sense of and are worthy of commemorating as enterprising
interventions in a racist and sexist globalised media culture
that otherwise repressed and denigrated black women'.[77]
According to Alicja Sowinska: 'Shaking her scantily dressed
behind on stage, Baker exploited European eroticisation of the

black body only to deconstruct this self-constructed image on the Parisian streets', where she dressed in the most elegant and sumptuous fashions of the time, cloaking rather than uncovering her body.[78] But, as far as Baker herself was concerned, there was no conflict between her life as a scantily clad performer and the pursuit of racial equality. Equal rights did not, in her view, stand or fall on women's bodily modesty. As she bluntly noted, 'the rear end exists [and] I see no reason to be ashamed of it. [Although] It's true there are rear ends so stupid, so pretentious, so insignificant that they're good only for sitting on.'[79] Despite the hoards of people attempting to shame her, Baker remained joyously unashamed.

According to the first wave of feminism, equal rights needed to be matched by an equal morality,[80] and this was to occur not through the sexual liberation of women but through the sexual repression of men. Modesty was for men as well as for women. In the words of Christabel Pankhurst, the demand was for 'Votes for Women; Chastity for Men'.[81] Immodest women were an embarrassment to the cause; unless, that is, they were victims or subversives.

Socialist Feminists

For the Saint-Simoniennes, sexual freedom was in tune with, rather than inimical to, social harmony.[82] In stark contrast to the suffragettes, early utopian socialists argued that sexual repression was key to women's subordination. As Mari Jo Buhle writes, '[i]f the mainstream woman's movement of the nineteenth century had named man as the potential debaucher, socialists had substituted capitalism and its masters as the curse of maidenly virtue'.[83]

In their 1825 book titled *Appeal of One Half of the Human Race, Women, Against the Pretensions of the Other Half, Men*, Anna Wheeler and William Thompson argued that private property meant that women would be forever disadvantaged, as capitalism failed to recognise the domestic and reproductive contributions of women, leaving them economically dependent on men. Communal ownership was, they argued, key to ensuring free and equal relations between the sexes. Victoria Woodhull, who published the first American edition of the *Communist Manifesto*, campaigned for 'free love'.[84] The socialist writer Wilma Meikle called for a 'Sane Feminism', chastising Victorian feminists for demonising sex.[85] Emma Goldman (1869–1940), known as Red Emma, saw sexual liberation as a revolt against capitalism.[86] Victorian feminists were written off as 'prudes',[87] modesty was seen as 'bourgeois' and the whole notion of illegitimacy was, well, illegitimate.

But not all socialists were onboard with this vision of sexual freedom. When, in 1895, the 24-year-old socialist and feminist Edith Lanchester was committed to an asylum after announcing to her family that she would be cohabiting with her partner, many senior socialists, including Keir Hardie, were reluctant to speak in her favour, for fear that her 'sexual immorality' would tarnish the socialist cause.[88] Later, in post-revolution Soviet Russia, Alexandra Kollontai, the first female Minister for Social Welfare, defended the sexual liberalism that had set in as part of the revolutionary fervour, noting that sex was neither sinful nor shameful. But Lenin did not agree, describing casual sex as akin to drinking from the gutter, or from 'a glass whose edge has been greased by many lips'.[89]

Whatever its stance on sex and, perhaps in part because of its ambivalence, socialism proved increasingly popular as the twentieth century rumbled on. As the world plunged into the Great Depression, and as fascists responded with 'Kinder, Kuche, Kirche',[90] socialism offered hope. Even where they rejected full-scale revolution, feminists turned to socialism to improve the lives of working-class women. Maternal feminism, as a result, replaced purity feminism. In the UK, the then newly installed leader of the National Union of Societies for

Equal Citizenship (NUSEC), Eleanor Rathbone (1872–1946), campaigned for family allowances paid directly to women.[91] While this 'new' feminism addressed 'the real needs of large numbers of women',[92] according to some it too closely resembled anti-feminist pre-war visions of womanhood.[93] In 1926, Millicent Fawcett left the NUSEC, and the UK women's movement splintered.[94]

While few early twentieth-century women subscribed to a socialist form of 'free love', they did reject bourgeois purity feminism. The work of Clelia Duel Mosher, the women's sexuality pioneer who was decades ahead of Kinsey, helps to reveal what women really felt about sex and love at the turn of the century. Of the forty-five women she surveyed, thirty-five 'testified that they felt desire for sexual intercourse independent of their husband's interest', thirty-four experienced orgasm (a half of them regularly), and more than a half thought that sex was a pleasure for women as well as for men.[95]

According to Dora Russell (1894–1986), the 'important task' of feminism was now to 'bury the lie ... that the body is a hindrance to the mind, and sex a necessary evil'; she wanted '[t]o understand sex – to bring it to dignity'.[96] Alongside this, rather than rejecting birth control, the new breed of feminists threw their weight behind it.[97] While chastity was the goal of many Victorian feminists, for the post-war generation 'good sexual intercourse was the aim'.[98]

Sheila Jeffreys argues that this was the point when 'feminism lost its vital spark': that what the new feminism offered was 'sexual first aid' with a vision of 'sexual freedom' that was limited to heterosexuality; moreover, that '[t]he new feminists, in their eagerness to promote the joy of sex, avoided or ignored the unpleasant realities that earlier feminists had been fighting'.[99] For Jeffreys, the 'spark' returned with her own breed of feminism – radical feminism – in the 1970s.

Radical Feminists

In June 1975, more than a hundred sex workers barricaded themselves in Saint Nizier church in Lyon for eight days in protest at their treatment by the police, which included multiple arrests the week before. Local people brought food and clothing as a show of support. When the police responded with force, similar sit-ins spread to churches in other French cities. Hostility to the protests was visible in both conservative and feminist circles. The French Women's Rights Minister refused to set up a meeting with the sex workers involved,[100] and as one member of a local French feminist group recounts:

> What the women of Saint-Nizier wanted was not what we wanted. We didn't really know if we should support the prostitutes' struggle . . . or whether we should express our own positions on prostitution, accepting that the two were contradictory. In sum, they wanted to be able to practise their occupation in good conditions, and we, even though we didn't actually say it, wanted that occupation to disappear.[101]

Despite the hostility, the sex worker movement gathered steam in the 1970s, bringing individual sex workers together from across the globe to campaign for rights and respect. The international activism culminated in 1985 in the first World Whores' Congress, when a *World Charter for Prostitutes' Rights* was published, calling for the decriminalisation of sex work and 'to change social attitudes which stigmatise and discriminate against prostitutes and ex-prostitutes of any race, gender or nationality'.[102] A year later, at the invitation of the 'Green Alternatives', the European Parliament in Brussels hosted the second World Whores' Congress. Conservative members of the parliament disparaged it as a 'prostitutes' jamboree' and called for a 'full investigation' of the event. Many feminists were also left squirming. On the last day, the Italian

feminist group Femministe i Rivolta sneaked into the conference, pushed forward to the speakers, and shouted 'sex with
men is rape' while throwing coins at the sex workers present.[103]

Prostitution and pornography, the two P's, were splitting
women's rights campaigners down the middle, in a battle that
became known as the Feminist Sex Wars. And, just as Victorian
feminists failed to invite sex workers into their movement,[104]
and were 'indignant when confronted with an unrepentant
prostitute who refused to be reformed or rescued',[105] radical
feminists were making the same mistakes. They argued that
prostitution was exploitative for *all* women involved, that it
rendered every woman (prostitute or not) a sex object, and
that only through its abolition could the feminist utopia be
achieved. Just as Marxism did not believe that economic
exploitation could be resolved without tackling class, radical
feminists did not believe that the exploitation of women could
be resolved without confronting sex: 'Sexuality is considered as
the primary dynamic in the ordering of society' and 'prostitution' is seen as playing an important role in 'maintaining the
dynamic'.[106] According to Catherine MacKinnon, pornography
is used 'to train women to sexual submission' and, according to
Andrea Dworkin, '[p]rostitution in and of itself is an abuse of a
woman's body' and exists as a reflection of male supremacy.[107]

On the other side of the debate, Margo St James, who
had herself been arrested under allegations of sex work and
who became a leading force in the sex worker rights movement, argued that criminalisation and abolition did nothing
to resolve the harms that sex workers faced, or the reasons
they ended up selling sex in the first place.[108] Rather than supporting a crackdown on prostitution, St James demanded an
immediate end to the arrest of sex workers, writing that 'there
is no immorality in prostitution. The immorality is the arrest of
women . . . for a service that's demanded of them by society.'[109]

In the modern day, the descendants of radical feminism,
known as sex work abolitionists, are busily campaigning for

the 'abolition' of sex work, driving policy change in a direction that sex worker unions argue is making their lives less safe. The 'Abolitionist Principles' of the European Women's Lobby include the statement that prostitution 'constitutes a fundamental violation of women's human rights and a serious form of male violence against women'.[110] Similarly, the Nordic Model Now! group argues that 'the system of prostitution perpetuates the archaic practice of female sexual submission for male entertainment' that 'feeds the punter's sense of entitlement and the sense that she has no rights'.[111] The resultant Nordic Model 'end-demand' policy approach, which criminalises the clients of sex workers, was first introduced in Scandinavia, spreading from Sweden to Norway (2009), Iceland (2009), Canada (2014), France (2016), Ireland (2017) and Israel (2020). Northern Ireland adopted the Nordic Model in 2015, while elsewhere in the UK it has received the backing of both the Women's Equality Party and the Fawcett Society, and has the approval of the All-Party Parliamentary Group on Prostitution.[112] In December 2020, Labour MP Dame Diana Johnson put forward an associated Private Members' Bill to the UK parliament. It claims to be 'radical in spirit and feminist in practice'.[113] The European Parliament had already passed a motion encouraging member countries to adopt this kind of approach. In the United States, FOSTA and SESTA legislation (passed in 2018) limits the ability of sex workers' to have their own bank accounts, to accept payments, and to advertise online.

Despite the broad popularity of this abolitionist approach, the World Health Organization, Amnesty International, and the Royal College of Nursing have all expressed concerns, with growing evidence suggesting that criminalising the purchaser of sex, even when the seller of sex is not themselves criminalised, puts sex workers in greater danger. After Ireland implemented the Nordic Model in 2017, violent attacks on sex workers increased by 50 per cent.[114] A recent overview of the numerous quantitative studies published between 1990 and 2018 and covering a range of countries found that sex workers are twice as likely to have an STD and three times more likely to be victims of violence under a system of criminalisation.[115] A synthesis of the qualitative evidence provided by more than ninety publications over the same time period suggests that this is because 'in contexts of criminalisation, the threat and enactment of police harassment and arrest of sex workers or their clients displaced sex workers into isolated work locations, disrupting peer support networks and service access, and limiting risk reduction opportunities. It discouraged sex workers from carrying condoms and exacerbated existing inequalities experienced by transgender, migrant, and drug-using sex workers.'[116] To quote one Canadian sex worker:

> They couldn't have designed a law better to make it less safe, even if they sat for years! It's like you have to hide out, you can't talk to a guy, and there's no discussion about what you're willing to do and for how much. The negotiation has to take place afterwards, which is always so much scarier . . . it's designed to set it up to be dangerous. I don't think it was the original intention, but that's what it does.[117]

So why, despite the evidence, and despite the protestations of sex workers, do feminist groups persist with the 'end-demand' approach? It is because, according to radical feminists, more is at stake than the wellbeing of individual sex workers: it is, they believe, the fate of all women. As Heather Berg highlights, in the framework of radical feminism the 'problem' with sex work is not just about 'damage' to sex workers' own welfare 'but rather what happens when men impose this same treatment on respectable women outside the home and the brothel . . . The sex worker is not a person with her own claims for respectful, negotiated working conditions, but rather a metaphor to dramatise the harms' that other women face.[118] Eliminating sex work is seen as central to dispelling the notion that all women are sex objects.[119]

But, in addition to being considered sex objects, women are also commonly assumed to be the default caregivers within society. Indeed, Feminist Economics identifies care work, rather than sex work, as being central to gender inequality, particularly the expectation that women take on the role of caring for children and elderly parents, an expectation that in turn affects their ability to earn and save. Since it is this unpaid (as opposed to paid) care that is seen as responsible for 'branding' women as the carers of society, it raises a question: why, in parallel terms, do sex work abolitionists focus on paid (rather than unpaid) sex as being the 'problem' – as being key to women being branded 'sex objects'? Why is it that radical feminists support the remuneration of unpaid care, along with better pay and conditions for paid care workers, but not the equivalent when it comes to sex? And why, in response to the exploitation within the sex industry, do radical feminists not apply the same policy approach that is used in regard to tackling exploitation in domestic labour: improving rights and conditions, while tackling domestic slavery alongside (as opposed to a blanket approach of criminalisation and abolition)? A comparison of care work and sex work helps to reveal what is really behind the radical feminist approach to sex work: logic or, instead, the cult of female modesty.

Perhaps the most glaring concern of all when it comes to sex work is exploitation. Exploitation, in one form or another, has, sadly, long been a feature of not only sex work but also of domestic labour. In 1975, an international campaign known as 'Wages for Housework' served a notice to all governments: 'We clean your homes and factories. We raise the next generation of workers for you. Whatever else we may do, we are the housewives of the world. ... We are serving notice to you that we intend to be paid for the work we do.'[120] According to the International Labour Organization, the amount of unpaid care conducted globally is the equivalent of two billion people working full-time for nothing, and three-quarters of this unpaid care is carried out by women.[121] The fact that care is considered a female responsibility affects the educational and work opportunities of women and girls, their ability to progress in the workplace, and their overall degree of financial independence. Not only are highly gendered expectations in terms of who conducts unpaid care central to the gap in earnings between men and women, so too is the way in which even paid care or domestic work is poorly remunerated, in part because of its characterisation as 'women's work'. In the UK, it is estimated that almost half of care workers earn below 'the living wage', which is more than double that in the economy as a whole.[122]

Care and domestic labour is also associated with forms of exploitation that go beyond the financial. Indeed, LaShawn Harris argues that in the USA some domestic workers historically moved into sex work to escape the physical, sexual and racist abuse they suffered while cleaning and caring in white homes.[123] Not only is there a long history of physical and sexual abuse within domestic work, it remains a problem today.[124] Some of this is a result of modern-day slavery.[125] While much of the discussion of international trafficking tends to focus on sex work, domestic slavery is also significant. Global estimates of modern slavery suggest that 40 million people are victims of slavery, 25 million of whom are in forced labour and 15 million of whom are in forced marriage. Of the 25 million in forced labour, 4.8 million are estimated to be in forced sexual exploitation and 16 million in other forms of private sector labour exploitation, including domestic work, agriculture and construction.[126] Sex work and domestic labour therefore share a lot in common. But, despite the similarities in terms of the potential for exploitation, radical feminism calls to abolish sex work, rather than adopting a policy approach that parallels that used in regard to domestic labour, one of tackling domestic slavery but while also improving the rights, pay and conditions for those who do enter the industry through something other than force.

Of course, you might well have doubts as to the degree to which people really do enter the sex industry 'by choice'. Sex work certainly can be forced, coerced or involve little choice, but at the root of that is poverty, which abolitionist policies simply do not address. This is something that sex-worker unions, such as the English Collective of Prostitutes, 'have been shouting from the rooftops for years', demanding that politicians 'outlaw poverty not prostitutes'.[127] According to Martha Nussbaum, radical feminists' refusal to hear this cry suggests that '[radical] feminist theory may be insufficiently grounded in the reality of working-class lives and too focused on sexuality as an issue in its own right, as if it could be extricated from the fabric of poor people's attempts to survive'.[128] For Nussbaum, when sex work becomes concerning is where the economic situation faced restricts choice: 'This seems to me the truly important issue raised by prostitution' she concludes.[129] Not only does 'end-demand' not address the underlying economic issues, it worsens the situation by pushing sex workers into the margins and by making it more difficult for sex workers to collectivise.[130]

Nussbaum and others have also noted the way in which sex work crosses a cultural wall. Two centuries ago, so did receiving payment for a whole range of tasks, including acting, singing and poetry, all of which were considered unsavoury when performed for money. Nussbaum identifies two contributing factors to this disapproval of the exchange of a service for money: 'aristocratic class prejudice and fear of the body and its passions'.[131] With it, accepting money made any service 'dirty' and less 'pure', while a display of the body and its passions was considered vulgar. However, while it is now deemed respectable to accept money in return for acting, singing and poetry, sex work remains taboo. To understand why, Nussbaum compares sex work with other jobs in which women 'take money for bodily services', including plucking chickens, cleaning, singing in a nightclub, being a skilled masseuse and working as a hypothetical 'colonoscopy artist' (using your colon as a testing ground for the latest medical developments).[132] Many feminists who campaign to abolish sex work argue that the inside of a woman's body is not a place of work.[133] In that sense, perhaps the closest comparator for sex work would be the colonoscopy artist, as it involves intimate, anal, bodily intrusion. But, despite it, few of us would see being a colonoscopy artist as a 'bad' form of employment, and we certainly would not stigmatise those involved. Nussbaum thereby concludes that, when it comes to sex work, 'the biggest difference' compared with other forms of work is not either exploitation or bodily intrusion, but 'the fact that it is, today, more widely stigmatised'.[134]

Some might argue that a further difference is that the work of the colonoscopy artist, together with care, is both necessary and is 'helping others'. By contrast, when it comes to sex work, abolitionist literature is clear that sex work is not necessary; that the idea that people have 'sexual needs' that require fulfilment is a poor argument for maintaining sex work.[135] In comparison with sex work, often we cannot survive unless someone takes on jobs involving care. Dependency is a natural state of human existence: at some point we all need help from others. Hence, a policy of 'ending demand' for carers (akin to 'ending demand' for sex work) would greatly impact the ability of millions of people to survive.

But, on these terms, we must then ask: should an industry that is 'unnecessary', as feminists claim is the case with the sex industry, be criminalised? You don't have to think for long before realising that our answer must, inevitably, be 'of course not'. After all, it would otherwise mean criminalising not only those who purchase sex but also, alongside, people who purchase cars (rather than use public transport), those who buy fancy shoes, and those who go out for nice meals. The claim that sex work is unnecessary is, therefore, insufficient to justify those who wish to criminalise and abolish it.

Of course, even if something is not necessary, it does not mean that it is not valuable; sex creates pleasure, and that is worth a lot to the person concerned. A life where only needs, not wants and desires, are met, would be a poor existence. If someone freely chooses to meet the associated demand for sexual stimulation, what is the problem? This brings us to the major difference between sex work and caring that – as far as some feminists are concerned – could 'justify' the abolition of the former but not the latter. According to the radical feminist Carole Pateman, sex work is 'morally undesirable'.[136] 'Shifting the Burden', the UK All-Party Parliamentary Group Report, argues that '[l]egislation on prostitution is not value-free' and that it 'sends a signal about what is, and what is not, acceptable'.[137] Radical feminists, along with other supporters of sex work abolition, wish to send the signal that the exchange of sex for money is not morally acceptable.

Unlike sex work, and nowadays at least, cleaning and caring are not commonly considered 'immoral', at either the selling or buying end of the trade. Cleanliness is, of course, 'next to godliness', and care is, well, caring. Neither can easily be seen as morally 'wrong'. Despite the similarities between female care work and sex work in terms of gendered stereotypes, care work is considered both necessary and morally 'good'. It is here, therefore, that we can find the crucial difference in terms of the seemingly hypocritical stance that radical feminists take towards these two forms of 'work'. If sex workers were judged to be conducting valuable and respectable work, as is the case with care workers, radical feminists would no longer be pursuing an approach of 'end-demand' and abolition. While radical feminism attempts to escape the old-fashioned notion that individual sex workers are themselves immoral, it actually aligns itself with the archaic view that sex work is morally undesirable.

Interestingly, there was, in fact, a time when paying someone to take care of your children and your elderly relatives was
deemed 'immoral'. Perhaps some still take that view today. In
such a situation, would you be happy to be rendered a criminal
for placing your elderly parent in a care home, or for purchasing at-home care or cleaning services? Of course, if radical
feminists were to apply the same 'end-demand' approach to
care, criminalising those who purchase care, it would leave
many people (on both the buying and selling sides of these
exchanges) up in arms today. In the modern world, women go
out to work and there are fewer siblings to share elderly care,
making paying for care 'necessary'. Alongside, and given both
the extent of demand for it and the labour intensity involved,
the workforce in the care sector is huge and growing. It has
been estimated that there are around 72,800 sex workers in the
UK, the vast majority of whom are female.[138] By contrast, there
are more than 1.6 million people in the UK working in social
care alone; 74 per cent of these are directly providing care.[139]
As with sex work, the vast majority are female: more than 80
per cent of adult social-care jobs are held by women.[140] It is
clear therefore that, in contrast to care workers, sex workers
are in a minority within the workforce and, as such, radical
feminists find it much easier to campaign for policies that 'end-
demand' for their services. By contrast, when it comes to care
work and domestic services, the number of women working
in the industry is not only sizeable, but women are also big
buyers. Berg therefore has her own cynical answer for why
many feminists are inconsistent in their policies towards sex
work and care work: 'because white women have always been
bosses' in the realm of domestic and caring labour, the idea of
criminalising it would be like turkeys voting for Christmas.[141]

Comparing sex work with care work reveals that implicit
to the 'end-demand' approach is not only an element of self-
interest but also a long-standing set of moral beliefs. If, as
a society, we were entirely comfortable with sex and happy

for people to choose to monetise their bodies as well as their
brains, it is difficult to imagine why a policy approach that
involves criminalising those who pay for sex, strangling the
client-base of those who choose to sell sex, would be appealing. Moreover, if we really were concerned about people
being forced into sex work through poverty, then we would
be emphasising worker rights and encouraging workers to
collectivise, as well as tackling the inflexibility of the welfare
state, and the lack of access to adult education and employment opportunities, rather than pushing for abolition (which
does nothing to address poverty). And, if we were concerned
with trafficking, which occurs both within and beyond the sex
trade, including in the form of domestic slavery, we would
be, for example, rethinking our border policies.[142] The fact
that the policy approach favoured by radical feminists is to
entirely eliminate demand for sex work is, therefore, indicative of a view that women should not be selling sex, and that
sex should not be open for purchase. Society would, apparently, be better off without the exchange of sex for money, and
gender equality would be better served without, rather than
with, sex workers.

    An associated lack of respect for sex workers is clear in the
writings of radical feminists and abolitionists. Exotic dancers
and sex workers are regularly described in dehumanising ways,
such as 'implants wrapped around a pole', 'pieces of meat' and
'broken dolls'.[143] And throughout radical feminist and abolitionist discussion of sex work one finds use of the phrase
'buying women'. Carole Pateman writes that 'when a prostitute
contracts out the use of her body she is . . . selling herself in a
very real way'.[144] Alison Jaggar writes that 'since, unlike a man,
she [a woman] is defined largely in sexual terms, when she
sells her sexuality she sells herself'.[145] Not only does this notion
that buying sex involves 'buying a woman' fall into the trap of
assuming that a woman is nothing more than sex but, as one
UK sex worker 'accused of destroying the feminist cause' has

noted, 'feminists have to realise that all work involves selling some part of your body. You might sell your brain, you might sell your back, you might sell your fingers for typewriting. Whatever it is that you do you are selling one part of your body. I choose to sell my body the way I want to and I choose to sell my vagina.'[146]

As Julia Laite notes, the 'end-demand' approach is 'an ideal way to appear to crack down on prostitution without appearing to crack down on the women involved'. In reality, though, while '[t]he legal stigma of selling sex might be removed by a law that criminalises clients and only clients . . . the social stigma of engaging in the sex industry, even if it is claimed to be a choice made by an adult woman, still remains' and, as such, abolitionism still 'maintains the age-old position that prostitution is inherently morally wrong'.[147]

While radical feminism claims to reject the idea that a woman's worth hangs on her body, it nevertheless judges women based on what they do with that body, seeing gender inequality as the result of using that body in 'immodest' ways. Of course, so as not to appear as if they are blaming women themselves for the resultant gender inequality, immodest women have to be cast as unwilling victims. In their view, it is inconceivable that any woman would choose to be a sex worker. But, once we escape the 'cult of female modesty', sex workers' voices start to make sense, and the idea of 'abolishing' them is revealed for what it really is: a morally driven and intellectually elitist project in which women who monetise their brains are denying other women, often on the margins of societies, equivalent rights and freedoms.

Radical feminists today may, like the Victorian moralists, feel a warm moral glow by throwing their weight behind the 'abolition' of sex work, but warm glows do not compensate for the harm imposed on real people. Not only does feminist resistance to decriminalisation increase, as opposed to reduce, the harm that sex workers face, it also, by perpetuating whorephobia, contributes to the harm that the 'cult of female modesty' inflicts on all women in society.

Gail Pheterson's *A Vindication of the Rights of Whores* (published in 1989) carried with it an insistence that Mary Wollstonecraft's teachings were as applicable to sex workers as they were to all women. Sex workers should, in other words, be entitled to the same rights and respect as everyone else. But, just as Wollstonecraft had herself been rendered a whore, banished from existence by the Victorian feminists who were desperately trying to uphold their reputation for respectability, the sex-worker rights movement has similarly been banished into oblivion by modern-day radical feminism. And, as we will see next, not only have sex workers been the target of feminist criticism, so too have immodest women more generally.

Naked Feminists

In 1975, the artist Hannah Wilke was invited to submit a piece of work for the 'What is Feminist Art?' exhibition. Her submission, titled 'Marxism and Art: Beware of Fascist Feminism', contained at its centre the artist posing provocatively, her shirt wide open to her low-cut jeans, with a tie hanging between her breasts, and her largely topless torso covered in miniature vulva formed from chewing gum. It was a direct response to the 'chorus of critical voices' from within feminism in relation to her previous sexually suggestive performances.[148] According to Jeanette Kohl, 'ideological feminism did not approve of the double game of a self-aware Venus who was both a Muse *and* an artist, a beauty *and* a feminist, subject *and* manipulator of (male) desire'.[149] Wilke was accused of objectifying herself and of reinforcing, rather than subverting, traditional depictions of women.[150] Her submission, part of a wider series, highlights the way in which 'women who are beautiful, witty, and success-ful are usually accused of conspiring with men against other women'[151] and 'that a feminism that prescribes how a woman should look or behave is as harmful as the objectifying values that feminism seeks to redress'.[152] She 'warned of the dangers of feminist puritanism that militated against women themselves, their sensuality and the pleasure of their own bodies'.[153]

Barbara T. Smith's 'Feed Me' performance is another artwork that has faced feminist disapproval, with her naked display being described as a 'peep show' that reinforces misogyny. Alongside, Annie Sprinkle, who, by placing her own cervix on public display, has pushed 'the boundaries of propriety more than any other performance artist', has faced 'claims that she is complicit in misogyny'.[154]

Not only have feminist artists been declared 'unfeminist', so too have feminist protesters. In 2011, Aliaa Elmahdy, an Egyptian art student, 'launched her nude body into the blogosphere', bringing 'sex to Tahrir Square', by uploading a nude photo of herself to her blog, 'A Rebel's Diary'.[155] It was an act that violated the public/private dichotomy, challenging the 'dualisms of secular and religious, erotic and sacred, real and virtual'.[156] And, since her full frontal nude was accompanied by stockings, red shoes and a flower in her hair, it was erotic and sexually charged. Within the first week, her blog had received 1.5 million hits, and 'incited discourse and rage'. Many feminists jumped to criticise Elmahdy for claiming that her nudity was liberation. She was, instead, told that she was playing to the ideal of women as ornamental and sexual creatures, reinforcing the 'pernicious toxic Western aesthetic codes of man as surveyor/subject and woman as surveyed/object of the gaze'.[157] Some defended her on the basis of subversion, noting Egypt's 'milieu of sexual harassment, gang rape, forced virginity testing, and public shaming of women'.[158] Facing rape and death threats, Elmahdy fled Egypt and was granted political asylum in Sweden. There she collaborated with Femen, protesting naked outside the Egyptian Embassy in Stockholm, and later joining their 'International Topless Jihad Day' (ITJD).[159] It was a collaboration that intensified the criticism that Elmahdy had already received, causing some of the feminists who had previously supported her to defect to the ranks of critics.

At issue wasn't only the way that Elmahdy had sexualised her body, but the way it was felt to play into colonial narratives, with Femen's protests being described as 'racist colonial feminism'.[160] Karina Eileraas Karakuş writes that '[b]y allying with Femen, an organisation that uniformly equates nudity with empowerment and hijab with oppression Elmahdy short-circuits the complexities of her political message. Her liaison with Femen invites us to reflect on the dangers of neocolonial feminism.'[161] 'Muslim Women Against Femen' posted an open letter to say that that they were 'fed up and tired of hearing from women of privilege perpetuating the stereotype that Muslim women, women of colour and women from the Global South are submissive, helpless and in need of Western "progress"'.[162] In striking comparison with Femen's own images, they posted images of themselves modestly dressed, holding up signs with messages such as: 'Nudity DOES NOT liberate me and I DO NOT need saving'; 'Shame on you Femen, hijab is my right'; and, 'You do not represent me!'[163] Unlike Femen, I have never penned an objection to, or protested against, the hijab, but that doesn't mean that I have been immune to this same form of criticism. As one feminist tweeted in response to my own naked activism '[a]s a Middle Eastern woman, I find nudity oppressive and signifies Western intrusion'.[164]

Nakedness is, however, certainly not a Western invention. As Maryam Kazeem asks: 'Have we forgotten the naked protests that have taken place in Nigeria, Liberia, Kenya and Uganda for over a century?'[165] In 1929, thousands of Igbo Nigerian women used their bodies in a show of resistance to colonial authority, sparked by a newly imposed tax on women's economic activities, in what became known as 'the Women's War'. Alongside attacking symbols of colonisation, such as cutting telegraph wires and attacking post offices, they used 'lewd gestures', and

they danced and they sang.[166] On numerous other occasions,
African women have used naked protest to fight violence,
corruption and multinational oil companies, facing criticism
well before any modern-day naked protesters.[167] As Tricia
Twasiima writes:

> Nudity as a form of protest upsets the very ideas of what
> respectable womyn should be. What better way to resist then
> than to deploy the same tools that have been previously con-
> trolled and policed. The belief that womyn's bodies must be
> clothed, until decided otherwise, is why womyn's nudity as a
> form of resistance is exceptionally remarkable. The reclaiming
> of our bodies, and the self-determination of what they will be
> used for, undermines the patriarchal narrative which makes it
> even more powerful . . . By freeing ourselves from the limits
> of what is acceptable, we give room to new ways of resisting
> and ultimately new ways of liberation. I would challenge us to
> begin to reimagine what this freedom truly looks like. One of
> the ways to do this is by reclaiming our bodies and determining
> for ourselves what we will use them for. This of course is dif-
> ficult considering the consequences dealt to those who reject
> the set standards, but perhaps we can begin by unlearning our
> own biases and internalisations about our bodies. Questioning
> ourselves, and pushing back against the narratives that take
> self-determination away from us is a good place to start.[168]

Nevertheless, prominent Arab feminists, including Nawal al-
Saadawi, have noted their 'disgust' with 'the degradation of
women implied in the public display' of their bodies.[169] Gabby
Aossey argues that while '[w]omen who wear hijab have freed
themselves from a man's and a society's judgemental gaze; the
Free the Nipplers have not . . . [t]hey have fallen deep into the
man's world, believing that this trend will garner respect'.[170]
Following a series of my own naked protests, a member of a
Sheffield Radical Feminist group tweeted: 'does it not even

make you pause for thought when you realise that men over-whelmingly support your feminism'. Many women offer a comment along these same lines: aren't you just giving men precisely what they want?

But to resist naked protesting, or another form of nudity, so as to avoid the male gaze is, to my mind, allowing the male gaze to dictate what I do or do not do with my own body. I am perfectly capable of respecting myself and confident enough to pursue my goals, irrespective of what men might think or feel in response to my naked body. I have made a concerted choice not to let anyone who might 'ogle' or make crude comments stand in my way. For women to live their lives in a way that is *limited* by the male gaze as a means of *escaping* the male gaze would seem to be at best a pyrrhic victory. Surely it can be feminist to ignore, rather than be constrained by, the male gaze.

In my view, the solution to women being viewed as 'sex objects' is to be found in changing the way we as a society judge women, rather than changing (and restricting) women's behaviour. When I employ someone to move my heavy aca-demic books, it is typically a man who arrives at my door, but that does not mean that I objectify men as existing to fulfil my muscle-based needs. If I were to see men as carthorses, that would be my fault, not the fault of the removal men. Similarly, where men choose to see women as sexual objects, it is they and not women who are to blame. Just because some women do not cover their bodies is no excuse for men to think that women are 'just bodies', and just because some women sell sex is no excuse for men to think that women are 'sexual objects'. I am perfectly able to respect a man whatever he is or is not wearing; it would, to my mind, be superficial to judge another person based on their state of dress. And I, for one, am also perfectly capable of respecting people who sell sex, irrespective of their gender. Similarly, just because a woman makes you a coffee in a cafe, or makes your hotel bed, it does not mean that you should assume that all women exist to serve your basic needs. If men feel sexually entitled to women's bodies and if women's respect and worth hangs on something as flimsy as a piece of cloth, this is a serious problem, but that problem is not semi-naked women or sex workers. Feminists need to stop problematising what they see as immodest women and instead switch their focus to challenging, rather than reinforcing, the belief that a woman's worth and respect hangs on her bodily modesty.

Perhaps this argument was best made in a letter which was sent to the American group Women Against Pornography:

> I recently heard one of your members say that porn films caused rape. I work in sex films. I don't think that women who appear sexy, either in film or in person are to blame for rape. The blame lies with the rapist – so let's not make excuses for his crime . . . To say that looking at a sexy picture makes a normal, healthy man go out and rape is crazy. Most of the men I meet would not force themselves on me, and the ones who would, would do so even if they never saw an X-rated film.[171]

As Coco Khan writes in regard to modesty culture within her own community, '[t]oo tempting, everything is too bloody tempting, what happened to self-control? Like it's our fault they're creeps! Heaven forbid a woman should have a life outside the house and start getting crazy ideas about independence.'[172] The problem is not immodest women; the problem is that those deemed 'whores' are expected to shoulder the sins of men. A woman's respect should not have to rest on her state of bodily coverage, and we should all be capable of giving every woman, veiled or scantily clad, the respect she deserves.

Living Dolls?

Not only have feminist artists and naked protesters faced the
wrath of puritanical feminism, so too have those engaging in
the practice of 'beauty' (including makeup and fashion) and
what Ariel Levy has christened 'raunch culture'.[173] While
important critiques exist of both beauty and raunch culture,
they frequently speak in derogative tones towards those they
describe as being 'living dolls', 'narcissistic' and 'artificial'.[174]
Even and perhaps especially among feminists, '[w]omen who
parade their beauty or sexuality are belittled as stupid, lacking
in intellect, and other 'meaningful' social attributes'.[175] Implicit
within feminism's dismissal of 'beautiful' or 'hot' women is the
idea that the body is inferior to the brain, something which
follows in a long tradition.

While the intellectuals who write and commentate on
women and society clearly value mental efforts and endeavours (including their own), they have a tendency to devalue
bodily efforts, particularly those revolving around beauty and
sexuality. To address this double standard, Catherine Hakim
coins the term 'erotic capital' to include beauty, sexual attrac-
tiveness, charm, vivaciousness and sexual skill, and points out
that, like human capital, it 'requires some basic level of talent
and ability, but can be trained, developed, and learnt, so that
the final quantum goes far beyond any initial talent'.[176] But
the notion of valuing and respecting those who invest in and
develop their 'erotic capital' remains taboo among feminists.
While there is little criticism of women who 'show off' or
'pimp' their brain, if you hone your erotic skills and sell sexual
stimulation for a living, that is somehow considered wrong.
Hakim explains this double standard in terms of a 'puritan
Anglo-Saxon antipathy to beauty and sexuality' that, rather
than valuing the body, assumes that 'taking any account of
someone's appearance should be outlawed, effectively making
the valorisation of erotic capital unlawful'.[177]

According to nineteenth-century liberal thinkers such as John Stuart Mill, the mind and the body were at odds with one another, and human achievement depended on suppressing 'the animal instinct'; the body, unlike the brain, was demonised.[178] Since the Enlightenment, there has been a tendency to view 'clever' people as superior to those seen as 'just bodies'. Historically, this thinking has incorporated an implicit gender element: the association of the brain with men and the body with women. Since the body has been traditionally associated with women, and since women have traditionally been seen as inferior to men, then by default it has been assumed that 'showing off' or making money from the body is less respectable than 'showing off' or making money from the brain. And, of course, it has been in the interest of men to leave models, dancers and sex workers in a vulnerable position, unprotected by the law, and scorned by society. Too many feminists fall into this same trap; one which devalues women who earn income from their looks or their sexuality; in fact, not only devaluing them, but aiming to eradicate them. While there is something seriously wrong with a world in which women's only means of survival operates via their body, there is similarly something wrong with a world in which women are free to make the most of their brains, but not of their bodies: a world in which the women who make use of their brains have rights and respect, but those who make use of their bodies are denied the same. In fact, not only has the body been derided, the brain has come to be seen as disembodied – as separate, and superior, to the body.[179] It is worth reminding ourselves, as Judith Butler noted, '[t]here is no writing without the body'.[180]

The derision of women who reveal or monetise their bodies extends to those who embrace 'femininity'. The 'feminine' look is seen as a product of patriarchy, leading, famously, to twentieth-century feminists adopting trousers, short hair and plain clothes as a show of resistance.[181] While there is absolutely nothing wrong with making such choices, the associated

notion that women who choose to appear 'feminine' are brainwashed by patriarchy is offensive and patronising. As a young
female academic, I had to navigate my need to signal serious-
ness with a concern that being seen as feminine could detract
from it. Other academics experienced the same tension, as
Ngaire Donaghue's study of their style blogs highlights:

> Bloggers were well-aware that dressing in their preferred, nor-
> mative feminine styles could (and sometimes did) lead others
> to question both their seriousness as scholars and their feminist
> politics. Yet at the same time, they challenged the legitimacy of
> this reading and frequently argued that it is politically neces-
> sary for feminists to embody a range of modes of femininity in
> order to lay to rest the notion that femininity is incompatible
> with intellectual seriousness.[182]

Hannah McCann argues that femininity should be valued as
an element of self-expression, and the notion that it is 'consumerist' and 'anti-feminist' ignores the pleasure and identity
of those appearing, embodying and performing femininity.[183]
Queerness and transsexuality suggests that femininity is not
simply a process of socialisation and sexualisation; you can
have a feminine identity without it necessarily being forcibly
imposed on you by society. By interviewing those working in
beauty salons, McCann confronts feminist ideas with the emotional 'boost' and 'good feelings' involved. For many women, a
visit to the salon is an occasion that offers 'me time', a chance
to unload emotionally, and an opportunity to escape caring
commitments and 'feel yourself again'. Beauty is, she argues,
'beyond skin deep'.[184] Ternikar notes that pious fashion is
also 'used as a way to create community and partnership' for
women in the American Muslim diaspora, while McCann has
brought to light the way in which, as sites of emotional rev-
elation between client and worker, salons can act as a source
of support and information about, for example, domestic

violence.[185] Nevertheless, attempts to revalue, as opposed to deride, femininity and beauty face criticism for having 'ignored' the concerns of earlier feminists, and are even dismissed as 'unsophisticated'.[186]

In addition to deriding beauty and femininity, feminism has a particular tendency to deride sexiness. The actress and model Emily Ratajkowski has spoken out about the shame she has been made to feel 'for playing with sexiness'.[187] 'There's this idea that if a man enjoys a photograph of a nude woman or if he likes your short skirt, he's taking something away from you.'[188] She also notes the same in regard to sex: 'A woman talks about having sex, and it's like, well, a guy got to have sex with you, so you're stupid. You've given something up.'[189] She notes that many people 'were outraged that the naked girl from the viral music video [Ratajkowski] . . . had dared to call herself a feminist'.[190]

While sexiness and sexism can and do sometimes overlap, it need not be the case. The reality is that women can be 'sexy' without it being sexist. In their book *Objectification: On the difference between sex and sexism*, Susanna Paasonen et al. argue that too many feminists have conflated sex with sexism; that sexual representation and sexist representation are two different things. They note that 'while there may be more *sexual* depiction than ever, *sexist* representations have grown less socially acceptable, and it is productive to ply these two concepts apart'.[191] Contrary to those who argue that sexy images of women are a key driver of sexism, Brian McNair notes that women's rights and gay rights have progressed 'further and faster in liberal democratic societies of the type where cultural sexualisation and pornographication have been most visible'.[192] While in recent years there has been a marriage of anti-porn feminists and anti-porn Christians, McNair points out that being blanket anti-porn (or pro-porn) makes little sense, as porn can be 'empowering and fascinating' as well as 'destructive and injurious', which should therefore encourage us to be more nuanced: in other words, 'just as there can be no pro-/anti-prose fiction position, or pro-/anti-narrative film or TV drama position', '[t]here is no meaningful "pro-" or "anti-porn" position'.[193] Nevertheless porn, and the sexual depiction of women more generally, has become a scapegoat, letting sexism off the hook. Alongside, while many feminists see 'objectification' and 'sexualisation' as central to gender inequality, it is worth noting that women, indeed people in general, can be objectified in ways unrelated to sex, that sexism can occur in contexts other than sexualised ones, and that '[o]ne can be sexually explicit without being sexist'.[194]

Women are too often made to feel that their body detracts from everything else and that, therefore, they must make a choice: between being a body or a brain. Ratajkowski recounts a comment she received on Instagram: 'stop showing your body and maybe someone will start listening to you', which was in turn mirrored by the advice she has been offered by professionals.[195] 'If you want people to think of you as a good actress, you're going to need to get ugly' noted one agent.[196] Hairstylists she worked with on a film set warned her that 'it was time to stop doing nude photo shoots now that I was no longer just a model and muse'.[197] Ratajkowski notes the way in which her female acquaintances and peers adopt more modest dress in order to command greater respect, even dyeing their hair brown 'to be considered serious', and asks whether it is 'fair' that they should be expected to do this.[198] She recalls the media asking Kim Kardashian why she was 'dressing less sexy', who in turn responded: 'I'm here in the White House and then the next day I was posting, like, a crazy bikini selfie. And I was thinking, I hope they don't see this, I have to go back there next week.'[199]

In her book *Living Dolls*, Natasha Walter writes that:

> When we talked about empowerment in the past, it was not a young woman in a thong gyrating around a pole that would

spring to mind, but the attempts by women to gain real political and economic equality.[200]

But, why assume that a pole dancer isn't at the same time interested in politics or standing for political office? Why should Kim Kardashian be expected to hide her body, or avoid being sexy, if she is to be listened to? And why can't Ratajkowski have her 'instagram hustle' while also 'being respected' for her 'ideas and politics'?[201] More generally, why can't women, if we so choose, be both an Athena and an Aphrodite?

The classicist Sarah Pomeroy may provide us with the answer:

> Unable to cope with a multiplicity of powers united in one female, men from antiquity to the present have envisioned women in 'either-or' roles. As a corollary of this anxiety, virginal females are considered helpful, while sexually mature women like Hera are destructive and evil . . . If the characteristics of the major goddesses were combined, a whole being with unlimited potential for development – a female equivalent of Zeus or Apollo – would emerge.[202]

And this would, of course, 'engender anxiety in the insecure male'.[203]

But the internalisation of the idea that women must choose between their body and their brain, ideally in favour of the latter, isn't the only problem within feminism. Ironically, some feminists are very happy for women to flaunt their bodies but only on the condition that they have proven their intelligence first. Rachel Khona writes that Kim Kardashian has 'reduced herself . . . to a vapid sex object'.[204] Khona does not, however, object to women who are both 'sexy' and 'smart', and so insists that 'Kim . . . should also show us she's smart, interesting, and funny as well'. Even putting aside the question of Kim Kardashian's intelligence, the idea that a woman is only entitled to be 'sexy' if she also proves her worth in some other way is intellectually elitist and unfair. Respectable immodesty should not be reserved for the privileged few.

In addition to women in possession of brain-power, economic and class privilege similarly makes it easier for some women to escape the classification of being 'slutty'. The reality is that women who display 'middle-classness' are less likely to be judged 'slutty' when appearing sexy, particularly where they are white. As Monique Mulholland writes, drawing on the work of Beverley Skeggs, what form of 'raunch' is considered acceptable as opposed to 'slutty' 'can be seen as a continuation of bourgeois signifiers of respectability', with 'class-based judgements' representing a 'continued attempt to *control* the illicit by deciding in whose hands the raunchy best resides'.[205] This has 'invidious consequences for working-class girls'; at the same time, upper-class women are able to 'flaunt' their bodies – including by wearing sexy clothes – while maintaining a degree of respectability.[206]

As the exotic dancer Josephine Baker knew well, the judgements that Black women face make the situation even worse. Comparing young people's reactions to Lady Gaga and Beyoncé music videos, Mulholland notes that different standards are applied when it comes to categorising white and Black women as 'hot' versus 'slutty'. She writes that people find it 'surprising and notable when a 'white' girl displays raunchy sexuality because of the historical trajectory *not to do so* . . . [whereas] black female sexuality is pervasively essentialised as intrinsically sexual'.[207]

Jade LB's *Keisha the Sket*, written in 2005 when the author was herself a teenage girl, follows a 17-year-old London girl navigating her sex life against a backdrop of both raunch culture and a history of Black women being deemed 'jezebels'.[208] As Kadish Morris sums it up:

Even when partaking in her own sexualisation, repeatedly commenting on the smallness of her waist and the bigness of her breasts, Keisha understands that a woman's purity is her currency. In order to receive love from Ricardo and respect in society, she must slut-shame herself back to virginity. 'Ive slept around abit aswel, but ive used protection at least 90% of da tym. I aint proud of da tingz i bin up 2 . . . I wish I cud turn bck da clock [sic]'.[209]

The way in which feminist writers problematise women who make erotic use of their bodies (including for money), along with women who live their lives in lipstick and short skirts, or who simply choose not to cover all their flesh (for comfort or for naked protest), is revealing of who they do and do not respect. Given the long history of white middle-class women rendering working-class women and women of colour unrespectable, it is especially troubling.[210] Feminism increasingly appears to be a group of 'clever' women talking down to those they see as 'selling themselves': a feminism of brain versus body, where only those with privilege, whether in the form of education, class or race, are entitled to a respectable body.

Why Modesty is not the Answer

'You know, men have no respect for women anymore. I can't even get guys to wear condoms . . . after three dates when I wouldn't sleep with him, he dumped me . . . If you ask me, it's because it's way too easy for them. Why should they waste time with a girl like me when they can get it for free.'[211] Those were the words of a 33-year-old woman which are at the heart of Wendy Shalit's book making the case for *A Return to Modesty*. For Aossey, '[h]ip Feminist campaigns like Free the Nipple only encourage a gullible behavior of disrespect for our own bodies, leading to everyone else around us disrespecting our bodies as well'. Like Shalit, she also makes the case for a more modest form of feminism, pointing to Muslim feminists for inspiration.[212]

As these two examples show, immodest women are to the feminist movement what scabs are to the trade union movement. Feminist critiques of immodesty and of naked feminism in its most literal form can be boiled down to the argument that immodest women not only hurt themselves but also impose a cost on other women: that even if immodest women really were displaying or monetising their bodies in a way that was freely chosen, the costs to other women would be large enough to render such behaviour unacceptable; that the modesty cult is, in other words, not a cult, but a form of collective wisdom – one that individual women renege on to the peril of the wider sisterhood.

So, is there any logic in the argument that modesty culture really can be in women's collective best interest? Helpfully, this question is one that has been researched by a group of academics that have come to be known as Social Exchange Theorists, and their findings are revealing. They show that modesty can indeed work in women's collective best interests – but only if sex is the key thing that women have to offer.[213] When women are locked out of education, work and politics, it can be in women's collective best interest to restrict the supply of sex so as to achieve a higher 'price' for the one thing they do have to offer (whether in monetary or non-monetary terms). If sex is all a husband is interested in (i.e. if he doesn't value his wife for anything but sex), then reducing the supply of sexual stimulation (by cracking down on immodest women) can prevent the husband from 'wandering'. In response, wives can demand better treatment from their husbands in return for the sex they have to offer them, safe in the knowledge that their husband won't be able to access sexual stimulation elsewhere. They can, in a sense, hold their husband to ransom, in the style of 'give me what I want or I'll go on sex strike'. Whereas, when men can get sex elsewhere, the threat of a sex strike is an empty threat and that's a problem if sex is the only thing that women have to bargain with. Hence, in a situation in which sex really is the only thing women have to offer, it could indeed be argued that immodesty 'cheapens' women, whereas modesty makes them more valuable.

Roy Baumeister and Kathleen Vohs draw a parallel with the cartel that controls the global supply of oil:

> Similar to how OPEC seeks to maintain a high price for oil on the world market by restricting the supply, women have often sought to maintain a high price for sex by restricting each other's willingness to supply men with what men want.[214]

But even in a society where sex really is the key thing that women have to offer, perhaps the modesty cult is as much about intra-female competition as it is about conspiring with other women to increase the price of sex. By living your life to the tune of the cult of female modesty, you can climb the social hierarchy by signalling your purity. Covering up and 'saving yourself' for the 'right' man can, if achievable, be an optimal strategy in a world in which women's worth and survival depends on men's judgement of them. But, to get the best outcome for yourself, you have to outdo other women in terms of modesty, pointing out where you are doing better, and where they have 'fallen'. Modesty is a relative thing; for one woman to be modest, another must be deemed immodest. It is one of the reasons women slut-shame: to signal that they do not approve of, or engage in, immodest behaviour, taking the opportunity to mark themselves out as more 'worthy'. In other words, modesty is not necessarily enforced by the sisterhood in order to 'protect' one another, it can also be the outcome of intra-female competition in a world in which making the best of a bad situation involves 'playing the game'.[215] Within modesty culture, there is no better way to trumpet your own 'virtue' than by putting another woman down; drawing attention to another woman's 'promiscuity'.

The idea that women should abide by the modesty cult is, therefore, dependent on a world in which all women have to offer is sex; a world in which women can offer little else to society than sexual access and the reproduction that comes with it. The more that women have been free to participate in education, paid work and politics, the more they have become seen as something other than 'sex' and the less they have needed to slut-shame one another. In that sense, sexual revolutions are the product of a world which is already working in the direction of gender equality.

Where women are no longer dependent on men and where sex is no longer a woman's only ace card, the notion that they should have to abide by the modesty cult appears perverse. Indeed, in a situation in which women have more to offer their societies than sex, the modesty cult works only to divide women, rather than bringing them together. It turns woman against woman, and, as with any strategy of divide and conquer, enhances the power of the patriarchy. As we saw in Chapter 2, the modesty cult is filled with dangers; the idea that it represents some form of feminist utopia bears little relation to reality. While there is nothing wrong with women choosing to be modest, there is a great deal wrong with judging women on the basis of that modesty.

An Appeal for Tolerance

I am not naive. The sexual revolution certainly did not offer all that it promised; there is still much work to be done. Women's sexual desires still come second to men's. We are still surrounded by unrealistic images of women.[216] And our sex education is all too often flimsy and impractical, sometimes steeped in shame and at other times gung-ho.

Critics of beauty and raunch culture have some valid concerns. If people really do equate every woman's worth with
the degree to which she is 'beautiful' or 'hot and sexy', it is,
like modesty culture, resting a woman's value on her body
alone. Shalit documents how difficult she has found life as a
modest women, being bullied and ostracised by her female
peers,[217] and how young women feel under pressure to dress a
certain way to avoid being labelled prudes: 'My daughter says
she doesn't like wearing tight clothing all the time, but she
says all the girls at school dress like that, so she's always saying
"Mom I *have* to!".'[218] Muslim women wearing head coverings
are also increasingly singled out, both by society and by the
force of law. By 2019, burqa bans were in place in all public
areas in France, Belgium, Denmark, Austria and Bulgaria, and
in at least some places or regions in Norway, the Netherlands,
Spain, Germany, Switzerland and Austria.[219] In Canada in
2021, Fatemeh Anvari, a teacher, was removed from the classroom for wearing a headscarf in front of her class.[220] The same
Canadian clothing constraints apply to police officers, lawyers
and judges, with women who wear headscarves barred from
public positions of authority.

At the other end of the spectrum, while billboards and
pornography may suggest that as a society we are entirely
comfortable with 'immodest' women, the reality is otherwise.
Women are still deemed 'whores' in Western society and mis-
treated and abused daily as a consequence. While being 'hot'
can now command respect, young people make a clear distinction between being 'hot' and being 'slutty', and, where a young
woman is categorised as the latter rather than the former, she
is, in the words of one teenage boy, offered 'zero respect'.[221]
As Monique Mulholland notes, 'displaying a femininity that
is hot but not slutty is tricky, and hard to navigate', and is also
riddled with class and racial prejudice, with the consequence
that some women are more readily categorised as 'slutty' than
others.[222] Women who are seen as 'slutty' are exploited and

abused, and sex workers are murdered at the hands of those who see them as unworthy, while having their voices disregarded by feminists who claim that they do not know their own minds. While, according to some, modesty culture is dead and buried, for others it could not be more obvious.

The reality is that both modest and immodest women alike get a raw deal today. In response, societies appear to be moving towards the two extremes: banning headscarves is seen by some as a movement towards gender equality, and modesty is championed by others as being the route to a feminist utopia.

Aossey urges her 'Free the Nipple gal pals to take a look at your Muslim sisters and collaborate with them to create a feminism that treats the female body as a temple and not as a toy. Let us see feminism in a different light – through modesty and the courage to savor our sugar. Let us call on the Muslim feminists of the world.'[223] As we have already seen, Shalit has also called for a 'return to modesty' in American society, and here in the UK, Louise Perry has made a similar call.[224] While for Aossey, Shalit and Perry, a more modest way of life is the route to respect, the lives of women in the past (as we saw in Chapter 1), and the lives of women today (as we saw in Chapter 2), suggest otherwise. At the same time, enforcing immodesty, such as through burqa bans, is also not the answer; laws which ban women from covering their hair are no better than laws which force them to cover up. Both raunch culture and modesty culture contain the same fundamental flaw: the mistreatment of women on the basis of their modesty is equally abhorrent to the mistreatment of women on the basis of their immodesty.

Rather than turning to either extreme, it would instead be better to aim for a world in which no woman was judged on the basis of her bodily modesty, so that modest and immodest women alike can co-exist, each feeling respect for themselves and for one another. As Katherine Bullock writes in regard to the stream of modesty feminism within Islam, tolerance

is needed on both sides: 'the "conservative" side of the spectrum needs to be careful of arrogance and denouncing those
who do not wish to wear hijab; as does the "progressive" side
in its denunciations of those who do wish to wear hijab or
niqab'.[225] The way we can truly gauge women's bodily freedom is through the degree of diversity we see around us, and
the open-mindedness and tolerance with which women treat
other women. A world in which women can be as immodest or
modest as they like is a far freer world than one in which we all
dress and behave the same, whether modestly or immodestly.
As Naomi Wolf notes, '[t]he real issue has nothing to do with
whether women wear makeup or don't, gain weight or lose it,
have surgery or shun it, dress up or down, make our clothing
and faces and bodies into works of art or ignore adornment
altogether. The real problem is our lack of choice.'[226]

Clearly, we still have a lot to do in terms of ensuring that *all*
women have choices and that women who choose to monetise
their bodies have the same rights and respect as those who
monetise their brain. We also, however, need to be more tolerant of the choices made by individual women, whether that
is to don a veil, to sit topless on the beach, to uncover their
hair, or to strip for money. Just as a world in which women are
forced to sell sex, or forced to uncover their bodies, can never
be a feminist utopia, a world that is intolerant of immodest
women cannot be one either.

The answer to our problems should not be to enforce conformity, but to challenge the whole notion of modesty norms;
to stop judging one another on the basis of our bodily modesty; to let every person dress as they wish; to not assume that
uncovered women are 'trashy' and can be treated as 'meat', or
that modest women are 'victims' and 'prudes'.

Like Wendy Shalit, when I was a teenage girl, I was bullied
for being a 'prude', and faced constant harassment from other
girls when wearing my long skirts and long socks. Ironically,
the abuse and mistreatment faced by modest women is in part

a product of modesty culture itself: a concern in the minds of individual women that modest women, relatively speaking, render them 'immodest' in comparison; that when someone covers more than you, you are the one left feeling 'naked'. Once we escape from the modesty cult, we also escape from the idea that modest as well as immodest women are to be feared. We can, at last, be respectful and tolerant of one another.

Conclusion

While you might imagine that women today would be free to do what they want with their own body, the reality is otherwise. Naked feminism is commonly seen as contradictory and hypocritical. Women who embrace nudity, along with sexiness, femininity and beauty, are seen as maidens of the patriarchy, and certainly not as 'real' feminists. The feminists who deride them think they have good cause. After all, as Gabby Aossey asks: 'Don't women deserve consistent respect and to actually be listened to without drools or criticisms over our bodies and looks?'[227] Many would like us to follow in the footsteps of the suffragettes, embracing not only their tricolour branding but the modesty messaging behind it. They spotlight their immodest sisters, holding them responsible for women being treated like sex objects. The stripper and the sex worker are at the tip of this immodesty iceberg, and must, apparently, be abolished if the society-wide abuse and mistreatment of women is to be brought to a close. Implicit is a view that while it is perfectly acceptable, even to be encouraged, for a woman to 'show off' and monetise her brain, it is not acceptable for her to do the same with her body. Any woman who does is assumed either to be selfish, or brainwashed by patriarchy, and must (apparently) be forced out of this mindset so as to prevent indignity and harm to other women. If only women covered up, stopped 'strutting their stuff', and monetised their brains rather than their bodies, sexism could, apparently, be made extinct.

I disagree. As we saw in Chapter 2, the modesty cult does not help women, it hurts women – and in multiple ways. While feminists who critique raunch and immodesty raise some valid concerns, those concerns, and our means of resolving them, should not come at the cost of demonising 'immodest' women. As the former stripper and author Lily Burana writes: 'Just because a girl has bleached blonde hair and high heels doesn't mean that she's going to sell the female gender down the river.'[228] However modest or not we choose to be, women share the same set of problems. When Sabica Khan and Mona Eltahawy shared their personal experiences of facing sexual abuse while at Mecca, the hashtag #MosqueMeToo went viral.[229] As Eltahawy later wrote, 'my body was groped, pinched and touched without my permission during the nine years that I wore hijab . . . sexual assault has nothing to do with how you're dressed.'[230] Similar stories also abound within Christian circles, as shared via the hashtag #ChurchToo.[231] While, in response to the Harvey Weinstein revelations, the actress Mayim Bialik initially suggested in the New York Times that by dressing modestly women could avoid such abuse, she later apologised.[232]

A return to puritanism has never helped women, and this time will be no different. The solution to the problems women collectively face is instead to be found in revolutionising the way we think about and value women. Challenge the cult of female modesty and the whorephobia that is so central to it and you challenge a system of beliefs that hampers the freedom and happiness of every woman.

Conclusion

When a London statue by the artist Maggi Hambling was unveiled in 2020 in honour of Mary Wollstonecraft, it rapidly became a 'feminist battle-ground'.[1] Emerging from the undulating and organic metal form was, at its peak, a tiny sculpture of a naked woman. Across social media, and in the press, feminists expressed their disapproval. As one journalist noted, '[m]any have asked why a statue of a thinker as pioneering as Wollstonecraft should draw attention to the physicality of the female body rather than to Wollstonecraft's work and ideas'.[2]

The fact that even modern-day feminists seem to believe that nudity and intellectual prowess are somehow incompatible suggests that we are still living in a society in which women are categorised as either 'brains' or 'bodies', when incontrovertibly everyone has both. This is something I attempt to challenge every time I place my own naked body in the public sphere. From my nude portrait, displayed at the Mall Galleries in London in 2014, to my naked performance at the Cambridge Junction Theatre in 2019, I aim to demonstrate that every woman (dressed *or* undressed) is a real thinking being, and that we should reject judging women on the basis of their bodily modesty.[3] In response, I am declared 'trashy', an 'idiot' and a 'whore'. This, of course, would not have surprised Wollstonecraft, who was herself posthumously attacked for her immodest behaviour, ultimately being branded a 'prostitute' by the press.[4] Indeed, according to the *Anti-Jacobin Review*, 'Mary's theory . . . is so far from being new, that it is as old as prostitution'; they later published a poem titled *The Vision of Liberty* that held her responsible for 'propagating w[hore]s'.[5] What is ironic is that, rather than challenging this archaic modesty cult, some of the feminist critics of Hambling's naked statue appear to have subscribed to it.

Women's bodies are one of the biggest battlegrounds we face today and – inside as well as outside feminism – it is the cult of female modesty that leads the charge. Across the world, women and girls are secluded, forcibly veiled, subjected to virginity tests, and face genital mutilation. From Mexico to the Pacific Islands, the modesty cult encourages men – and women – to harass and abuse those they judge to be 'whores', absolved from guilt, and instead warmed by the glow of believing that they are maintaining social order. Thousands of women are murdered by their own families in order to eradicate the perceived stain of immodesty. Millions have been denied the opportunity of education or of paid work in order to limit the risk of such a stain. In the West, modesty momentum fuels lobbies that seek to restrict women's free-dom to control their own fertility, resulting in the present day push to deny women access to abortion in America. While at first glance it might be easy to assume that the modesty cult has been consigned to history, I ask you this: find me a woman who has not faced being called a 'whore', who has not experienced embarrassment when accessing birth control or sexual health services, or who has not feared for her 'reputa-tion'. Although modesty culture manifests itself in different ways in different parts of the world, in all cases it inflicts great harm on immodest and modest women alike. It runs deeper and is more widespread than we like to imagine. And most importantly, we cannot tackle women's lack of bodily autonomy, or the broader problem of gender inequality, without breaking it.

An optimist might assume that society's obsession with women's bodily modesty naturally recedes with time. After all, from where I am sat in the West, we are now on the other side of the sexual revolution, and are told that we are living in a 'striptease culture' where sex is more visible than ever before, and porn stars 'are entering the world of mainstream celebrity'.[6] But history teaches us that a return to modesty is never far away. The cult of female modesty has ebbed and flowed across time, and, whenever it has seemingly been overcome, it has eventually risen like a phoenix from the ashes, reasserting itself with claims of being in the best interests of women and for the greater good of wider society. Wherever it has been liberated, women's sexuality has been seen as a threat to social order, with scantily clad and 'promiscuous' women blamed for everything from wars and plague to natural disasters. From single mothers to sex workers, 'immodest' women have been hunted, burned, drowned, committed to asylums and imprisoned in their thousands, if not millions. And, despite the obvious lessons from history, the pendulum is now swinging back towards modesty.

The Puritans are not a historical relic – they are making a comeback. Against a backdrop of raunch, modesty culture sells itself as our saviour, promising a refreshing change from female exposure and a 'sexed up' society. So the cult of female modesty grows. In America, 'purity culture' is on the rise, including in the form of virginity pledges and chastity balls. In Afghanistan, where women were once free to dress as they chose, they are now forced to veil, and, worryingly, clothing restrictions are spreading to more and more countries. In Israel, gender segregation has become increasingly popular as a means of 'protecting' women's modesty. And, across the world, strippers and glamour models, and women on a night out, are demonised and held responsible for the bad behaviour of men. Even within feminism itself, immodest women (and those who refuse to judge them) are portrayed not only as 'brainwashed' but as the enemy of womankind: as, to quote Ariel Levy, 'female chauvinist pigs'.[7]

Whatever the problems with raunch culture, modesty culture is not the solution. Rather than embracing it, we need to confront the damage it imposes on millions of women and girls across the globe. We need to reflect on our own lives, rejecting our own internal whorephobia and slut-shaming; we need to call out the same damaging attitudes and behaviours that are at the heart of the women's movement; and, in its place, we need feminism to position the concept of 'my body, my choice' in its broadest possible form, and with the tolerance on which it depends, at its heart. It is through these three steps that we can achieve real freedom for women, and create a truly equal society.

Step 1: Self-reflection

While on the Cairo metro in a headscarf, Mona Eltahawy was confronted by a woman wearing a niqab, who asked why she wasn't covering her face. 'Isn't what I'm wearing enough?', Eltahawy asked. The woman replied: 'If you want to eat a piece of candy, would you choose one that is in a wrapper or an unwrapped one?'[8] Now, there is absolutely nothing wrong with choosing to wear a niqab (just as there is equally nothing wrong with choosing not to). And there are plenty of women who are modest without internalising the modesty cult – without judging other women on the basis of their perceived immodesty.[9] But, in this case, the internalised 'male gaze' could not be more clear. Women are not 'pieces of candy' waiting on a shelf to be devoured by a man, and they should not have to live their lives desperately trying to avoid behaviours that might somehow repel men.

The internalisation of the modesty cult goes well beyond this particular Cairo confrontation. A recent survey of Egyptian attitudes revealed that not only do more than three-fifths of men believe that the victim of an honour killing 'usually deserves such punishment', so too do almost a half of women.[10] Women are also instrumental in female genital mutilation, just as they were in footbinding.[11] In the West, where forced veiling, honour killings and genital cutting are less common, many women nevertheless resort to slut-shaming[12] and have little tolerance for peers who reveal more flesh than they themselves do. Only a minority of UK women think that topless sunbathing is 'acceptable for both men and women',[13] while one in two think that non-sexualised naked protest is completely unacceptable.[14] And, on both sides of the Atlantic, feminist groups are actively excluding strippers and sex workers from their ranks, questioning their claims of agency and spearheading campaigns to close down their places of work.

So step one of our three-point plan is purging ourselves of whorephobia. For a long time, I myself played host to an internalised modesty cult and it has taken longer than I expected to shake it off. A decade ago, I would never have dreamed of life-modelling. I was brought up to believe that women who reveal their bodies to anyone other than a long-term partner were 'ruining' their reputation, rendering themselves less respectable in the eyes of others, and reducing their worth. It was only by coming to the personal realisation that my value as a human being should depend on much more important things than who had seen my body, that I was able to begin shedding the modesty cult, along with my clothes. But, as I later found out, this was only the start of the process. When the first nude image of me reached the public eye in 2014, in the form of an oil painting, some responded by saying that I was 'little better than a Page 3 girl'. My initial reaction was to devise a mental list of ways in which my naked act was different to the work of a glamour model – In other words, how I was somehow 'better' than them. My list included the fact that my nude was in a prestigious gallery alongside eminent public figures, rather than on the pages of a 'lads' mag'; that my image wasn't 'sexualised' or manipulated – it was 'just me' in its most natural form; and, of course, that I hadn't been paid for posing naked, that I had a 'proper' and 'respectable' job. But I soon realised that my defensiveness was not only unwarranted (what did I have to be ashamed of?), it was also a product of modesty culture. It was a response to the way in which we are, sadly, conditioned to look down on strippers, sex workers and topless models. Little wonder that I wanted to mark myself out as different – to be able to reveal my body while maintaining my reputation. Yet the truth is that whether I choose to pose naked or not, I am worth no more, and no less, than a glamour model. None of us is. My initial, and erroneous, thought process is, in retrospect, my one and only regret about posing naked. Having now fully broken my own internalisation of the modesty cult, I instead respond to accusations in a very different way, noting that glamour models, strippers and sex workers are some of the most genuine, understanding and wise people you could know, and that I am proud to sit, metaphorically and literally, alongside them.

Step 2: Reforming Feminism

After purging ourselves of our internal whorephobia, we also need to purge feminism of the same embedded attitudes to women's bodies. Only by joining forces with one another do women have the power to tackle gender inequality, but, sadly, the collective response of some women has been, and still is, to enforce rather than to challenge the modesty cult. The suffragettes were known for embracing 'purity' as part of their feminist message, represented by the white stripe of their famous tricolour branding. Today, too many feminists would like us to follow in their footsteps, adopting not only the colours but the attitudes of their predecessors. They pour scorn on immodest women, holding them responsible for womankind being treated like 'sex objects'. They mistakenly believe that the solution to sexism is to eradicate immodest women; that it is women, not men, who need to change. They conveniently sidestep the accusation of speaking down to other women by claiming that all women they deem to be immodest are brainwashed and so are incapable of adding to the feminist conversation, all while actively denying that there is any difference between sex work and involuntary prostitution, arguing that choice is either questionable or irrelevant. Ultimately, they cannot understand why any woman would, in her right mind, actually choose to be immodest. As a result, naked feminists like myself are condemned as no better than the scabs that cross a picket line. As one so-called feminist wrote to me: 'Why do u think women are not taken seriously or listened to and thought as sex objects? Because of silly tarts like you . . . You're a disgrace to all women!'

Some feminists are less vicious. They adopt the modesty cult not with a passion but with reluctance; as what they see as the only 'sensible' response to the biological reality women face – that of unwanted pregnancy, paternity uncertainty and rape. But if this biological reality determines our lives, why isn't history filled with curfews for men, male castration, and the demonisation of men's bodies, rather than the seclusion of women, female genital mutilation, and the vilification of women's bodies? As Golda Meir, the former Israeli Prime Minister, recalls:

> Once in the Cabinet we had to deal with the fact that there had been an outbreak of assaults on women at night. One minister (a member of an extreme religious party) suggested a curfew.

Women should stay at home after dark. I said: 'But it's the men who are attacking the women. If there's to be a curfew, let men stay at home, not the women.[15]

The fact that it is women's, and not men's, bodies that have always been the target of modesty culture is a reflection of the fact that it is men who have acquired religious, economic and political power throughout history. The cult of female modesty is not a biological inevitability; it can and should be broken. And the reality is that rather than helping women, it hurts women; modesty culture is not a form of self-protection, it is a form of self-harm. While there is absolutely nothing wrong with choosing modesty (and indeed I sometimes do myself), there *is* something wrong with being complicit in the belief that immodest women are disrespecting themselves and devaluing womankind.

According to Naheed Mustafa, 'women are not going to achieve equality with the right to bare their breasts in public' and, while I would agree that the right to bare breasts will not by itself deliver equality, condemning those who choose to do so will inevitably hinder the feminist cause.[16] When the Tunisian feminist activist Amira Yahyaoui, who was not wearing a headscarf, asked a member of the Tunisian Constituent Assembly a question during an interview, he told her that he does not speak to 'naked' women. In response, she began to undress and, in shock, he asked her what she was doing. She replied: 'I'm showing you what a naked woman looks like.'[17] It is not Yahyaoui's naked feminism that we should feel threatened by, but the ideology that she protests, one that insists that women must pass a test of bodily modesty in order to be heard and to be treated with respect.

Immodest women are not the enemy of womankind, and the last people who should be demonising them are feminists. After all, if 'immodest' women really are a central cause of gender inequality, why are countries like Iran, Afghanistan and

Pakistan not at the top of the gender equality rankings? And why, despite the fact that women's bodies are more visible than ever before in Western society, is that society significantly less sexist than it was fifty or a hundred years ago? It is because what causes the most damage to womankind is not women who choose to wear revealing clothing, who engage in casual sex, or who sell sex but, instead, the social belief that a woman's value, worth and respect rest on her physical modesty.

In response to one of my naked protests, an American Ivy League graduate initially focused her Twitter attacks on criticising my figure, tweeting that I was 'fat' and 'needed to lose weight', before following up with: 'The body is sacred until you decide to give it over to gawking, opinionated onlookers. Then you get what you deserve.' This attitude – one in which immodest women are fair game, not worthy of basic respect – is the ultimate problem, and it is a problem rooted in minds, not in immodesty. Only once all women, and particularly the feminist cause, cease their conscious, or subconscious, support of the modestly cult can we aim for a world in which women will be truly equal.

Step 3: Embrace 'my body, my choice'

For centuries, men have restricted what women can do with their bodies and with their brains. In recent years, women have made great strides in terms of their ability to use their brains as they wish. However, the same cannot be said for their bodies. Having progressed to achieve positions among the elite, women themselves are now using their intellectual and political power to deprive less privileged women of the most fundamental freedom of all: freedom over their own body. Show too much of that body, and they will be accused, as I often am, of objectifying and sexualising themselves and of 'setting feminism back a hundred years' while 'embarrassing' womankind. And, while making money from your brain is to be celebrated, making money from your body, for example as a glamour model, stripper or a sex worker, is not; instead you are shamed, stigmatised and attacked by the new feminist elite. Ultimately, is it not inconsistent to allow women to metaphorically uncover and make money from their brains but not to literally uncover and make money from their bodies? And is it not equally inconsistent to argue for 'my body, my choice' but only some of the time, or in other words, 'my body, sometimes my choice'? Shouldn't all women be free to use both their bodies and their brains as they themselves see fit and not as others tell them?

The reality is that a powerful and influential vein of modern-day feminism increasingly appears like a group of 'clever' women, who reveal and monetise their brains, ganging up to obstruct and marginalise those who do the same with their bodies. An intellectual elitism has taken hold within the movement, and an internalised 'male gaze' has created something akin to Orwellian doublethink: the notion that somehow restricting women's freedom will enhance women's freedom, particularly where the bodies of marginalised or minority women are concerned. Fittingly, George Orwell was himself sceptical of the ability of both liberals and intellectuals to resist incursions on personal liberty. He writes that 'it is the liberals who fear liberty'[18] and that 'perhaps when the pinch comes the common people will turn out to be more intelligent than the clever ones'.[19] In the case of women, those who society writes off as immodest are indeed the cleverest of all when it comes to understanding the path to equality, but they are dismissed as simply 'bodies' without brains, spoken down to and derided by feminists and the rest of society, their voices silenced.

As someone who has posed nude for works of art, and protested, performed and appeared on television naked, with numerous videos and photos of me available online, including, albeit without my permission, on porn sites, I would be a hypocrite to object to any woman who chooses to strip or sell glamour shots. While it is undeniable that a lack of well-paid jobs, a lack of access to childcare, the gender pay gap, and an inflexible welfare state all mean that too many women are pushed into situations in which they feel they have no choice but to monetise their body, be that by posing naked or selling sex, this does not mean that every woman who makes a living from her body does so because she has no choice. By assuming that no woman would ever actually choose to monetise her body, we are in turn assuming that immodest women are lacking in worth and respect; that no one could possibly choose to reveal their body or to sell sex. If our concern really is for women forced by financial constraint into selling their bodies, we should be 'outlawing poverty, not prostitutes' and joining the campaign for sex workers to have the same rights as everyone else.[20] After all, since when did the possibility of exploitation lead us to recommend fewer rather than more rights? The real problem is that those in positions of power with the ability to make a difference prefer to ignore this reality, and instead throw their weight behind the conveniently lower-cost agenda of 'abolition'. While it might generate a personal moralistic 'warm glow', abolition does not solve the problem of poverty and neither, therefore, will it solve the problem of exploitation. To ensure that every woman has choice, poverty must be tackled alongside the modesty cult.

'My body, my choice', in the broadest sense of the term, needs to replace the whorephobia that has for too long been at the heart of feminism. And, unlike in the past, it must not be applied solely to the issues of interest to women with intellectual and political power, but to all issues and to all women. Feminism must support the right of every woman to do what she wants with her own body, whether or not any of us, including the self-proclaimed intellectual elite, agree with her choice.

L et us stop and ask ourselves: What do we want our feminist utopia to look like? In my view, a feminist utopia that refuses entry to any woman, immodest or otherwise, is no utopia at all. Our utopia should instead be one in which every woman is truly free to do what she wants with her own body, and where those who do choose to reveal or monetise their body are free from stigma, and treated with the same respect as everyone else. As we have seen, the fate of every woman is intimately tied up with the fate of those deemed immodest. We cannot reach our feminist utopia without first breaking the cult of female modesty.

As is apparent in Afghanistan and Iran, naked feminism isn't just an abstract issue, and neither is it simply about the right to walk around undressed. Naked feminism certainly doesn't require you to be naked – it respects your right to choose modesty, just as it respects your right to choose otherwise. Naked feminism does, however, understand that women can only be free if their worth and respect is not conditional on something as superficial as the way they dress or whether their hymen is intact. It invites you to challenge modern-day social injustices: to break taboos about women's bodies, allowing women to talk about them without embarrassment, and thereby improve their health and enjoyment; to fight social practices and policies that seclude women, that forcibly cover their bodies, or that cut or kill; and to confront our hypocrisy in terms of women's ability to do what they want with their brains but not with their bodies, something which could have a transformative effect on some of society's most vulnerable women.

Despite what some may think, naked feminism isn't contradictory: its message is the recipe for liberation. Breaking the modesty cult frees women from the constant daily struggle against men who try to embarrass and demean them, along with state regulations that restrict their freedom in order to 'protect' their bodily 'honour'. It breaks the dislocation that can exist between a woman and her body, one which can make a woman feel that her body is a liability. It allows women to take back control in their bedroom, to be healthier and to feel happier in themselves. Naked feminism challenges the very thing that restricts the freedom of millions of women across the world.

As I've seen for myself, modest and immodest women alike are perfectly capable of recognising the value in one another: they can respect each other irrespective of their state of dress or their sexual history. It is time for everyone to do likewise. It is time for us all, however we choose to dress or live our lives, to come together and challenge the toxic notion that women's worth and respect hang on something as superficial as their bodily modesty.

Imagine what would happen if all of the time and energy invested in women's modest 'reputation' and 'honour' across the globe was instead invested in education, exploring the world, or simply enjoying life? Not only would women be happier, and able to achieve more, but the world would be full of joy.

Let's break the cult of female modesty – once and for all.

Notes

Preface

1 Indeed, as Brian McNair notes in his book *Porno? Chic!* (2002), part of the present day backlash against the sexual revolution is driven by a homophobic response to the increasing visibility of homosexuality and other forms of sexual identity.
2 Williams, 2007.
3 Morgan, 1980, quoted in Paasonen et al., 2021.

Introduction

1 El Feki et al., 2017, pp. 83, 137, 215.
2 Jayachandran, 2015.
3 Pew Research Center, 2014, p. 9. Also see Adamczyk and Hayes, 2012.
4 Tang, Bensman and Hatfield 2013.
5 Poushter, 2014.
6 On 'striptease culture', see McNair, 2002.
7 Berkowitz, 2012, p. 11.
8 Ibid., p. 12.
9 Blundy, 2014.
10 YouGov, 2020.
11 YouGov, 2019.

12 Mulholland, 2013, ch. 7. For the classic Australian text on whore-phobia and the Madonna/Whore dichotomy, see Summers, 2016 (first published in 1975).
13 Hyde and DeLamater, 2020, p. 296.
14 Higgins et al., 2010; Sprecher et al., 1995.
15 Hyde and DeLamater, 2020, p. 296.
16 Keane, 2016.
17 Roberts, 2017. Also Lloyd, 2020.
18 Emmers-Sommer et al., 2017.
19 Quoted in Keane, 2016.
20 Maguire, 2008, p. 4.
21 Farzan, 2019.
22 Buckingham et al., 2011.
23 O'Riordan, 2020.
24 Ibid.
25 O'Brien, 2020.
26 Ratajkowski, 2019.
27 Ibid.
28 Hakim, 2010.
29 Ratajkowski, 2019.
30 Levy, 2005; Attwood, 2009, p. xiii; McNair, 2002; Mulholland, 2013, p. 5; Barton, 2021.
31 Triger, 2013, p. 19.
32 Carvalho, 2013.
33 Bullock, 2007, ch. 5.
34 Aossey, 2017.
35 Stiller et al., 2015.
36 Lookadoo and DiMarco, 2003, p. 213.
37 Ibid.
38 Gresh, 1999; quoted in Klement and Sagarin, 2016.
39 Blank, 2007, p. 249.
40 Under Title V (section 510(b)) of the Personal Responsibility and Work Opportunity Reconciliation Act.
41 Blank, 2007, pp. 239–41.
42 Fahs, 2010, p. 118.

43 Ibid.
44 Hamad, 2020; LB, J., 2021; Levine, 2003, 2007, 2008; McClintock, 1995.
45 Gibbs et al., 2019.
46 El Feki et al., 2017, p. 85, p. 139, p. 186.
47 Bryson, 2016, p. 80.
48 Jumet, 2017, p. 96. Also see Jasper, 2018.
49 Górnicka, 2016.
50 On how people (wrongly) assume that immodest women are lacking in self-esteem, see, for example: Krems et al., 2021.
51 Alibhai-Brown, 2015.
52 Smith, 2013, p. 21.
53 Ibid., p. 28.
54 Walter, 2010; Levy, 2005, p. 4, p. 20, p. 93.
55 Ibid., pp. 25, 28, 90–1.
56 Barton, 2021.
57 Ibid., pp. 2–3.
58 Channell, 2014, p. 613. Also see Matich, Ashman and Parsons, 2019 and Rivers, 2017.
59 Aossey, 2017.
60 Mustafa, 2013.
61 Hobson, 2019; Samuel, 2019.
62 Barton, 2021.

1 The Modesty Cult: A History

1 Robb and Harris, 2013, p. 39; Riddell, 2021, p. 121; Stannard and Langley, 2020.
 2 Stannard and Langley, 2020.
 3 Gilligan, 2019, p. 5.
 4 Ibid.
 5 Mayhew and Hemyng, 1861, p. 33. Also see Lecky, 1905.
 6 Ibid., p. 44.
 7 Goelet, 1993.
 8 Ibid.
 9 Budin, 2016.

10 Brusasco, 2004; Stol, 1995, p. 124.
11 Stol, 1995, p. 137.
12 Brusasco, 2004.
13 Ibid., 2004.
14 Budin, 2016.
15 Brosius, 2016.
16 Ibid.
17 See, for example, The Met, *Female figure 1500–1100 B.C.*
18 Dossani, 2013.
19 Goelet, 1993.
20 Dossani, 2013.
21 Ibid.
22 Ibid.
23 Ibid.
24 Berkowitz, 2012
25 Budin, 2016.
26 Ibid.
27 Ibid.
28 Stol, 1995, p. 130.
29 Carr-Gomm, 2013, pp. 52–4.
30 Ibid., pp. 58–9.
31 Ibid., p. 68.
32 Galt, 1931.
33 Tumanov, 2011.
34 Pomeroy, 1975, pp. 8–9.
35 Ibid., p. 49.
36 Glazebrook, 2016.
37 Ibid.
38 Dossani, 2013; Galt, 1931.
39 Dossani, 2013.
40 O'Faolain and Martines, 1979, p. 46
41 Ibid.
42 Glazebrook, 2016.
43 Ibid.
44 Lister, 2020, p. 84.

45 Hemelrijk, 2016, p. 896.
46 Dossani, 2013.
47 Ibid.
48 Hemelrijk, 2016, p. 897.
49 Mayhew and Hemyng, 1861, pp. 53–4.
50 Potter, 2015, pp. 91–2.
51 Ibid., pp. 28, 55–6, 183.
52 Orthodox Church of America, *Lives of the Saints*, n.d.
53 Baumeister and Twenge, 2002, p. 194; Stark, 1996.
54 Pope John Paul II, 1979.
55 Lerner, 1993, pp. 6–7.
56 Thompson, 1988.
57 Dossani, 2013.
58 Power, 1996.
59 Dossani, 2013.
60 Palladius and Meyer, 1965, pp. 36–7.
61 Karras, 1998, p. 107.
62 Karras, 2017, pp. 45–6.
63 Tumanov, 2011.
64 Castelli, 1986; McNamara, 1976; Power, 1996.
65 Tumanov, 2011.
66 Keddie, 2007, p. 24.
67 Ibid., pp. 26–7.
68 Ibid., p. 27.
69 Dossani, 2013.
70 Guthrie, 2001.
71 Cohen, 2005.
72 Goitein, 1967.
73 Mernissi, 1991; Ahmed, 1992.
74 El Guindi, 1999.
75 Mernissi, 2011 [1975], pp. 12–14.
76 Ibid., p. 13.
77 Ibid., p. 18.
78 Ibid., p. 17.
79 Michalopoulos, Naghavi and Prarolo, 2017.

80 Tang, Bensman and Hatfield, 2013. Also Molony, Theiss and Choi, 2016, and Sechiyama, 2015.
81 Molony, Theiss and Choi, 2016, pp. 8–10.
82 Tang, Bensman and Hatfield, 2013.
83 Molony, Theiss and Choi, 2016, p. 48; Tang, Bensman and Hatfield, 2013, p. 232.
84 Molony, Theiss and Choi, 2016, pp. 17–18, 52, 54.
85 Ibid., p. 41.
86 Ibid., p. 43.
87 Jung, 2011.
88 Cho, 2017, p. 563.
89 Ibid.
90 Ibid.
91 Dabhoiwala, 2012, p. 10.
92 Solberg, 2018.
93 Ibid., p. 5; Riddell, 2021, p. 125.
94 Solberg, 2018, pp. 7–9.
95 Lister, 2020, p. 25.
96 Levine and Wrightson, 1980, pp. 169, 170–1; Wiesner-Hanks, 2008, pp. 44, 258.
97 Laslett, 1980, p. 60.
98 Macfarlane, 1980, p. 73; Hardwick, 2020; Strasser, 2007; Farr, 1995.
99 Hardwick, 2020.
100 Laslett, 1980, p. 55, p. 57 fn.48.
101 Karras, 1998, p. 41.
102 Lister, 2020, p. 20.
103 Karras, 1998, p. 76.
104 Levine and Wrightson, 1980, p. 169, pp. 170–1.
105 Karras, 1998, p. 103.
106 Berkowitz, 2012, p. 191.
107 Wrightson, 1980, p. 180.
108 Levine and Wrightson, 1980, p. 173.
109 Ibid., p. 174.
110 Ibid., pp. 173–4.

111 Wrightson, 1980, p. 180.
112 Macfarlane, 1980, p. 77; Wiesner-Hanks, 2008, p. 66.
113 Wrightson, 1980, p. 181.
114 Levine and Wrightson, 1980, p. 161.
115 Berkowitz, 2012, p. 192.
116 Dabhoiwala, 2012, p. 15.
117 Berkowitz, 2012, p. 193.
118 Van der Heijden and Muurling, 2018; Cohen, 2008.
119 Wiesner-Hanks, 2008, p. 69.
120 Ibid., p. 68.
121 Ibid., 2008, p. 69.
122 Carr-Gomm, 2013, pp. 30–1.
123 Wiesner-Hanks, 2008, p. 253.
124 Ibid., p. 254.
125 D'Emilio and Freedman, 2012; Dabhoiwala, 2012, pp. 44, 78.
126 Fitzgerald, 2020.
127 Dabhoiwala, 2012, p. 78.
128 British Library, n.d., *A General History*; British Library, n.d., *The Rise of the Novel*.
129 Ibid.
130 Eberle, 2001.
131 Ibid., coda to ch1; and Johnson, 1988, xxiii.
132 Nekoei and Sinn, 2021.
133 Mullan, 2018.
134 British Library, n.d., *Evelina*.
135 Ibid.
136 Ibid.
137 Mullan, 2018.
138 Gatrell, 2007, pp. 348–9.
139 Ibid., p. 357.
140 Ibid., pp. 357–8.
141 Ibid., p. 366.
142 Ibid.
143 Ibid.

144 Ibid.
145 Dabhoiwala, 2012, pp. 55–71.
146 Ibid., pp. 55–71.
147 Ibid., p. 67.
148 Ibid., pp. 71–2.
149 Ibid., p. 54.
150 Ibid., p. 55.
151 Williams, 2018, p. 231.
152 Laslett, 1980, p. 54.
153 Ibid., p. 27; Flinn, 1981.
154 Smith, 1980, p. 370.
155 Laslett, 1980, p. 27.
156 British Library, n.d, *Harris's List*.
157 Tuckniss, 1967 [1861], pp. xxxiv–xxxv.
158 Ibid., pp. xxxvi–xxxvii.
159 Lister, 2020, pp. 31, 34.
160 Skeggs, 1997, p. 3. Also, Tyler, 2020.
161 Jeffreys, 1985, p. 7.
162 Levine, 2018, pp. 146–7.
163 Jeffreys, 1985, p. 8.
164 Ibid., p. 10.
165 Ibid., p. 17.
166 Ibid., p. 13.
167 Kalsem, 2004.
168 Banks, 1954.
169 Mort, 2000 [1987].
170 Levine, 2007.
171 Lister, 2020, p. 60.
172 Scull and Favreau, 1986, pp. 248–50.
173 Ibid., pp. 250–1.
174 Ibid., p. 254; Levine-Clark, 2014, p. 218.
175 Scull and Favreau, 1986, p. 255.
176 Angel, 2010.
177 Lister, 2020, pp. 166–7.
178 Ibid., p. 110.

179 Smith, 1980, p. 370.
180 Quoted in Gilligan, 2019, p. 11.
181 Ibid., p. 15.
182 Watson, 1998, p. 2.
183 Quoted in Gilligan, 2019, p. 12.
184 Hamad, 2020; LB, 2021; Levine, 2003, 2007, 2008; McClintock, 1995.
185 Levine, 2003, p. 182.
186 Patel, 2012, p. 300; Cronin, 2014, p. 9, p. 16.
187 Ibid., p. 20.
188 Ibid., p. 23; Northrop, 2004.
189 Edgar, 2003, p. 132. Also Kamp, 2006.
190 Cronin, 2014, p. 21.
191 Kamp, 2014, p. 217.
192 Cronin, 2014, ch. 1.
193 Cho, 2017.
194 Ibid.
195 Patel, 2012, p. 300.
196 Cronin, 2014, ch. 1.
197 Patel, 2012, p. 300; Cronin, 2014, p. 26.
198 Hoffman-Ladd, 1987, pp. 23–4.
199 Eltahawy, 2015, pp. 41–2.
200 Baumeister and Twenge, 2002, p. 184.
201 McLaren, 1999, p. 43; Szreter and Fisher, 2011, p. 113. Also, Roberts, 1995.
202 Mclaren, 1999, p. 43.
203 Szreter and Fisher, 2011, pp. 138–9.
204 Ibid., p. 131.
205 Ibid., p. 141.
206 Ibid., p. 123.
207 Ibid., p. 156.
208 Ibid., p. 121.
209 Ibid., p. 122.
210 Szreter and Fisher, 2011, pp. 71–2.
211 Ibid., p. 161; Tinkler, 1995, p. 165.

212 Szreter and Fisher, 2011, p. 144.
213 Ibid., pp. 119–20.
214 Caslin in McCarthy et al., 2015.
215 Ibid.
216 Ibid.
217 Barton, 2021.
218 Kleinplatz, 2018, pp. 35–6. Kinsey et al., 1953. For the British equivalent report, see Chesser, 1956.
219 Ibid., p. 35.
220 Blank, 2007, pp. 226–7.
221 Sprecher et al., 2013, p. 1397; Baumeister and Twenge, 2002, p. 184.
222 Ibid., p. 185.
223 Vance, 1993.
224 Attwood, 2009; McNair, 2002.
225 Barton, 2021.
226 Levy, 2005, p. 5.
227 Valenti, 2010.
228 Uecker, 2008.
229 Fahs, 2010, p. 118.
230 Valenti, 2010, p. 13.
231 Ibid., p. 32.
232 Eltahawy, 2015, p. 43.
233 Hoffman-Ladd, 1987, p. 24.
234 Ibid.
235 Patel, 2012, pp. 310–13.
236 Triger, 2013.
237 Bronstein, 2011.
238 Dalgety, 2022. On Bristol, see Wall, 2021.
239 https://twitter.com/unitedswers/status/153740830597016 7810?s=21&t=AaLi_MEOdo-FBSSfDPrdmA.
240 Karras, 2017, p. 48.
241 Lister, 2020, p. 229.
242 Ibid., pp. 42–3.
243 Ibid., p. 48.

244 Ibid., p. 49.
245 Ibid., pp. 50–1.
246 Ibid., pp. 60–3.
247 Ibid., p. 229.
248 Ibid., pp. 230–2.
249 Ibid., p. 233.
250 Ibid., p. 237.
251 Laslett, 1980, pp. 14–19.
252 Ibid., pp. 6, 60.
253 Ibid., p. 60.
254 Ibid.

2 The Modesty Cult: The Dangers

1 Shalit, 2014.
2 Eltahawy, 2015, p. 60.
3 Ibid., p. 123.
4 Gibbs et al., 2019.
5 Wollstonecraft, 1988 [1792], p. 133.
6 Eberle, 2001.
7 Wollstonecraft, 1988 [1792], p. 63.
8 Ibid., p. 110.
9 Ibid., p. 192.
10 Johnson, 2018.
11 Rostek, 2021, p. 194.
12 UNESCO, 2020a.
13 UNESCO Institute for Statistics (UIS) and UNICEF, 2015, p. 56.
14 UNESCO, 2020a.
15 UNESCO Institute for Statistics (UIS) and UNICEF, 2015, p. 61.
16 Ibid., pp. 70–2.
17 Data Sources: UNESCO Institute for Statistics and the World Bank, n.d.; Barber, 2018; Diamant, 2020.
18 All the countries for which data are available are included in the chart (and similarly for the subsequent charts).

19 The exceptions (such as Egypt) – the small handful of countries which have high levels of disapproval of premarital sex but nevertheless achieve reasonably high levels of secondary school completion for girls – include those in which modesty requirements are met at the school level through gender segregation.
20 BBC News, 2021; UN Women, 2021.
21 BBC News, 2021.
22 UNICEF, 2019, p. 10.
23 World Economic Forum, 2021, p. 18.
24 UNESCO, 2019, p. 4.
25 UNFPA and UNICEF, 2018; Girls Not Brides, n.d.
26 UNFPA and UNICEF, 2018; UNESCO Institute for Statistics (UIS) and UNICEF, 2015.
27 Field and Ambrus, 2008.
28 Torchlight Collective, 2022, p. 5.
29 Ibid., p. 15.
30 Source: UNICEF Child Marriage Country Profiles https://data.unicef.org/resources/child-marriage-country-profiles/.
31 Diamond, 2022, p. 31 (note: this completion rate data, which comes from UNICEF, is based on all girls in the relevant age group, rather than – as in the UNESCO data – trying to measure completion as a proportion of those who start lower secondary school).
32 Diamond, 2022, p. 33.
33 UNESCO Institute for Statistics (UIS) and UNICEF, 2015, pp. 60–1.
34 Onoyase, 2018.
35 Diamond, 2022, p. 35.
36 UNFPA and UNICEF, 2018, p. 4.
37 Diamond, 2022, pp. 21–3.
38 Ibid., p. 43.
39 Ibid., p. 42.
40 Ibid., p. 26.

41 Source: UNICEF Child Marriage Country Profiles https:// data.unicef.org/resources/child-marriage-country-profi les/.
42 UNESCO Institute for Statistics (UIS) and UNICEF, 2015, p. 65.
43 Diamond, 2022, p. 38.
44 UNESCO Institute for Statistics (UIS) and UNICEF, 2015, p. 59; UNICEF, 2019, p. 14.
45 UNESCO Institute for Statistics (UIS) and UNICEF, 2015.
46 Jayachandran, 2015.
47 Source: World Bank and International Labour Organization (modelled estimates), n.d.: https://data.worldbank.org/in dicator/SL.TLF.CACT.FE.ZS. Figures for 2019.
48 Ibid.; UNESCO Institute for Statistics and the World Bank, n.d.
49 Source: World Bank and International Labour Organization (modelled estimates), n.d.: https://data.worldbank.org /indicator/SL.TLF.CACT.FE.ZS. Figures for 2019.; Barber, 2018; Diamant, 2020.
50 World Bank, 2013, p. 8.
51 Ibid., p. 12 and ch. 2.
52 See, for example, Joslin and Nordvik, 2021.
53 Inglehart and Norris, 2003, p. 49.
54 Bayanpourtehrani and Sylwester, 2012.
55 World Bank, 2013, p. 43.
56 Chamlou et al., 2011; Chamlou et al., 2016; also Atasoy, 2016.
57 Thomas, 2019, p. 15.
58 World Bank, 2013, p. 27.
59 Joslin and Nordvik, 2021.
60 World Bank, 2013, pp. 16–17.
61 As also noted in Jayachandran, 2015.
62 World Bank, 2013, p. 69.
63 Bursztyn et al., 2018.
64 Ibid.

65 Labib, 2020, p. 15.
66 Ibid., p. 16.
67 Patel, 2012.
68 Jayachandran, 2015.
69 Sarkar, Sahoo and Klasen, 2019, p. 292.
70 Ibid.
71 Source: World Bank and International Labour Organization (modelled estimates), n.d.: https://data.worldbank.org/indicator/SL.TLF.CACT.FE.ZS. Figures for 2019. Figures for 2019.
72 Ibid.
73 Ibid.; Naqvi and Shahnaz, 2002.
74 Naqvi and Shahnaz, 2002, pp. 506 and 510.
75 Ibid., p. 510.
76 On demand for female labour driving the entry of Portuguese women into the workforce, see Cardoso and Morin 2018.
77 Evans, 2021a; Xue, 2018.
78 Evans, 2021a.
79 For a summary and critique see Abdelhadi and England, 2019.
80 Enfield, 2019; Adeyem et al., 2016.
81 Pastore and Tenaglia, 2013.
82 Abdelhadi and England, 2019, p. 1530.
83 Bulut, 2016; Read, 2004.
84 UK Government, 2021; Turner and Wigfield, 2013, p. 643; Commission on Race and Ethnic Disparities, 2021, p. 108.
85 UK Government, 2021.
86 Turner and Wigfield, 2013, p. 653.
87 Ibid., p. 658.
88 House of Commons Women and Equalities Committee, 2016, p. 17. Also see Begum, 2008.
89 Turner and Wigfield, 2013; Tariq and Syed, 2017.
90 Once gender traditionalism is included in data analysis, Islam no longer works well as a predictor of women's lack of

engagement in the workforce. See Abdelhadi and England, 2019; Read, 2004; Bayanpourtehrani and Sylwester, 2012.
91 Cheung, 2014; Heath and Martin, 2014.
92 House of Commons Women and Equalities Committee, 2016, pp. 19–20.
93 Turner and Wigfield, 2013, p. 647.
94 Cheung, 2014, p. 147.
95 Source: World Bank and Inter-Parliamentary Union, n.d.
96 World Bank, 2013, pp. 9–10.
97 Source: World Bank and Inter-Parliamentary Union, n.d.
98 Thomas, 2019.
99 Kandar, 2020, p. 70.
100 Bardhan and Foss, 2020, p. 271.
101 Afary, 2009.
102 Ibid., p. 192.
103 Ibid.
104 Ibid.
105 Amnesty International UK, 2019.
106 Tsujigami, 2020, p. 342.
107 Folke and Rickne, 2022.
108 Data sources: Barber, 2018; Diamant, 2020.
109 WHO, 2021.
110 Bruce-Lockhart, 2016. For India, also see Bishnoi, 2021. On the methodology of measurement, see Vera-Gray, 2016.
111 Ipsos, 2018.
112 Ibid.
113 Bruce-Lockhart, 2016.
114 El Feki et al., 2017, p. 85, p. 139, p. 186.
115 WHO, 2021, p. VI; Thomson Reuters Foundation with YouGov (reproduced in Bruce-Lockhart, 2016).
116 Jourdan and Labbé, 2020.
117 Ibid.
118 Jalal, 2009, p. 21.
119 Chaturvedi and Niaz, 2019.

120 El Feki et al., 2017, p. 15.
121 Oxfam, 2018.
122 Heslop, 2016, p. 3.
123 Ibid.
124 Diamond, 2022, p. 42.
125 Ibid.
126 Klement and Sagarin, 2016.
127 Lookadoo and DiMarco, 2003, p. 109.
128 Fahs, 2010, p. 121.
129 Collins, 2015.
130 Klement and Sagarin, 2016.
131 Anderson, 2013. Also, Klement and Sagarin, 2016; Moon and Reger, 2014; Owens, Hall and Anderson, 2020.
132 Triger, 2013.
133 Ibid., p. 19.
134 Summers, 2008. 'Easy targets' for predators. BBC News.
135 Roberts, 1992; Lowman, 2000; Sanders et al., 2017.
136 Kinnell, 2008.
137 Laverte, 2017.
138 El Feki et al., 2017, p. 83.
139 Brooks-Gordon, 2016.
140 Zakaria et al., 2020.
141 Feather, 2020, p. 54.
142 El Feki et al., 2017, p. 82, p. 138.
143 Johnson, 2021.
144 Zakaria et al., 2020.
145 For a fictional and powerful account, see Sidhwa, 2015.
146 Menon and Bhasin, 1998.
147 Saikia, 2021.
148 Hundal, 2007.
149 Ibid.
150 Navarro-Tejero, 2019.
151 Butalia, 2014.
152 Jalal, 2009, p. 22.
153 WHO, 2021.

154 Jalal, 2009, p. 22.
155 UN News, 2018.
156 Ibid.
157 El Feki et al., 2017, p. 138.
158 Lister, 2020, p. 80.
159 Mortimer, 2015.
160 Bardhan and Foss, 2020, p. 270.
161 BBC Newsbeat, 2020 on the UK; Crosby et al., 2020, on the USA.
162 Gibbs et al., 2019.
163 Ibid.
164 Ibid.
165 UNFPA, 2021, p. 45; Gibbs et al., 2019; Selby 2016.
166 El Feki et al., 2017, pp. 83, 137, 185, 215.
167 Gibbs et al., 2019.
168 Quawas, 2020, p. 22.
169 Mackie, 1996.
170 Batyra et al., 2020.
171 WHO Africa, n.d.
172 Ahinkorah et al., 2020.
173 Eltahawy, 2015, pp. 129–35.
174 Van Der Kwaak, 1992; Shell-Duncan et al., 2016; Mohammed et al., 2014; Cetorelli et al., 2020.
175 UNFPA, 2021, p. 46.
176 Shell-Duncan et al., 2016. Also see Lightfoot-Klein, 1989.
177 This is the approach of Convention Theorists. See Grose et al., 2019; Mackie and LeJeune, 2009.
178 Grose et al., 2019.
179 See Hayford, 2005, and Grose et al. 2019, for a summary of the different sociological theories of FGM/C.
180 Batyra et al., 2020.
181 Eltahawy, 2015, p. 122; Mohammed et al., 2014.
182 Khan, C., 2019, pp. 18–19.
183 Alomair et al., 2021a, 2021b.
184 Ibid., 2021a, 2021b.

185 Fahs, 2010, p. 119.
186 Ibid., p. 118.
187 Ibid., p. 119.
188 UNFPA, 2021, p. 116.
189 Ibid., p. 106, p. 120 (based on the 75 countries for which data is available).
190 Ibid., p. 10 (based on the 57 countries for which data is available).
191 Glasier et al., 2006; Emmers-Sommer et al., 2017.
192 Tolman, 2005, p. 6.
193 Ibid., p. 2.
194 Ibid., p. 3.
195 Fahs, 2010, p. 123–4; Manlove et al., 2003.
196 Fahs, 2010, p. 117.
197 Fine, 1988. Also, Fine and McClelland, 2006.
198 Emmers-Sommer et al., 2017.
199 Tolman, 2005, p. 12.
200 Ibid.
201 Holland et al., 1998.
202 Mulholland, 2013, p. 124.
203 Abdolsalehi-Najafi and Beckman, 2013.
204 Rees, 2017a, p. xiv.
205 Chan et al., 2019, p. 6; Dsouza et al., 2020.
206 Crawford et al., 2015, p. 127.
207 Ibid., p. 145.
208 Ibid., p. 146.
209 Dsouza et al., 2020.
210 Ibid., p. 2211.
211 Ibid., p. 2212.
212 Ibid., p. 2212.
213 Tolman, 2005, p. 51–5.
214 Roberts, 2017.
215 Kleinplatz, 2018, p. 47.
216 NHS, 2021.
217 Hyde and Delamater, 2020, p. 419.

218 Ibid., p. 418.
219 Ibid.
220 Ibid.
221 Cryle, 2009.
222 Désormeaux, 1905, p. 38; quoted in Cryle, 2009, p. 61.
223 Quoted in ibid., p. 49.
224 Angel, 2010.
225 Cryle, 2009, p. 50.
226 Kleinplatz, 2018, p. 37; Masters and Johnson, 1970.
227 Tolman, 2005, p. 1.
228 Ibid.
229 Ibid., p. 12.
230 Ibid., p. 5.
231 Ibid., p. 14.
232 Ibid., p. 6.
233 Emmers-Sommer et al., 2017.
234 Ibid., pp. 427–8.
235 Abdolsalehi-Najafi and Beckman, 2013.
236 Davidson, Moore and Ullstrup, 2004; also see Emmers-Sommer et al., 2017.
237 Garceau and Ronis, 2017.
238 Emmers-Sommer et al., 2017.
239 Ortiz et al., 2021.
240 Uecker, 2008, p. 736.
241 Emmers-Sommer et al., 2017, p. 428.
242 Abdolsalehi-Najafi and Beckman, 2013.
243 Ibid.
244 Tolman, 2005, p. 20.
245 Proudman, 2022, p. 32.
246 UNFPA, 2021, p. 47.
247 Lister, 2020.
248 Tolman, 2005, p. 13.
249 See also ibid., p. 19.
250 MacKinnon, 1989, p. 110.
251 Eberle, 2001, p. 2.

3 The Modesty Cult: The Causes

1 Lister, 2021, p. 29.
2 Bone, 2016.
3 Lister, 2020, p. 80.
4 Bardhan and Foss, 2020, p. 270.
5 BBC, 2012; Feather, 2020, p. 54.
6 Eltahawy, 2015, p. 15.
7 Amnesty International UK, 2019.
8 Farzan, 2019.
9 Bryson, 2016, p. 39.
10 Ternikar, 2009.
11 Iyer, 2016.
12 Pew Research Center, 2012.
13 Lipka and Hackett, 2017; Pew Research Center, 2015.
14 Kazeem, 2019.
15 Stiller et al., 2015.
16 Adamczyk and Hayes, 2012; Inglehart and Norris, 2003; Pastore and Tenaglia, 2013; Adeyem et al., 2016; Joslin and Nordvik, 2021; though also see Bayanpourtehrani and Sylwester, 2012; Meyersson, 2014; Abdelhadi and England, 2019; Read, 2004.
17 Evans, 2021c. Also Mir-Hosseini, 2006.
18 Also see Read and Bartkowski, 2000, pp. 400–1; Ternikar, 2009.
19 Triger, 2013, p. 23.
20 Lerner, 1993, p. 5.
21 Klement and Sagarin, 2016.
22 Feldhahn and Rice, 2009, p. 162.
23 Collins, 2015.
24 Carr-Gomm, 2013, p. 75.
25 Ibid., p. 79.
26 Keddie, 2007, p. 17.
27 Ibid., pp. 15–17.
28 Feldhahn and Rice, 2009, p. 160.
29 Baumeister and Twenge, 2002.

30 Scelza et al., 2021.
31 Ibid.
32 Symons, 1979.
33 As summed up in Thornhill and Palmer, 2000, p. 62.
34 Brownmiller, 1975, p. 11.
35 Perry, 2022, p. 15, p. 188. Also Harrington, 2021.
36 Steeves, 1997.
37 UNESCO Institute for Statistics (UIS) and UNICEF, 2015, p. 59; Diamond, 2022, p. 29.
38 UNESCO Institute for Statistics (UIS) and UNICEF, 2015, p. 59.
39 Diamond, 2022, p. 29.
40 UNESCO, 2020b, pp. 53.
41 Diamond, 2022, p. 38.
42 For a recent example, see e.g. Perry, 2022.
43 Kokko and Jennions, 2008.
44 Alger et al., 2020.
45 Shenk et al., 2019.
46 Brodman, 2017.
47 Shenk et al., 2019.
48 Ibid.
49 Evans, 2021b.
50 Gibbs et al., 2019.
51 Ibid.
52 Henrich, 2020.
53 Scelza et al., 2021.
54 Ibid.
55 Ibid.
56 Ibid.
57 Smuts, 1995, p. 16.
58 Alesina et al., 2013. Also see Demie, 2018.
59 Morgan, 1877, argued that pastoralism was key to the shift from matriliny to patriliny; Aberle, 1961, provided a more holistic account spanning different types of agriculture, including the plough.

60 Becker, 2019.
61 Holden and Mace, 2003.
62 Vicente et al., 2021.
63 Scelza et al., 2021.
64 Becker, 2019.
65 Fan and Wu, 2019.
66 Beresford-Jones et al., 2018.
67 Engels, 2010 [1884]. For a classic critique, see Coontz and Henderson, 1986. For a modern day application to more recent history, see Smith 2020.
68 Shenk et al., 2019.
69 Korotayev and Kazankov, 2003; Schlegel, 1991.
70 Quoted in Mariani, 2012; also see Goethals, 1971.
71 Bryson, 2016, p. 63.
72 Northrop, 2004.
73 Mattison, 2010; Scelza et al., 2019.
74 Evans, 2021b; Brown and Satterthwaite-Phillips, 2018.
75 Boserup, 1970; Alesina et al., 2013; Becker, 2019; Qian, 2008; Xue, 2018.
76 Brown and Satterthwaite-Phillips, 2018.
77 Evans, 2021b.
78 Schlegel, 1991, p. 724.
79 Foucault, 2020 [1976], p. 120.
80 Ibid.
81 Haboush, 1990.
82 Cronin, 2014, p. 5.
83 Evans, 2021a.
84 Mariani, 2012.
85 Fan and Wu, 2019. For an equivalent discussion applied to FGM/C, see Chesnokova and Vaithianathan, 2010; and, on female seclusion, see Rai and Sengupta, 2013.
86 Mariani, 2012, p. 336.
87 According to Lawerence Stone, 1990, the expansion of the propertyless class during the eighteenth century helps to explain the greater sexual permissiveness in this era.

88 Albanesi and Olivetti, 2007.
89 See e.g. Akerlof et al., 1996; Greenwood and Guner, 2010; Fernández-Villaverde, Greenwood and Guner, 2014.
90 Tyler, 2008. On the associated broader social trends, see Lewis and Kiernan, 1996.
91 On when, how and why nation states take charge of repro-duction, with extensive historical coverage, see Togman, 2019.
92 On China, see Wang, 2022.
93 Murdock, 1949, p. 207.
94 Ember and Ember, 1971, p. 584.
95 For supportive evidence, see Shenk et al., 2019.
96 Carvalho, 2013.
97 Evans, 2021c; Kumar, 2016.
98 Brownmiller, 1975, p. 15.
99 Smith-Spark, 2009.
100 Phipps, 2020.
101 Quoted in Kent, 2004 [1987], p. 12.
102 Smuts, 1995, pp. 9–10.
103 Ibid., p. 12.
104 Ibid., p. 11.
105 Karras, 1998, p. 108.
106 Mernissi, 1991.
107 Bateman, 2019, p. 131.
108 Pleijt et al., 2019.
109 Smuts, 1995, p. 17.
110 Rubin, 2018. Also see: Charrad, 2001; Htun and Weldon, 2015.
111 Dabhoiwala, 2012, p. 9.
112 Ibid., ch. 1.
113 As an example, see e.g. Evans, 2015.
114 For an example, see Manktelow, 2018.
115 Castillo, 2013.
116 Carvalho, 2013.
117 Macleod, 1993.

118 Baumeister and Twenge, 2002.
119 The extensive studies conducted by anthropologists have served to reveal that 'sexual permissiveness' is 'associated with the simpler subsistence technologies, absence of stratification, smaller communities, matrilineal descent, matrilocal residence, absence of belief in high gods' together with 'high female economic contribution, little or no property exchange at marriage, and ascribed rather than achieved status' (Schlegel, 1991). Shenk et al., 2019, find that agriculture and property are the two most important factors determining shifts from matriliny to patriliny.
120 This includes models embodying increasing-returns and tipping-points (see e.g. Schelling, 1978; Kuran, 1995, 1998).
121 Mackie 1996; Blaydes and Linzer, 2008; Chesnokova and Vaithianathan, 2010; Rai and Sengupta, 2013; Lindskog et al., 2022.
122 Baumeister and Mendoza, 2011.
123 Schlegel, 1991, p. 732.
124 Mariani, 2012.
125 As Schlegel, 1991, p. 732, writes: 'Technology alone, without significant changes in social relations, is not enough to alter such deep-seated cultural values as the value on virginity.'
126 Mariani, 2012.

4 Beware Puritanical Feminism

1 Bateman, 2019.
2 Baumeister and Twenge, 2002; Baumeister and Vohs, 2012; Manne, 2018.
3 Poos, 1995.
4 Baumeister and Twenge, 2002, p. 181; King et al., 1977.
5 Bartlett et al., 2014; Speed, 2016.
6 Baumeister and Twenge, 2002, p. 179; Coleman, 1961; Tolman, 2005; Milhausen and Herold, 1999; Honkatukia and Keskinen, 2018.

7   Payne, 2010.

8   Moses, 1998, p. 140, quoted in Bryson, 2016, p. 26.

9   Bryson, 2016, p. 25.

10   BBC Sport, 2018.

11   Beauvoir, 2011 [1949], p. 7.

12   Mackie, 1996; Patel, 2012; Blaydes and Linzer, 2008; Chesnokova and Vaithianathan, 2010; Rai and Sengupta, 2013; Lindskog et al., 2022.

13   Bayat, 2007, p. 158.

14   Carvalho, 2013, p. 354. Also, Ternikar, 2009.

15   Mule and Barthel, 1992.

16   Beauvoir, 2015, p. 7.

17   Ibid., xxi; for an application of socialisation in regard to Hindu girls, see Dube, 1988.

18   Holland et al., 1998.

19   Winch, 2013, p. 5, pp. 10–12; Ringrose, 2013, p. 95.

20   Ibid., p. 93; quoted in Winch, 2013, p. 12.

21   Lerner, 1993, p. 6.

22   Honkatukia and Keskinen, 2018, p. 147.

23   Payne, 2010, p. 320.

24   Lerner, 1993. Also see Lerner, 1986.

25   Beauvoir, 2015, p. 30.

26   Evans, 2020, p. 53.

27   Ibid.

28   Ibid., p. 63.

29   Ibid., p. 87.

30   Ibid., p. 63.

31   Wolf, 1990, p. 2.

32   Ibid., p. 1.

33   Faludi, 1991; Wolf, 1990; Tasker and Negra, 2007.

34   Grogan, 1998.

35   Jha, 2016; Tate, 2017.

36   Elias et al., 2017.

37   Cronin, 2014, p. 24.

38   Bullock, 2007, ch. 5.

39 Jones, 2010; Bucar, 2016.
40 Ternikar, 2022.
41 Evans, 2020, p. 92.
42 Attwood, 2009, pp. xiii–xv.
43 Barton, 2021, p. 3.
44 Degler, 1974, p. 1473.
45 Chertsey Museum, n.d.
46 Levine, 2018 [1987], p. 161.
47 Kent, 2004 [1987], p. 33.
48 Levine, 2018 [1987], pp. 129–30.
49 Ibid., p. 129; Kent, 2004 [1987], pp. 60–2.
50 Degler, 1974, p. 1468.
51 Kent, 2004 [1987], pp. 62–3.
52 Ibid., p. 60.
53 Levine, 2018 [1987], pp. 133–6.
54 Jeffreys, 1985, p. 33; also see Degler, 1974, p. 1468; Bryson, 2016, pp. 37, 97.
55 Levine, 2018 [1987], p. 140,
56 Ibid., p. 145,
57 Ibid., p. 147,
58 Quoted in Jeffreys, 1985, p. 33,
59 Kent, 2004 [1987], p. 159,
60 Levine, 2018 [1987], p. 150. Also see Bland, 1995.
61 Wilma Meikle, quoted in Kent, 2004 [1987], p. 159,
62 See Kent, 2004 [1987], pp. 161–2, which also notes that not all feminists were in agreement on this point.
63 Levine, 2018 [1987], p. 130,
64 Jeffreys, 1985, p. 29.
65 Holton, 1994, p. 214.
66 Jeffreys, 1985, p. 31.
67 Levine, 2018 [1987], p. 149.
68 Ibid., p. 150; Jeffreys, 1985, pp. 41–5.
69 Ibid., p. 32.
70 Quoted in Jeffreys, 1985, pp. 41–2.
71 Ibid., p. 44.

72 Evans, 1977; Banks, 1981.
73 Bryson, 2016, p. 36.
74 Degler, 1974, p. 1467.
75 Bryson, 2016, p. 32.
76 Sowinska, 2005, p. 132. Also see Boittin, 2010, p. 30 (and ch. 5).
77 Boisseau, 2015.
78 Sowinska, 2005, p. 132.
79 Ibid., p. 132.
80 Kent, 2004 [1987].
81 Bryson, 2016, p. 80.
82 Smart, 2005.
83 Buhle, 1981, p. 253, quoted in Bryson, 2016, p. 96.
84 Bryson, 2016, p. 37.
85 Jeffreys, 1985, p. 150.
86 Bryson, 2016, p. 100.
87 A suspicion of sex existed not only within mainstream feminism but also within liberal circles more generally (Bryson, 2016, p. 52). On the use of the term 'prude', see Jeffreys, 1985, ch. 10.
88 Hunt, K., 2002, p. 102; Freeman, 2011, p. 199.
89 Quoted in Bryson, 2016, p. 117.
90 Kent, 2004 [1987], p. 224.
91 Ibid., p. 225.
92 Bryson, 2016, p. 87.
93 Kent, 2004 [1987], p. 226.
94 Kent, 2004 [1987], p. 226.
95 Degler, 1974, pp. 1483–6.
96 Quoted in Jeffreys, 1985, p. 158.
97 Ibid., pp. 157–60.
98 Ibid., p. 158.
99 Ibid., pp. 158–9, 190.
100 N.S.W.P., n.d.; Farnsworth, 1975.
101 Mathieu, 2001, p. 126.
102 Weiss, 2018, p. 304.

103 Pheterson, 1989, p. 46.
104 Ibid., p. 11.
105 Walkowitz, 1980, p. 7.
106 Scoular, 2004, p. 345.
107 MacKinnon, 1987, p. 188; Dworkin, 1993.
108 St James, 1989.
109 *The Irish Times*, 2021.
110 European Women's Lobby, 2011.
111 Nordic Model Now!, 2016, p. 8, p. 11.
112 All-Party Parliamentary Group on Prostitution and the Global Sex Trade, 2014. Shifting the Burden.
113 Laite, 2020.
114 Casey, 2018.
115 Platt et al., 2018.
116 Ibid., pp. 1–2.
117 Quoted in Platt et al., 2018, p. 39 – see my paper.
118 Berg, 2020, p. 273.
119 The next few paragraphs are drawn from Bateman, 2021.
120 New York Wages for Housework Committee, 1975; Federici, 1975; Toupin, 2018.
121 ILO, 2018.
122 Dromey and Hochlaf, 2018.
123 Harris, 2016.
124 Berg, 2020.
125 On modern slavery, see Kenway, 2021.
126 International Labour Organization, 2017.
127 See https://prostitutescollective.net/outlaw-poverty-not-prostitutes/.
128 Nussbaum, 1999, p. 278.
129 Ibid., p. 296.
130 Zatz, 1997.
131 Nussbaum, 1999, pp. 278–9.
132 Ibid., p. 281.
133 Bindel, 2017.
134 Nussbaum, 1999, p. 288.

135 Banyard, 2016. Also see McIntosh, 1978.
136 Pateman, 1983, p. 56.
137 All-Party Parliamentary Group on Prostitution and the Global Sex Trade, 2014, p. 47.
138 Brooks-Gordon et al., 2015.
139 Skills for Care, 2011, 2020.
140 Skills for Care, 2020.
141 Berg, 2020, p. 269.
142 For this and other policy ideas, see Mac and Smith, 2018, and Kenway, 2021.
143 On the latter, see Hyde, 2018. Also Nagle, 2010 and Roberts, 1992.
144 Pateman, 1988, p. 207.
145 Jaggar, 1991, p. 274. Also see Macleod et al., 2008.
146 Quoted in Pheterson, 1989, pp. 145–6.
147 Laite in McCarthy et al., 2015.
148 Kohl, 2015, p. 81.
149 Ibid., p. 82.
150 Ibid.
151 Ibid., p. 97.
152 Manchester, 2008.
153 Goldberg, 1988, p. 175.
154 Rees, 2017a, pp. 229–36.
155 Karakuş, 2020, p. 161.
156 Ibid., pp. 162–3.
157 Ibid., p. 165.
158 Ibid., p. 167.
159 Ibid., p. 168.
160 Mourad, 2013; Nagarajan, 2013.
161 Karakuş, 2020, p. 169.
162 Nelson, 2013.
163 Karakuş, 2020, p. 169.
164 https://twitter.com/likeplastic_/status/1372460305075216384?s=20.
165 Kazeem, 2013.

166 Manktelow, 2018.
167 Kazeem, 2013.
168 Twasiima, 2019.
169 Hoffman-Ladd, 1987, p. 24. Also see Mohammadi, 2019.
170 Aossey, 2017.
171 This letter was exhibited at the Museum of the City of New York in 2018, courtesy of Schlesinger Library, Radcliffe Institute, Harvard University.
172 Khan, C., 2019, p. 19.
173 Levy, 2005.
174 Walter, 2010; Smith, 2013. As Noah Zatz notes, 'attributions of false consciousness . . . are radically undemocratic, setting up a privileged group (usually intellectuals) to interpret the experience of others for them' (Zatz, 1997, p. 296).
175 Hakim, 2010, p. 510.
176 Ibid., p. 512.
177 Ibid., pp. 511–12.
178 Bryson, 2016, p. 52.
179 Quoted in Rees, 2017b.
180 Ibid.
181 Delap, 2020, ch. 5.
182 Donaghue, 2017, p. 243.
183 McCann, 2019.
184 Ibid., n.d.
185 Ternikar, 2022; McCann, n.d.
186 Donaghue, 2017, p. 244.
187 Ratajkowski, 2019.
188 Emily Ratajkowski, quoted in Wolf, 2016.
189 Ibid.
190 Ratajkowski, 2021, p. 3.
191 Paasonen et al., 2021, p. 11.
192 McNair, 2013, p. 7.
193 Ibid., p. 106, p. 11.
194 Paasonen et al., 2021, p. 80. Also see Cahill, 2011.

195 Ratajkowski, 2021, p. 96.
196 Ibid., p. 93.
197 Ibid., p. 216.
198 Ibid., pp. 95–8.
199 Ibid., p. 97.
200 Walter, 2010.
201 Ratajkowski, 2021, pp. 88–9.
202 Pomeroy, 1975, pp. 8–9.
203 Ibid., p. 8.
204 Khona, 2016.
205 Mulholland, 2013, p. 135.
206 Buckingham et al., 2011.
207 Mulholland, 2013, pp. 138–9.
208 LB, 2021.
209 Morris, 2021.
210 Ringrose, 2013, ch. 4, notes the 'middle-classness' of social panics surrounding the 'sexualisation' of women and girls.
211 Shalit, 2014, p. 112.
212 Aossey, 2017.
213 Baumeister and Twenge, 2002.
214 Baumeister and Vohs, 2012.
215 On intra-female competition, also see Manne, 2018.
216 Evidence reveals that being exposed to a wider and more varied range of body types boosts (rather than diminishes) body confidence (West, 2020; West 2021).
217 Shalit, 2014, p. xiii.
218 Quoted in ibid., p. 73.
219 *The Economist*, 2019.
220 Cecco, 2021.
221 Mulholland, 2013, p. 134.
222 Ibid., p. 141.
223 Aossey, 2017.
224 Perry, 2022.
225 Bullock, 2007.
226 Wolf, 1990.

227 Aossey, 2017.
228 Quoted in McNair, 2013, p. 104.
229 Khan, M., 2019, p. 112.
230 Eltahawy, 2018.
231 Allison, 2021.
232 Khan, M., 2019, pp. 111–12.

Conclusion
 1 Peirson-Hagger, 2020.
 2 Ibid.; also see: Brown, 2020; Coslett, 2020; Freeman, 2020.
 3 Bateman, 2014.
 4 Eberle, 2001.
 5 Ibid.
 6 McNair, 2002; Attwood, 2009, p. xiv.
 7 Levy, 2005.
 8 Eltahawy, 2015, p. 34.
 9 Abu-Lughod, 2009.
10 El Feki et al., 2017, p. 83.
11 See e.g. Shell-Duncan et al., 2016.
12 Baumeister and Twenge, 2002, p. 179; Coleman, 1961; King et al., 1977; Tolman, 2005; Milhausen and Herold, 1999; Honkatukia and Keskinen, 2018; Bartlett et al., 2014; Speed, 2016.
13 YouGov, 2020.
14 YouGov, 2019.
15 Quoted in Triger, 2013, p. 26.
16 Quoted in Bullock, 2007, ch. 5.
17 Eltahawy, 2015, p. 72.
18 Orwell and Shamsie, 2018, p. 118.
19 Ibid., 2018, p. 73.
20 https://prostitutescollective.net/outlaw-poverty-not-prosti tutes/.

References

Abdelhadi, E. and England, P., 2019. Do values explain the low employment levels of Muslim women around the world? A within- and between-country analysis. *British Journal of Sociology*, 70(4), 1510–38.

Abdolsalehi-Najafi, E. and Beckman, L., 2013. Sex guilt and life satisfaction in Iranian-American women. *Archives of Sexual Behavior*, 42(6), 1063–71.

Aberle, D., 1961. Matrilineal descent in cross-cultural perspective. In D. Schneider and K. Gough, eds, *Matrilineal Kinship*. University of California Press.

Abu-Lughod, L., 2009. *Remaking Women*. Princeton University Press.

Adamczyk, A. and Hayes, B., 2012. Religion and sexual behaviors. *American Sociological Review*, 77(5), 723–46.

Adeyem, O., Odusina, K. and Akintoye, A., 2016. Religion and labour force participation in Nigeria: Is there any inequality among women? *African Journal of Reproductive Health*, 20(3), pp. 75–84.

Afary, J., 2009. *Sexual Politics in Modern Iran*. Cambridge University Press.

Ahinkorah, B., Hagan, J., Ameyaw, E., Seidu, A., Budu, E., Sambah, F., Yaya, S., Torgbenu, E. and Schack, T., 2020. Socio-economic and demographic determinants of female genital mutilation in sub-

Saharan Africa: Analysis of data from demographic and health surveys. *Reproductive Health*, 17(1).

Ahmed, L., 1992. *Women and Gender in Islam.* Yale University Press.

Akerlof, G., Yellen, J. and Katz, M., 1996. An analysis of out-of-wedlock childbearing in the United States. *Quarterly Journal of Economics*, 111(2), 277–317.

Albanesi, S. and Olivetti, C., 2007. Gender roles and technological progress. NBER Working Paper Series 13179.

Alesina, A., Giuliano, P. and Nunn, N., 2013. On the origins of gender roles: Women and the plough. *Quarterly Journal of Economics*, 128(2), 469–530.

Alger, I., Hooper, P., Cox, D., Stieglitz, J. and Kaplan, H., 2020. Paternal provisioning results from ecological change. *Proceedings of the National Academy of Sciences*, 117(20), 10746–54.

Alibhai-Brown, Y., 2015. As a Muslim woman, I see the veil as a rejection of progressive values. *Guardian.*

Allison, E., 2021. *#ChurchToo.* Broadleaf Books.

All-Party Parliamentary Group on Prostitution and the Global Sex Trade, 2014. Shifting the Burden. UK Parliament.

Alomair, N., Alageel, S., Davies, N. and Bailey, J., 2021a. Factors influencing sexual and reproductive health of Muslim women: A systematic review. *Reproductive Health*, 17(1).

Alomair, N., Alageel, S., Davies, N. and Bailey, J., 2021b. Barriers to sexual and reproductive wellbeing among Saudi women: A qualitative study. *Sexuality Research and Social Policy.*

Amnesty International UK, 2019. Iran: 30+ years in prison for protesting forced veiling laws. [Blog] *Amnesty International.*

Anderson, D., 2013. Purity culture as rape culture: Why the theological is political. [Blog] *Rewire News Group.*

Angel, K., 2010. The history of 'Female Sexual Dysfunction' as a mental disorder in the 20th century. *Current Opinion in Psychiatry*, 23(6), 536–41.

Aossey, G., 2017. Muslims are the true feminists. [Blog] *Huffington Post.*

Armstrong L., 2020. *Sex Work and the New Zealand Model.* Polity.

Atasoy, B., 2016. Female labour force participation in Turkey: The role of traditionalism. *European Journal of Development Research*, 29(4), pp. 675–706.

Attwood, F., 2009. *Mainstreaming Sex.* I.B.Tauris.

Banks, J., 1954. *Prosperity and Parenthood, A Study of Family Planning Among the Victorian Middle Classes.* Routledge & Kegan Paul.

Banyard, K., 2016. *Pimp State.* Faber & Faber.

Barber, N., 2018. Cross-national variation in attitudes to premarital sex: Economic development, disease risk, and marriage strength. *Cross-Cultural Research*, 52(3), 259–73.

Bardhan, S. and Foss, K., 2020. Revolutionary graffiti and Cairene women. In R. Stephan and M. Charrad, eds, *Women Rising.* New York University Press.

Bartlett, J., Norrie, R., Patel, S., Rumpel, R. and Wibberley, S., 2014. *Misogyny on Twitter.* Demos.

Barton, B., 2021. *The Pornification of America.* New York University Press.

Barton, L., 2021. The clitoris, pain and pap smears: How our bodies, ourselves redefined women's health. *Guardian.*

Bateman, V., 2014. Why I posed naked and natural. *Guardian.*

Bateman, V., 2019. *The Sex Factor.* Polity.

Bateman, V., 2021. How decriminalisation reduces harm within and beyond sex work: Sex work abolitionism as the 'cult of female modesty' in feminist form. *Sexuality Research and Social Policy*, 18, 819–36.

Batyra, E., Coast, E., Wilson, B. and Cetorelli, V., 2020. The socio-economic dynamics of trends in female genital mutilation/cutting across Africa. *BMJ Global Health*, 5(10), e003088.

Baumeister, R. and Mendoza, J., 2011. Cultural variations in the sexual marketplace: Gender equality correlates with more sexual activity. *Journal of Social Psychology*, 151(3), 350–60.

Baumeister, R. and Twenge, J., 2002. Cultural suppression of female sexuality. *Review of General Psychology*, 6(2), 166–203.

Baumeister, R. and Vohs, K., 2012. Sexual economics, culture, men, and modern sexual trends. *Society*, 49(6), 520–4.

Bayanpourtehrani, G. and Sylwester, K., 2012. Female labour force participation and religion: A cross-country analysis. *Bulletin of Economic Research*, 65(2), 107–33.

Bayat, A., 2007. *Making Islam Democratic*. Stanford.

BBC News, 2021. Afghanistan: Taliban announce new rules for female students. BBC.

BBC Newsbeat, 2020. Controversial 'virginity tests' sold by UK clinics. BBC News.

BBC Sport, 2018. Formula 1: 'Grid girls' will not be used at races this season. BBC.

BBC, 2012. Morocco protest after raped Amina Filali kills herself. BBC News.

Beauvoir, S. de, 2011. *The Second Sex*. Vintage.

Beauvoir, S. de, 2015. *Extracts from: The Second Sex*. Vintage.

Becker, A., 2019. On the economic origins of restrictions on women's sexuality. CESifo Working Paper No. 7770.

Begum, H., 2008. Geographies of inclusion/exclusion: British muslim women in the east end of London. *Sociological Research Online*, 13(5), 91–101.

Beresford-Jones, D., Pullen, A., Chauca, G., Cadwallader, L., García, M., Salvatierra, I., Whaley, O., Vásquez, V., Arce, S., Lane, K. and French, C., 2018. Refining the maritime foundations of Andean civilization: How plant fiber technology drove social complexity during the preceramic period. *Journal of Archaeological Method and Theory*, 25(2), 393–425.

Berg, H., 2020. Left of #MeToo. *Feminist Studies*, 46(2).

Berg, R. and Denison, E., 2013. A tradition in transition: Factors perpetuating and hindering the continuance of female genital mutilation/cutting (FGM/C) summarised in a systematic review. *Health Care for Women International*, 34(10), 837–59.

Berkowitz, E., 2012. *Sex and Punishment*. Westborne Press.

Bindel, J., 2017. *The Pimping of Prostitution*. Palgrave.

Bishnoi, Y., 2021. Prevalence of incidents of street sexual harassment against women in Delhi. *Paripex Indian Journal of Research*, 172–74.

Blank, H., 2007. *Virgin.* Bloomsbury.

Blaydes, L. and Linzer, D., 2008. The political economy of women's support for fundamentalist Islam. *World Politics,* 60(4), 576–609.

Blundy, R., 2014. Painting of woman showing pubic hair which was banned from central London exhibition set to be displayed in another London gallery. *The Evening Standard.*

Boisseau, T., 2015. Josephine Baker and the Rainbow Tribe, by Matthew Pratt Guterl. *Canadian Journal of History,* 50(1).

Boittin, J., 2010. *Colonial Metropolis: The Urban Grounds of Anti-Imperialism and Feminism in Interwar Paris.* University of Nebraska Press.

Bone, J., 2016. *The Curse of Beauty.* Regan Arts.

Boserup, E., 1970. *Woman's Role in Economic Development.* Allen & Unwin.

Boston Women's Health Book Collective, 1973. *Our Bodies, Ourselves.* Touchstone Book/Simon & Schuster.

British Library, n.d. *A General History of the Lives and Adventures of the Most Famous Highwaymen, Murderers, Street-Robbers.*

British Library, n.d. *Evelina.*

British Library, n.d. *Harris's List of Covent-Garden Ladies: An 18th-Century Guide to Prostitutes.*

British Library, n.d. *The Rise of the Novel.*

Brodman, J., 2017. *Sex Rules!* Mango.

Bronstein, C., 2011. *Battling Pornography: The American Feminist Anti-Pornography Movement 1976–1986.* Cambridge University Press.

Brooks-Gordon, B., 2016. Written evidence submitted by Dr Belinda Brooks-Gordon. UK Government.

Brooks-Gordon, B., Mai, N., Perry, G. and Sanders, T., 2015. Production, income, and expenditure from commercial sexual activity as a measure of GDP in the UK National Accounts. Report for Office of National Statistics (ONS).

Brosius, M., 2016. No reason to hide: Women in the Neo-Elamite and Persian periods. In S. Budin and J. Turfa, eds, *Women in Antiquity.* Routledge.

Brown, M., 2020. Mary Wollstonecraft statue becomes one of 2020's most polarising artworks. *Guardian.*

Brown, M. and Satterthwaite-Phillips, D., 2018. Economic correlates of footbinding: Implications for the importance of Chinese daughters' labor. *PLOS ONE*, 13(9), e0201337.

Brownmiller, S., 1975. *Against Our Will.* Simon & Schuster.

Bruce-Lockhart, A., 2016. Which cities have the most dangerous transport systems for women? [Blog] World Economic Forum.

Brusasco, P., 2004. Theory and practice in the study of Mesopotamian domestic space. *Antiquity*, 78(299), 142–57.

Bryson, V., 2016. *Feminist Political Theory.* Palgrave.

Bucar, E., 2016. Secular fashion, religious dress, and modest ambiguity: The visual ethics of Indonesian fashion-veiling. *Journal of Religious Ethics*, 44(1), 68–91.

Buckingham, D., Bragg, S., Russell, R., and Willet, R., 2011. Too much, too soon? *Sex Education*, 11(3), 279–92.

Budin, S., 2016. Female sexuality in Mesopotamia. In S. Budin and J. Turfa, eds, *Women in Antiquity.* Routledge.

Buhle, M., 1981. *Women and American Socialism*, 1780–1920. University of Illinois Press.

Bullock, K., 2007. Rethinking Muslim women and the veil. International Institute of Islamic Thought.

Bulut, E., 2016. The labor force participation of Arab women in the United States. *Women's Studies International Forum*, 55, 10–17.

Bursztyn, L., Gonzzlez, A. and Yanagizawa-Drott, D., 2018. Misperceived social norms: Female labor force participation in Saudi Arabia. NBER Working Paper Series 24736.

Butalia, U., 2014. *The Other Side of Silence.* Penguin Books.

Cahill, A.J, 2011. *Overcoming Objectification.* Routledge.

Cardoso, A. and Morin, L., 2018. Can economic pressure overcome social norms? The case of female labor force participation. Barcelona School of Economics Working Paper 1051.

Carr-Gomm, P., 2013. *A Brief History of Nakedness.* Reaktion Books.

Carvalho, J., 2013. Veiling. *Quarterly Journal of Economics*, 128(1), 337–70.

Casey, R., 2018. Does the Nordic model work? What happened when Ireland criminalised buying sex. *The New Statesman*.

Castelli, E., 1986. Virginity and its meaning for women's sexuality in Early Christianity. *Journal of Feminist Studies in Religion*, 2(1).

Castillo, A., 2013. The economics of 'slut-shaming'. [Blog] *The Ümlaut*.

CBE International, 1989. Defining biblical gender equality: Men, women, and biblical equality.

Cecco, L., 2021. Outrage as Quebec teacher removed from classroom for wearing hijab. *Guardian*.

Cetorelli, V., Wilson, B., Batyra, E. and Coast, E., 2020. Female genital mutilation/cutting in Mali and Mauritania: Understanding trends and evaluating policies. *Studies in Family Planning*, 51(1), 51–69.

Chamlou, N., Muni, S. and Ahmed, H., 2016. The determinants of female labor force participation in the Middle East and North Africa Region. In N. Chamlou and M. Karshenas, eds, *Women, Work and Welfare in the Middle East and North Africa*. World Scientific Publishing.

Chamlou, N., Muzi, S. and Ahmed, H., 2011. Understanding the determinants of female labor force participation in the Middle East and North Africa region: The role of education and social norms in Amman. AlmaLaurea Inter-University Consortium Working Paper.

Chan, D., So, W., Choi, K. and Gurung, S., 2019. Development of an explanatory model to explore cervical cancer screening behaviour among South Asian women: The influence of multilevel factors. *European Journal of Oncology Nursing*, 40, 2–9.

Channell, E., 2014. Is sextremism the new feminism? Perspectives from Pussy Riot and Femen. *Nationalities Papers*, 42(4), 611–14.

Charrad, M., 2001. *States and Women's Rights*. University of California Press.

Chaturvedi, A. and Niaz, L., 2019. Parallels in gender violence in India and Pakistan. [Blog] LSE South East Centre.

Chertsey Museum, n.d. Dress and the suffragettes. [Blog] Chertsey Museum.

Chesnokova, T. and Vaithianathan, R., 2010. The economics of female genital cutting. *B.E. Journal of Economic Analysis and Policy*, 10(1).

Chesser, E., 1956. *The Sexual, Marital and Family Relationships of the English Woman*. Hutchinson's Medical Publications.

Cheung, S., 2014. Ethno-religious minorities and labour market integration: Generational advancement or decline? *Ethnic and Racial Studies*, 37(1), 140–60.

Cho, S., 2017. The ideology of Korean women's headdresses during the Chosŏn Dynasty. *Fashion Theory*, 21(5).

Cohen, E., 2008. To pray, to work, to hear, to speak: Women in Roman streets c.1600. *Journal of Early Modern History*, 12(3–4), 289–311.

Cohen, M., 2005. Feeding the poor and clothing the naked: The Cairo Geniza. *Journal of Interdisciplinary History*, 35(3), 407–21.

Coleman, J., 1961. *The Adolescent Society*. Free Press.

Collins, N., 2015. 7 Lies that purity culture teaches women. [Blog] CBE International.

Commission on Race and Ethnic Disparities, 2021. The Report. UK Government.

Coontz, S. and Henderson, P., 1986. *Women's Work, Men's Property*. Verso.

Coslett, R., 2020. Why I hate the Mary Wollstonecraft statue: Would a man be 'honoured' with his schlong out? *Guardian*.

Crawford, J., Ahmad, F., Beaton, D. and Bierman, A., 2015. Cancer screening behaviours among South Asian immigrants in the UK, US and Canada: A scoping study. *Health and Social Care in the Community*, 24(2), 123–53.

Cronin, S., 2014. *Anti-Veiling Campaigns in the Muslim World*. Routledge.

Crosby, S.S., Oleng, N., Volpellier, M.M., and Mishori, R., 2020. Virginity testing: Recommendations for primary care physicians in Europe and North America. *BMJ Global Health*, 5(1).

Cruickshank, D., 2010. *The Secret History of Georgian London.* Windmill Books.

Cryle, P., 2009. 'A terrible ordeal from every point of view': (Not) managing female sexuality on the wedding night. *Journal of the History of Sexuality*, 18(1), 44–64.

Dabhoiwala, F., 2012. *The Origins of Sex.* Penguin.

Dalgety, S., 2022. Sex work is not a healthy career choice. *Edinburgh Evening News.*

Davidson, J., Moore, N. and Ullstrup, K., 2004. Religiosity and sexual responsibility: Relationships of choice. *American Journal of Health Behavior*, 28(4), 335–46.

Degler, C., 1974. What ought to be and what was: Women's sexuality in the nineteenth century. *American Historical Review*, 79(5), 1467.

Delap, L., 2020. *Feminisms.* Penguin.

Demie, M., 2018. Cereals and gender roles: A historical perspective. *SSRN Electronic Journal.*

D'Emilio, J. and Freedman, E., 2012. *Intimate Matters: A History of Sexuality in America.* University of Chicago Press.

Désormeaux, R., 1905. *L'impuissance et la stérilité.* P. Fort, L. Chaubard.

Diamant, J., 2020. Half of US Christians say casual sex between consenting adults is sometimes or always acceptable. [Blog] Pew Research Center.

Diamond, G., 2022. Social norms and girls' education: A study of eight sub-Saharan African countries Gender at the Centre Initiative (GCI) Policy Paper. *UNGEI.*

Donaghue, N., 2017. Seriously stylish. In S. Elias, R. Gill and C. Scharff, eds, *Aesthetic Labour.* Palgrave Macmillan.

Dossani, K., 2013. Virtue and veiling: Perspectives from ancient to Abbasid times. Master's Thesis. San Jose State University.

Dromey, J. and Hochlaf, D., 2018. Fair care: A workforce strategy for social care. *IPPR.*

Dsouza, J., Van den Broucke, S., Pattanshetty, S. and Dhoore, W., 2020. Exploring the barriers to cervical cancer screening through the lens of implementers and beneficiaries of the national screening program: A multi-contextual study. *Asian Pacific Journal of Cancer Prevention*, 21(8), 2209–15.

Dube, L., 1988. On the construction of gender: Hindu girls in patrilineal India. *Economic and Political Weekly*, 23(18).

Dworkin, A., 1993. Prostitution and male supremacy. *Michigan Journal of Gender and Law*, 1(1), 1–12.

Eberle, R., 2001. *Chastity, Transgression and Women's Writings 1792–1897*. Basingstoke: Palgrave Macmillan.

Economist, The, 2019. Burqa bans have proliferated in western Europe. *The Economist*.

Edgar, A., 2003. Emancipation of the unveiled: Turkmen women under Soviet rule, 1924–29. *Russian Review*, 62(1), 132–49.

El Feki, S., Heilman, B. and Barker, G., 2017. Understanding masculinities: Results from the International Men and Gender Equality Survey (IMAGES) – Middle East and North Africa. UN Women and Promundo-US.

El Guindi, F., 1999. *Veil: Modesty, Privacy, and Resistance (Dress, Body, Culture)*. Berg Publishers.

Elias, A., Gill, R. and Scharff, C., 2017. Aesthetic labour: Beauty politics in neoliberalism. In A. Elias, R. Gill and C. Scharff, eds, *Aesthetic Labour*. Palgrave Macmillan.

Eltahawy, M., 2015. *Headscarves and Hymens: Why the Middle East Needs a Sexual Revolution*. W&N.

Eltahawy, M., 2018. #MosqueMeToo: What happened when I was sexually assaulted during the hajj. *Washington Post*.

Ember, M. and Ember, C., 1971. The conditions favoring matrilocal versus patrilocal residence. *American Anthropologist*, 73(3), 571–94.

Emmers-Sommer, T., Allen, M., Schoenbauer, K. and Burrell, N., 2017. Implications of sex guilt: A meta-analysis. *Marriage and Family Review*, 54(5), 417–37.

Enfield, S., 2019. Gender roles and inequalities in the Nigerian labour market. K4D Helpdesk Report. UK Department for International Development.

Engels, F., 2010. *The Origin of the Family, Private Property and the State*. Penguin Classics.

European Women's Lobby, 2011. Abolitionist principles: Values and principles. [online]

Evans, A., 2015. History lessons for gender equality from the Zambian Copperbelt, 1900–1990. *Gender, Place and Culture*, 22(3), 344–62.

Evans, A., 2021a. How did East Asia overtake South Asia? [Blog] *The Great Gender Divergence.*

Evans, A., 2021b. How women in East Asia became much freer than their sisters in South Asia in just a century. [Blog] *Scroll In.*

Evans, A., 2021c. Will the BJP save Muslim women? [Blog] *The Great Gender Divergence.*

Evans, M., 2020. *Making Respectable Women*. Palgrave Pivot.

Evans, R., 1977. *The Feminist Women's Emancipation Movements in Europe, America and Australasia*. Croom Helm.

Fahs, B., 2010. Daddy's little girls: On the perils of chastity clubs, purity balls, and ritualized abstinence. *Frontiers: A Journal of Women Studies*, 31(3), 116.

Faludi, S., 1991. *Backlash*. Crown.

Fan, X. and Wu, L., 2019. The economic motives for footbinding. HKBU Working Paper.

Farnsworth, C., 1975. 200 prostitutes of Lyons in siege at church. *New York Times.*

Farr, J., 1995. *Authority and Sexuality in Early Modern Burgundy*. Oxford University Press.

Farzan, A., 2019. A 'curvier' high school swimmer won – only to be disqualified because of a 'suit wedgie'. *Washington Post.*

Feather, G., 2020. 'Ne touche pas mes enfants!' In R. Stephan and M. Charrad, eds, *Women Rising*. New York University Press.

Federici, S., 1975. *Wages Against Housework*. Falling Wall Press.

Feldhahn, S. and Rice, L., 2009. *For Young Women Only: What You Need to Know About How Guys Think*. Multnomah Publishers.

Fernández-Villaverde, J., Greenwood, J. and Guner, N., 2014. From shame to game in one hundred years: An economic model of the rise in premarital sex and its de-stigmatization. *Journal of the European Economic Association*, 12(1), 25–61.

Field, E. and Ambrus, A., 2008. Early marriage, age of menarche, and female schooling attainment in Bangladesh. *Journal of Political Economy*, 116(5), 881–930.

Fine, M. and McClelland, S., 2006. Sexuality education and desire: Still missing after all these years. *Harvard Educational Review*, 76(3), 297–338.

Fine, M., 1988. Sexuality, schooling, and adolescent females: The missing discourse of desire. *Harvard Educational Review*, 58(1), 29–54.

Fitzgerald, M., 2020. *Puritans Behaving Badly*. Cambridge University Press.

Flinn, M., 1981. *The European Demographic System* 1500–1820. Baltimore: Johns Hopkins University Press.

Folke, O. and Rickne, J., 2022. Sexual harassment and gender inequality in the labor market. *Quarterly Journal of Economics*, 137(4), 2163–212.

Foucault, M., 2020. *The History of Sexuality*, vol. 1. Penguin.

Freeman, L., 2020. London's new Mary Wollstonecraft statue is a flimsy, Barbie-like embarrassment. *The Telegraph*.

Freeman, N., 2011. 1895. *Drama, Disaster and Disgrace in Late Victorian Britain*. Edinburgh University Press.

Galt, C., 1931. Veiled ladies. *American Journal of Archaeology*, 35(4), 373–93.

Garceau, C. and Ronis, S., 2017. The interface between young adults' religious values and their sexual experiences before age 16. *Canadian Journal of Human Sexuality*, 26(2), 142–50.

Gatrell, V., 2007. *City of Laughter*. Atlantic Books.

Gibbs, A., Said, N., Corboz, J. and Jewkes, R., 2019. Factors associated with 'honour killing' in Afghanistan and the occupied Palestinian Territories: Two cross-sectional studies. *PLOS ONE*, 14(8), e0219125.

Gilligan, I., 2019. *Climate, Clothing, and Agriculture in Prehistory*. Cambridge University Press.

270 References

Girls Not Brides, n.d. Top 20 countries with the highest prevalence rates of child marriage. [online].

Glasier, A., Gülmezoglu, A., Schmid, G., Moreno, C. and Van Look, P., 2006. Sexual and reproductive health: A matter of life and death. *The Lancet*, 368(9547), 1595–607.

Glazebrook, A., 2016. Prostitutes, women, and gender in Ancient Greece. In S. Budin and J. Turfa, eds, *Women in Antiquity*. Routledge.

Goelet, O., 1993. Nudity in Ancient Egypt. *Notes in the History of Art*, 12(2), 20–31.

Goethals, G., 1971. Factors affecting permissive and non-permissive rules regarding premarital sex. In J. Henslin, ed., *Sociology of Sex*.

Goitein, S., 1967. *A Mediterranean Society*. Berkeley: University of California.

Goldberg, R., 1988. *Performance Art: From Futurism to the Present*. Thames & Hudson.

Górnicka, B., 2016. *Nakedness, Shame, and Embarrassment*. Springer.

Greenwood, J. and Guner, N., 2010. Social change: The sexual revolution. *International Economic Review*, 51(4), 893–923.

Gresh, D., 1999. *And the Bride Wore White*. Moody Publishers.

Grogan, S., 1998. *Body Image*. Routledge.

Grose, R., Hayford, S., Cheong, Y., Garver, S., Kandala, N. and Yount, K., 2019. Community influences on female genital mutilation/cutting in Kenya: Norms, opportunities, and ethnic diversity. *Journal of Health and Social Behavior*, 60(1), 84–100.

Guthrie, S., 2001. Arab *Social Life in the Middle Ages*. Saqi.

Haboush, J., 1990. The Confucianization of Korean society. In G. Rozman, ed., *The East Asian Region*. Princeton.

Hakim, C., 2010. Erotic capital. *European Sociological Review*, 26(5), 499–518.

Hamad, R., 2020. *White Tears/Brown Scars*. Catapult.

Hardwick, J., 2020. *Sex in an Old Regime City*. Oxford University Press.

Harrington, M., 2021. The sexual revolution killed feminism. *UnHerd.*

Harris, L., 2016. Sex Workers, Psychics, and Numbers Runners. University of Illinois Press.

Hayford, S., 2005. Conformity and change: Community effects on female genital cutting in Kenya. *Journal of Health and Social Behavior,* 46(2), 121–40.

Heath, A. and Martin, J., 2014. Can religious affiliation explain 'ethnic' inequalities in the labour market? *Ethnic and Racial Studies,* 36(6), 1005–27.

Hemelrijk, E., 2016. Women's daily life in the Roman West. In S. Budin and J. Turfa, eds, *Women in Antiquity.* Routledge.

Henrich, J., 2020. *The Weirdest People in the World.* Penguin.

Heslop, J., 2016. Technical brief: Engaging communities in dialogue on gender norms to tackle sexual violence in and around schools. Global Working Group to end school-related gender-based violence.

Higgins, J., Trussell, J., Moore, N. and Davidson, J., 2010. Virginity lost, satisfaction gained? Physiological and psychological sexual satisfaction at heterosexual debut. *Journal of Sex Research,* 47(4), 384–94.

Hobson, T., 2019. Victoria Bateman's naked Brexit stunt isn't feminist. *The Spectator.*

Hoffman-Ladd, V., 1987. Polemics on the modesty and segregation of women in contemporary Egypt. *International Journal of Middle East Studies,* 19(1), 23–50.

Holden, C. and Mace, R., 2003. Spread of cattle led to the loss of matrilineal descent in Africa: A coevolutionary analysis. *Proceedings of the Royal Society of London. Series B: Biological Sciences,* 270(1532), 2425–33.

Holland, J., Ramazanoglu, C., Sharpe, S. and Thomson, R., 1998. *The Male in the Head.* Tufnell.

Honkatukia, P. and Keskinen, S., 2018. The social control of young women's clothing and bodies: A perspective of differences on racialization and sexualization. *Ethnicities,* 18(1), 142–61.

House of Commons Women and Equalities Committee, 2016.

Employment opportunities for Muslims in the UK Second Report of Session 2016–17. House of Commons.

Htun, M. and Weldon, S., 2015. Religious power, the state, women's rights, and family law. *Politics and Gender*, 11(03), 451–77.

Hundal, S., 2007. The sexual politics of partition. *Guardian*.

Hunt, K., 2002. *Equivocal Feminists*. Cambridge University Press.

Hyde, J. and DeLamater, J., 2020. *Understanding Human Sexuality*. McGraw-Hill Education.

Hyde, N., 2018. Why a Leeds woman is making sculptures out of prostitutes' rubbish. Leeds Live.

ILO, 2018. Care work and care jobs for the future of work. ILO.

Inglehart, R. and Norris, P., 2003. *Rising Tide: Gender Equality and Cultural Change Around the World*. Cambridge University Press.

International Labour Organization (ILO), 2017. Global estimates of modern slavery. ILO.

Ipsos, 2018. International Women's Day: Global misperceptions of equality and the need to press for progress. [Blog].

Irish Times, The. 2021. Margo St James obituary: Advocate for sex workers. *The Irish Times*.

Iyer, S., 2016. The New economics of religion. *Journal of Economic Literature*, 54(2), 395–441.

Jaggar, A., 1991. Prostitution. In A. Soble, ed., *The Philosophy of Sex: Contemporary Readings*. Rowan and Littlefield.

Jalal, I., 2009. Harmful practices against women in Pacific Island countries. United Nations Division for the Advancement of Women.

Jasper, J., 2018. *The Emotions of Protest*. University of Chicago Press.

Jayachandran, S., 2015. The roots of gender inequality in developing countries. *Annual Review of Economics*, 7(1), 63–88.

Jeffreys, S., 1985. *The Spinster and Her Enemies*. Pandora.

Jha, M., 2016. *The Global Beauty Industry*. Routledge.

Johnson, C.L., 1988. *Jane Austen*. Chicago University Press.

Johnson, S., 2018. Celebrating *Priscilla Wakefield: Financial Inclusion Heroine and Forgotten Feminist Economist*. [Blog] University of Bath, Centre for Development Studies.

Johnson, S., 2021. 'Marry your rapist' laws in 20 countries still allow perpetrators to escape justice. *Guardian*.

Jones, C., 2010. Materializing piety: Gendered anxieties about faithful consumption in contemporary urban Indonesia. *American Ethnologist*, 37(4), 617–37.

Joslin, K. and Nordvik, F., 2021. Does religion curtail women during booms? Evidence from resource discoveries. *Journal of Economic Behavior and Organization*, 187, 205–24.

Jourdan, C. and Labbé, F., 2020. Urban women and the transformations of Braedpraes in Honiara. *Oceania*, 90(3).

Jumet, K., 2017. *Contesting the Repressive State.* Cambridge University Press.

Jung, J., 2011. Questions concerning widows' social status and remarriage in late Chosŏn. In Y. Kim and M. Pettid, eds, *Women and Confucianism in Choson Korea: New Perspectives*. SUNY Press.

Kalsem, K., 2004. Law, literature, and libel: Victorian censorship of 'dirty filthy' books on birth control. *William and Mary Journal of Women and the Law*, 10(3).

Kamp, M., 2006. *The New Woman in Uzbekistan: Islam, Modernity, and Unveiling Under Communism*. University of Washington Press.

Kandar, A., 2020. Refusing the backseat. In R. Stephan and M. Charrad, eds, *Women Rising*. New York University Press.

Karakuş, K., 2020. Aliaa Elmahdy, nude protest, and transnational feminist body politics. In R. Stephan and M. Charrad, eds, *Women Rising: In and Beyond the Arab Spring*. New York University Press.

Karras, R., 1998. *Common Women*. Oxford University Press.

Karras, R., 2017. *Sexuality in Medieval Europe*. 3rd edn. Routledge.

Kazeem, M., 2013. Bodies that matter: The African history of naked protest, FEMEN Aside. Okayafrica.

Kazeem, Y., 2019. Africa is set to be the global center of Christianity for the next 50 years. [Blog] *Quartz Africa*.

Keane, P., 2016. 100 Women 2016: Researching the female orgasm. BBC News.

Keddie, N., 2007. *Women in the Middle East*. Princeton University Press.

Kent, S., 2004 [1987]. *Sex and Suffrage in Britain* 1860–1914. Routledge.

Kenway, E., 2021. *The Truth about Modern Slavery*. Pluto Books.

Khan, C., 2019. Immodesty is the best policy. In M. Khan, ed., *It's Not About the Burqa*.

Khan, M., 2019. *It's Not About the Burqa*. Picador.

Khona, R., 2016. Kim K, It's NOT 'empowerment' if being sexy is all you're good at. Your Tango.

King, K., Balswick, J. and Robinson, I., 1977. The continuing premarital sexual revolution among college females. *Journal of Marriage and the Family*, 39(3), 455–9.

Kinnell, H., 2008. *Violence and Sex Work in Britain*. Willan Publishing.

Kinsey, A., Pomeroy, W., Martin, C. and Gebhard, P., 1953. *Sexual Behavior in the Human Female*. W.B. Saunders.

Kleinplatz, P., 2018. History of the treatment of female sexual dysfunction(s). *Annual Review of Clinical Psychology*, 14(1), 29–54.

Klement, K. and Sagarin, B., 2016. Nobody wants to date a whore: Rape-supportive messages in women-directed Christian dating books. *Sexuality and Culture*, 21(1), 205–23.

Kohl, J., 2015. Intra-Venus. In H. Berressem, G. Blamberger and S. Goth, eds, *Venus as Muse*. Brill.

Kokko, H. and Jennions, M., 2008. Parental investment, sexual selection and sex ratios. *Journal of Evolutionary Biology*, 21(4), 919–48.

Korotayev, A. and Kazankov, A., 2003. Factors of sexual freedom among foragers in cross-cultural perspective. *Cross-Cultural Research*, 37(1), 29–61.

Krems, J., Ko, A., Moon, J. and Varnum, M., 2021. Lay beliefs about gender and sexual behavior: First evidence for a pervasive, robust (but seemingly unfounded) stereotype. *Psychological Science*, 32(6), 871–89.

Kumar, M., 2016. *Communalism and Sexual Violence in India*. I.B. Tauris.

Kuran, T., 1995. *Private Truths, Public Lies*. Harvard.

Kuran, T., 1998. Ethnic norms and their transformation through reputational cascades. *Journal of Legal Studies*, 27(S2), 623–59.

Labib, N., 2020. Implementation of Beijing education commitments at national level, 1995–2020: School counselling and career education programmes to improve girls' and women's access to secondary TVET and STEM in higher education in the United Arab Emirates. UNESCO.

Laite, J., 2020. 'An equality of injustice': The sex buyers' bill and lessons from history. [Blog] *History Workshop.*

Laslett, P., 1980. Introduction. In P. Laslett, K. Oosterveen and R. Smith, eds, *Bastardy and its Comparative History.* Harvard University Press.

Laverte, M., 2017. Sexual violence and prostitution: The problem is your image of us. [Blog] *Die Tageszeitung.*

LB, J., 2021. *Keisha the Sket.* Penguin.

Lecky, W., 1905. *History of European Morals.* Longman Green.

Lerner, G., 1986. *The Creation of Patriarchy.* Oxford University Press.

Lerner, G., 1993. *The Creation of Feminist Consciousness.* Oxford University Press.

Levine, D. and Wrightson, K., 1980. The social context of illegitimacy in early modern England. In P. Laslett, K. Oosterveen and R. Smith, eds, *Bastardy and its Comparative History.* Harvard University Press.

Levine, P., 2003. *Prostitution, Race, and Politics.* Routledge.

Levine, P., 2007. Sexuality, gender and empire. In P. Levine, ed., *Gender and Empire.* Oxford University Press.

Levine, P., 2008. States of undress: Nakedness and the colonial imagination. *Victorian Studies*, 50(2), 189–219.

Levine, P., 2018. *Victorian Feminism, 1850–1900.* University Press of Florida.

Levine-Clark, M., 2014. 'I always prefer the scissors': Isaac Baker Brown and feminist histories of medicine. In T. Jones, D. Wear and L. Friedman, eds, *Health Humanities Reader.* Rutgers University Press.

Levy, A., 2005. *Female Chauvinist Pigs*. Simon and Schuster.

Lewis, J. and Kiernan, K., 1996. The boundaries between marriage, nonmarriage, and parenthood: Changes in behavior and policy in postwar Britain. *Journal of Family History*, 21(3), 372–87.

Lightfoot-Klein, H., 1989. *Prisoners of Ritual*. Haworth Press.

Lindskog, A., Congdon Fors, H. and Isaksson, A., 2022. Harmful norms: Can social convention theory explain the persistence of female genital cutting in Africa? *SSRN Electronic Journal*.

Lipka, M. and Hackett, C., 2017. Why Muslims are the world's fastest-growing religious group. Pew Research Center.

Lister, K., 2020. *A Curious History of Sex*. Unbound.

Lister, K., 2021. *Harlots, Whores and Hackabouts*. Thames and Hudson.

Lloyd, K., 2020. 'It destroys lives': Why the razor-blade pain of vaginismus is so misunderstood. *Guardian*.

Lookadoo, J. and DiMarco, H., 2003. *Dateable*. Fleming H. Revell.

Lowman, J., 2000. Violence and the outlaw status of (street) prostitution in Canada. *Violence Against Women*, 6(9), 987–1011.

Mac, J. and Smith, M., 2018. *Revolting Prostitutes*. Verso Books.

McCann, H., 2019. *Queering Femininity*. Routledge.

McCann, H., n.d. Beyond Skin-Deep Project: https://www.beautysalonproject.com/.

McCarthy, H., Caslin, S. and Laite, J., 2015. Prostitution and the law in historical perspective: A dialogue. *History and Policy*.

McClintock, A., 1995. *Imperial Leather*. Routledge.

Macfarlane, A., 1980. Illegitimacy and illegitimates in English history. In P. Laslett, K. Oosterveen and R. Smith, eds, *Bastardy and its Comparative History*. Harvard University Press.

McIntosh, M., 1978. Who needs prostitutes? The ideology of male sexual needs. In C. Smart and B. Smart, eds, *Women, Sexuality, and Social Control*. Routledge, pp. 53–64.

Mackie, G., 1996. Ending footbinding and infibulation: A convention account. *American Sociological Review*, 61(6), 999.

Mackie, G. and LeJeune, J., 2009. Social Dynamics of Abandonment of Harmful Practices: A new look at theory. *UNICEF Special Series on Social Norms and Harmful Practices*.

MacKinnon, C., 1987. *Feminism Unmodified*. Harvard.

MacKinnon, C., 1989. *Toward a Feminist Theory of the State*. Cambridge, Mass: Harvard University Press.

McLaren, A., 1999. *Twentieth-Century Sexuality*. Wiley.

Macleod, A., 1993. *Accommodating Protest*. Columbia University Press.

Macleod, J., Farley, M., Anderson, L. and Golding, J., 2008. A research report based on interviews with 110 men who bought women in prostitution. *Women's Support Project*.

McNair, B., 2002. *Striptease Culture*. Routledge.

McNair, B., 2013. *Porno? Chic!* Routledge.

McNamara, J., 1976. Sexual equality and the cult of virginity in early Christian thought. *Feminist Studies*, 3(3/4), 145.

Maguire, E., 2008. *Princesses and Pornstars*. Text Publishing.

Malinowski, B., 1932. *Sexual Life of Savages in Northwestern Melanesia*. Routledge.

Manchester, E., 2008. Marxism and art: Beware of fascist feminism. [Blog] *Tate*.

Manktelow, E., 2018. The women's war *1929*. [Blog] School of History, University of Kent.

Manlove, J., Ryan, S. and Franzetta, K., 2003. Patterns of contraceptive use within teenagers' first sexual relationships. *Perspectives on Sexual and Reproductive Health*, 35(05), 246–55.

Manne, K., 2018. *Down Girl*. Penguin.

Mariani, F., 2012. The economic value of virtue. *Journal of Economic Growth*, 17(4), 323–56.

Marwick, A., 2012. *The Sixties*. Bloomsbury Reader.

Masters, W. and Johnson, V., 1970. *Human Sexual Inadequacy*. Little, Brown and Company.

Mathieu, L., 2001. An unlikely mobilization: The occupation of Saint-Nizier church by the prostitutes of Lyon. *Revue Française de Sociologie*, 42, 107.

Matich, M., Ashman, R. and Parsons, E., 2019. #freethenipple – digital activism and embodiment in the contemporary feminist movement. *Consumption Markets and Culture*, 22(4), 337–62.

Mattison, S., 2010. Economic impacts of tourism and erosion of the visiting system among the Mosuo of Lugu Lake. *Asia Pacific Journal of Anthropology*, 11(2), 159–76.

Mayhew, H. and Hemyng, B., 1861. Prostitution in ancient states. In H. Mayhew, ed., *London Labour and the London Poor*, vol. 4. Frank Cass & Co [1967 reprint].

Menon, R. and Bhasin, K., 1998. *Borders and Boundaries: Women in India's Partition*. Kali for Women.

Mernissi, F., 1991. *The Veil and the Male Elite*. BASIC Books.

Mernissi, F., 2011 [1975]. *Beyond the Veil*. Saqi.

Met, The, 2022. Female figure ca. 1500–1100 B.C. Elamite. [Blog] The Met.

Meyersson, E., 2014. Islamic rule and the empowerment of the poor and pious. *Econometrica*, 82(1), 229–69.

Michalopoulos, S., Naghavi, A. and Prarolo, G., 2017. Trade and geography in the spread of Islam. *Economic Journal*, 128(616), 3210–41.

Milhausen, R. and Herold, E., 1999. Does the sexual double standard still exist? Perceptions of university women. *Journal of Sex Research*, 36(4), 361–8.

Mir-Hosseini, 2006. Muslim women's quest for equality: Between Islamic law and feminism. *Critical Inquiry*, 32(4), 629.

Mohammadi, M., 2019. *The Iranian Reform Movement*. Palgrave.

Mohammed, G., Hassan, M. and Eyada, M., 2014. Female genital mutilation/cutting: Will it continue? *Journal of Sexual Medicine*, 11(11), 2756–63.

Molony, B., Theiss, J. and Choi, H., 2016. *Gender in Modern East Asia*. Westview Press.

Moon, S. and Reger, J., 2014. 'You are not your own': Rape, sexual assault, and consent in Evangelical Christian dating books. *Journal of Integrated Social Sciences*, 4(1).

Morgan, L., 1877. *Ancient Society*. Henry Holt & Co.

Morgan, R., 1980. Theory and practice: Pornography and rape. In Lederer, L., ed., *Take Back the Night*. New York.

Morris, K., 2021. *Keisha the Sket* by Jade LB review – 'the literary version of the Black nod'. *Guardian*.

Mort, F., 2000. *Dangerous Sexualities*. Routledge.

Mort, F., 2010. *Capital Affairs*. Yale University Press.

Mortimer, C., 2015. Swedish doctors 'give teenage girls virginity tests' against their will. *Independent*.

Moses, C., 1998. French utopians. In T. Akkerman and S. Stuurnam, eds, *Perspectives on Feminist Political Thought*. Routledge.

Mourad, S., 2013. *The Naked Bodies of Alia*. [Blog] Jadaliyya.

Mule, P. and Barthel, D., 1992. The return to the veil: Individual autonomy vs. social esteem. *Sociological Forum*, 7(2), 323–32.

Mullan, J., 2018. The rise of the novel. [Blog] The British Library.

Mulholland, M., 2013. *Young People and Pornography: Negotiating Pornification*. Palgrave Macmillan.

Murdock, G., 1949. *Social Structure*. Palgrave Macmillan.

Mustafa, N., 2013. Naheed Mustafa: Put your shirts back on, ladies of Femen's Topless Jihad. *The Seattle Times*.

Nagarajan, C., 2013. Femen's obsession with nudity feeds a racist colonial feminism. *Guardian*.

Nagle, J., 2010. *Whores and other Feminists*. Routledge.

Naqvi, Z. and Shahnaz, L., 2002. How do women decide to work in Pakistan? *Pakistan Development Review*, 41(4II), 495–513.

Navarro-Tejero, A., 2019. Sacks of mutilated breasts: Violence and body politics in South Asian partition literature. *Journal of International Women's Studies*, 20(3).

Nekoei, A. and Sinn, F., 2021. The origin of the gender gap. VoxEU.

Nelson, S., 2013. Inna Shevchenko responds to Muslim women against Femen's open letter in wake of Amina Tyler topless jihad. *Huffington Post*.

New York Wages for Housework Committee, 1975. Wages for Housework.

NHS, 2021. Vaginismus. NHS: Health A to Z.

Nordic Model Now!, 2016. Submission to the Liberal Democrats 'sex work' policy consultation.

Northrop, D., 2004. *Veiled Empire.* Cornell University Press.

N.S.W.P., n.d. Occupation of St-Nizier Church. [Blog] Global Network of Sex Work Projects.

Nussbaum, M., 1999. *Sex and Social Justice.* Oxford University Press.

O'Brien, S., 2020. Carlow school principal denies female students were told not to wear tight-fighting clothes. *Irish Central.*

O'Faolain, J. and Martines, L., 1979. *Not in God's Image.* Virago.

Onoyase, A., 2018. Attitude of parents toward female-child secondary education in Sokoto state, Nigeria: Implications for counselling. *Journal of Educational and Social Research,* 8(2), 21–7.

O'Riordan, K., 2020. Students at a Carlow secondary school have been told by the school not to wear tight-fitting clothing to PE. *NewsTalk.*

Orthodox Church of America, n.d. Saint Theodora the Empress. [online] *Lives of the Saints.*

Ortiz, A., Hall, M., Anderson, T. and Muehlhoff, J., 2021. Marital status at first intercourse in married Christian women: Relationships with guilt, sanctification of sexuality, and marital satisfaction. *Journal of Psychology and Theology,* 50(4).

Orwell, G. and Shamsie, K., 2018. *Orwell on Freedom.* Penguin.

Owens, B., Hall, M. and Anderson, T., 2020. The relationship between purity culture and rape myth acceptance. *Journal of Psychology and Theology,* 49(4).

Oxfam, 2018. Young people in Latin America still think violence against women is 'normal': Oxfam. [Blog] Oxfam International.

Paasonen, S., Attwood, F., McKee, A., Mercer, J., and Smith, C., 2021. *Objectification: On the Difference Between Sex and Sexism.* Routledge.

Palladius and Meyer, R. (tr.), 1965. *The Lausiac History.* Paulist Press.

Pastore, F. and Tenaglia, S., 2013. Ora et non labora? A test of the impact of religion on female labor supply. IZA Discussion Paper Series.

Patel, D., 2012. Concealing to reveal: The informational role of Islamic dress. *Rationality and Society*, 24(3), 295–323.

Pateman, C., 1983. Defending prostitution: Charges against Ericsson. *Ethics*, 93(3), 561–5.

Pateman, C., 1988. *The Sexual Contract*. Polity.

Payne, E., 2010. Sluts: Heteronormative policing in the stories of lesbian youth. *Educational Studies*, 46(3), 317–36.

Peirson-Hagger, E., 2020. How a Mary Wollstonecraft statue became a feminist battleground. *The New Statesman*.

Perry, L., 2022. *The Case against the Sexual Revolution*. Polity.

Pew Research Center, 2012. The global religious landscape. [Blog] Pew Research Center.

Pew Research Center, 2014. Morality Interactive: Top line results. [online]

Pew Research Center, 2015. The future of world religions: Population growth projections, 2010–2050. [online]

Pheterson, G., 1989. *A Vindication of the Rights of Whores*. Seal.

Phipps, A., 2020. *#MeToo Not You*. Manchester University Press.

Platt, L., Grenfell, P., Meiksin, R., Elmes, J., Sherman, S., Sanders, T., Mwangi, P. and Crago, A., 2018. Associations between sex work laws and sex workers' health: A systematic review and meta-analysis of quantitative and qualitative studies. *PLOS Medicine*, 15(12), 1002680.

Pleijt, A., Zanden, J. and Carmichael, S., 2019. Gender relations and economic development: Hypotheses about the reversal of fortune in Eurasia. In C. Diebolt, A. Rijpma, S. Carmichael, S. Dilli and C. Störmer, ed., *Cliometrics of the Family*. Springer.

Pomeroy, S., 1975. *Goddesses, Whores, Wives, and Slaves*. Random House.

Poos, L., 1995. Sex, lies, and the church courts of pre-Reformation England. *Journal of Interdisciplinary History*, 25(4), 585.

Pope John Paul II, 1979. Thoughts on Women. Address to Italian Maids.

Potter, D., 2015. *Theodora*. Oxford University Press.

Poushter, J., 2014. What's morally acceptable? It Depends on where in the world you live. [Blog] Pew Research Center.

Power, K., 1996. *Veiled Desire*. Continuum.

Proudman, C., 2022. *Female Genital Mutilation: When Culture and Law Clash*. Oxford.

Qian, N., 2008. Missing women and the price of tea in China: The effect of sex-specific earnings on sex imbalance. *Quarterly Journal of Economics*, 123(3).

Quawas, R., 2020. Barefoot feminist classes. In R. Stephan and M. Charrad, eds, *Women Rising*. New York University.

Rai, B. and Sengupta, K., 2013. Pre-marital confinement of women: A signaling and matching approach. *Journal of Development Economics*, 105, 48–63.

Ratajkowski, E., 2019. Emily Ratajkowski explores what it means to be hyper feminine. *Harpers Bazaar*.

Ratajkowski, E., 2021. *My Body*. Quercus.

Read, J. and Bartkowski, J., 2000. To veil or not to veil? *Gender and Society*, 14(3), 395–417.

Read, J., 2004. Cultural Influences on immigrant women's labor force participation: The Arab-American case. *International Migration Review*, 38(1), 52–77.

Rees, E., 2017a. *The Vagina*. Bloomsbury.

Rees, E., 2017b. Varieties of embodiment and 'corporeal style'. In E. Rees, ed., *Talking Bodies*. Palgrave Macmillan.

Riddell, F., 2021. *Sex: Lessons from History*. Hodder and Stoughton.

Ringrose, J., 2013. *Postfeminist Education*? Routledge.

Rivers, N., 2017. Femen: Postfeminist playfulness or reinforcing sexualized stereotypes? In N. Rivers, ed., *Postfeminism(s) and the Arrival of the Fourth Wave*. Palgrave Macmillan, pp. 79–105.

Robb, J. and Harris, O., 2013. *The Body in History*. Cambridge University Press.

Roberts, E., 1995. *A Woman's Place*. Blackwell.

Roberts, M., 2017. Sex is painful for nearly one in 10 women, study finds. BBC News.

Roberts, N., 1992. *Whores in History.* Harper.

Rostek, J. 2021. *Women's Economic Thought in the Romantic Age.* Routledge.

Roth, M., 2001. Reading Mesopotamian law cases PBS 5 100: A question of filiation. *Journal of the Economic and Social History of the Orient,* 44(3), 243–92.

Rubin, J., 2018. *Rulers, Religion and Riches.* Cambridge.

Saikia, Y., 2021. The untold stories of the Independence War in Bangladesh. *Jacobin Magazine.*

Samuel, J., 2019. Victoria Bateman's nudity strips her arguments of force. *The Telegraph.*

Sanders, T., Cunningham, S., Platt, L., Grenfell, P. and Macioti, P., 2017. Reviewing the occupational risks of sex workers in comparison to other 'risky' professions. LSE Working Paper.

Sarkar, S., Sahoo, S. and Klasen, S., 2019. Employment transitions of women in India: A panel analysis. *World Development,* 115, 291–309.

Scelza, B., Prall, S. and Levine, N., 2019. The disequilibrium of double descent: Changing inheritance norms among Himba pastoralists. *Philosophical Transactions of the Royal Society B: Biological Sciences,* 374(1780), 20180072.

Scelza, B., Prall, S. and Starkweather, K., 2021. The role of spousal separation on norms related to gender and sexuality among Himba pastoralists. *Social Sciences,* 10(5), 174.

Schelling, T., 1978. *Micromotives and Macrobehavior.* W.W. Norton.

Schlegel, A., 1991. Status, property, and the value on virginity. *American Ethnologist,* 18(4), 719–34.

Scoular, J., 2004. The 'subject' of prostitution. *Feminist Theory,* 5(3), 343–55.

Scull, A. and Favreau, D., 1986. The clitoridectomy craze. *Social Research,* 53(2).

Sechiyama, K., 2015. *Patriarchy in East Asia.* Brill.

Selby, D., 2016. Everything you should know about honor-based violence. *Global Citizen.*

Shalit, W., 2014. *A Return to Modesty: Discovering the Lost Virtue.* Free Press.

Shell-Duncan, B., Naik, R. and Feldman-Jacobs, C., 2016. A state-of-the-art synthesis on female genital mutilation/cutting: What do we know now? Population Council.

Shenk, M., Begley, R., Nolin, D. and Swiatek, A., 2019. When does matriliny fail? *Philosophical Transactions of the Royal Society B: Biological Sciences*, 374(1780), 20190006.

Sidhwa, B., 2015. *Cracking India.* Milkweed Editions.

Skeggs, B., 1997. *Formations of Class and Gender.* Sage.

Skills for Care, 2011. The size and structure of the adult social care sector and workforce in England. Skills for Care.

Skills for Care, 2020. The state of the adult social care sector and workforce in England. Skills for Care.

Smart, A., 2005. The École Saint-Simonienne is outrage to public morals. *Nineteenth Century French Studies*, 33(3), 258–72.

Smith, D., 1980. The long cycle in American illegitimacy and pre-nuptial pregnancy. In P. Laslett, K. Oosterveen and R. Smith, eds, *Bastardy and its Comparative History.* Harvard University Press.

Smith, J., 2013. *The Public Woman.* The Westbourne Press.

Smith, N., 2020. *Capitalism's Sexual History.* Oxford University Press.

Smith-Spark, L., 2009. How did rape become a weapon of war? BBC News.

Smuts, B., 1995. The evolutionary origins of patriarchy. *Human Nature*, 6(1), 1–32.

Solberg, E., 2018. *Virgin Whore.* Cornell Press.

Sowinska, A., 2005. Dialectics of the banana skirt: The ambiguities of Josephine Baker's self-representation. *Michigan Feminist Studies*, 19.

Speed, B., 2016. Are 50 per cent of misogynistic tweets really sent by women? *The New Statesman.*

Sprecher, S., Barbee, A. and Schwartz, P., 1995. 'Was it good for you, too?': Gender differences in first sexual intercourse experiences. *Journal of Sex Research*, 32(1), 3–15.

Sprecher, S., Treger, S. and Sakaluk, J., 2013. Premarital sexual standards and sociosexuality: Gender, ethnicity, and cohort differences. *Archives of Sexual Behavior*, 42(8), 1395–405.

St James, M., 1989. Preface. In G. Pheterson, ed., *A Vindication of the Rights of Whores*. Seal.

Stannard, M. and Langley, M., 2020. The 40,000-year-old female figurine of Hohle Fels: Previous assumptions and new perspectives. *Cambridge Archaeological Journal*, 31(1), 21–33.

Stark, R., 1996. *The Rise of Christianity*. Princeton.

Steeves, H., 1997. *Gender Violence and the Press*. Ohio University Center for International Studies, Ohio University Press.

Stiller, B., Johnson, T., Stiller, K. and Hutchinson, M., 2015. *Evangelicals Around the World*. Rutledge Hill Press.

Stol, 1995. Women in Mesopotamia. *Journal of the Economic and Social History of the Orient*, 38(2), 123–44.

Stone, L., 1990. *The Family, Sex and Marriage in England 1500–1800*. Penguin.

Strasser, U., 2007. *State of Virginity*. University of Michigan Press.

Summers, A., 2016. *Damned Whores and God's Police*. NewSouth.

Symons, D., 1979. *The Evolution of Human Sexuality*. Oxford University Press.

Szreter, S. and Fisher, K., 2011. *Sex Before the Sexual Revolution*. Cambridge University Press.

Tang, N., Bensman, L. and Hatfield, E., 2013. Culture and sexual self-disclosure in intimate relationships. *Interpersona: An International Journal on Personal Relationships*, 7(2), 227–45.

Tariq, M. and Syed, J., 2017. Intersectionality at work. *Sex Roles*, 77, 510–522.

Tasker, Y. and Negra, D., 2007. *Interrogating Postfeminism*. Duke University Press.

Tate, S., 2017. Skin: Post-feminist bleaching culture and the political vulnerability of blackness. In A. Elias, R. Gill and C. Scharff, eds, *Aesthetic Labour*. Palgrave Macmillan.

Ternikar, F., 2009. Hijab and the Abrahamic traditions: A comparative analysis of the Muslim veil. *Sociology Compass*.

Ternikar, F., 2022. Beyond hijab and modest fashion: Muslim American women's negotiations of wardrobes and identities. *Fashion Studies Journal.*

Thomas, K., 2019. Women's rights in the Middle East and North Africa. Arab Barometer – Wave V.

Thompson, C., 1988. Hairstyles, head-coverings, and St Paul: Portraits from Roman Corinth. *The Biblical Archaeologist,* 51(2), 99–115.

Thompson, W. and Wheeler, A., 1825. *Appeal of One Half of the Human Race, Women, Against the Pretensions of the Other Half, Men, to Retain Them in Political, and Thence in Civil and Domestic, Slavery.* Longman.

Thornhill, R. and Palmer, C., 2000. *A Natural History of Rape.* MIT Press.

Tinkler, P., 1995. *Constructing Girlhood.* Taylor & Francis.

Togman, R., 2019. *Nationalizing Sex.* Oxford University Press.

Tolman, D., 2005. *Dilemmas of Desire.* Harvard University Press.

Torchlight Collective, 2022. Girls' sexuality and child, early, and forced marriages and unions: A conceptual framework. Torchlight Collective on behalf of CEFMU and Sexuality Working Group and collaborating organisations.

Toupin, L., 2018. *Wages for Housework.* Pluto Press.

Triger, Z., 2013. The self-defeating nature of 'modesty'-based gender segregation. *Israel Studies,* 18(3), 19.

Tsujigami, N., 2020. Driving campaigns. In R. Stephan and M. Charrad, eds, *Women Rising.* New York University Press.

Tuckniss, W., 1967. Introductory essay. In H. Mayhew, ed., *London Labour and the London Poor,* vol. 4. Frank Cass & Co.

Tumanov, V., 2011. Mary versus Eve: Paternal uncertainty and the Christian view of women. *Neophilologus,* 95(4), 507–21.

Turner, R. and Wigfield, A., 2013. South Asian women and the labour market in the UK: Attitudes, barriers, solutions. *Journal of Community Positive Practices,* 12.

Twasiima, T., 2019. Nudity and protest: Deploying our bodies against the patriarchy is legitimate. *African Feminism.*

Tyler, I., 2008. Chav mum chav scum. *Feminist Media Studies*, 8(1).

Tyler, I., 2020. *Stigma: The Machinery of Inequality.* Zed Books.

Uecker, J., 2008. Religion, pledging, and the premarital sexual behavior of married young adults. *Journal of Marriage and Family*, 70(3), 728–44.

UK Government, 2021. Employment (by ethnicity and gender). Ethnicity Facts and Figures. [online] UK Government.

UN News, 2018. 'Virginity testing': A human rights violation, with no scientific basis.

UN Women, 2021. Gender alert: Women's rights in Afghanistan: where are we now?

UNESCO Institute for Statistics (UIS) and UNICEF, 2015. Fixing the broken promise of education for all: Findings from the Global Initiative on Out-of-School Children. UIS.

UNESCO Institute for Statistics (UIS) and the World Bank, n.d. *Lower secondary completion rate, female.* [online] Available at: https://data.worldbank.org/indicator/SE.SEC.CMPT.LO.FE.ZS (& http://uis.unesco.org).

UNESCO, 2019. UIS Fact Sheet no. 56.

UNESCO, 2020a. #HerEducationOurFuture: The latest facts on gender equality in education. Fact sheet.

UNESCO, 2020b. A new generation: 25 years of efforts for gender equality in education.

UNFPA and UNICEF, 2018. Child marriage in west and central Africa at a glance.

UNFPA, 2021. My body is my own.

UNICEF, 2019. Afghanistan education equity profile for adolescent girls.

UNICEF, 2021a. Primary education. [online] UNICEF. Available at: https://data.unicef.org/topic/education/primary-education/.

UNICEF, 2021b. Secondary education. [online] UNICEF. Available at: https://data.unicef.org/topic/education/secondary-education/.

UNICEF, 2021c. Towards ending child marriage: Global trends and profiles of progress.

UNICEF, n.d. Child Marriage Country Profiles. [online] UNICEF.

Available at: https://data.unicef.org/resources/child-marriage-co untry-profiles/.

Valenti, J., 2010. *The Purity Myth.* Seal Press.

Van der Heijden, M. and Muurling, S., 2018. Violence and gender in eighteenth-century Bologna and Rotterdam. *Journal of Social History*, 51(4), 695–716.

Van der Kwaak, A., 1992. Female circumcision and gender identity: A questionable alliance? *Social Science and Medicine*, 35(6), 777–87.

Vance, C., 1993. More danger, more pleasure: A decade after the Barnard Sexuality Conference. *New York Law School Law Review*, 38, 289–315.

Vera-Gray, F., 2016. Men's stranger intrusions: Rethinking street harassment. *Women's Studies International Forum*, 58, 9–17.

Vicente, M., Lankheet, I., Russell, T., Hollfelder, N., Coetzee, V., Soodyall, H., Jongh, M. and Schlebusch, C., 2021. Male-biased migration from East Africa introduced pastoralism into southern Africa. *BMC Biology*, 19(1).

Walkowitz, J., 1980. *Prostitution and Victorian Society.* Cambridge University Press.

Wall, T., 2021. Gender equality activists hail Bristol council's vote on ban for strip clubs. *The Observer.*

Walter, N., 2010. *Living Dolls.* Virago.

Wang, Y., 2022. *The Rise and Fall of Imperial China.* Princeton.

Watson, I., 1998. Naked peoples: rules and regulations. *Law Text Culture*, 4.

Weiss, P., 2018. *Feminist Manifestos.* New York University Press.

West, K., 2020. A nudity-based intervention to improve body image, self-esteem, and life satisfaction. *International Journal of Happiness and Development*, 6(2), 162.

West, K., 2021. I feel better naked: Communal naked activity increases body appreciation by reducing social physique anxiety. *Journal of Sex Research*, 58(8), 958–66.

WHO Africa, n.d. Female genital mutilation, Factsheet.

WHO, 2021. Violence against women prevalence estimates 2018, Executive summary. Geneva.

Wiesner-Hanks, M., 2008. *Women and Gender in Early Modern Europe.* Cambridge University Press.

Williams, S., 2018. *Unmarried Motherhood in the Metropolis, 1700–1850: Pregnancy, the Poor Law and Provision.* Palgrave Macmillan.

Williams, Z., 2007. The market beyond porn. *Guardian.*

Winch, A., 2013. *Girlfriends and Postfeminist Sisterhood.* Palgrave Macmillan.

Wolf, N., 1990. *The Beauty Myth.* Vintage.

Wolf, N., 2016. *Emily Ratajkowski's Naked Ambition.* Harpers Bazaar.

Wollstonecraft, M., 1988 [1792]. *A Vindication of the Rights of Woman.* Norton.

World Bank, 2013. Opening doors: Gender equality and development in the Middle East and North Africa. World Bank.

World Bank and International Labour Organization (modelled estimates), n.d. Labour force participation rate, female. [online] Available at: https://data.worldbank.org/indicator/SL.TLF.CACT.FE.ZS.

World Bank and Inter-Parliamentary Union, n.d. Proportion of seats held by women in national parliaments. [online] Available at: https://data.worldbank.org/indicator/SG.GEN.PARL.ZS?view=chart.

World Economic Forum, 2021. Global Gender Gap Report 2021. World Economic Forum.

Wrightson, K., 1980. The nadir of English illegitimacy. In P. Laslett, K. Oosterveen and R. Smith, eds, *Bastardy and its Comparative History.* Harvard University Press.

Xue, M., 2018. High-value work and the rise of women: The cotton revolution and gender equality in China. Working Paper.

YouGov, 2019. Is it acceptable to use nudity to draw attention to a political issue? [Blog]

YouGov, 2020. Is topless sunbathing in the UK acceptable or unacceptable? [Blog]

Zakaria, A., Mughal, J. and Abi-Habib, M., 2020. Women face

dilemma in a war zone: Risk the blasts or sexual assault. *New York Times.*

Zatz, N., 1997. Sex work/sex act: Law, labor, and desire in construc-tions of prostitution. Signs. *Journal of Women in Culture and Society,* 22(2), 277–308.

Index

Free the Nipple campaign 17, 204, 209
Triger, Zvi 95–6, 122
Twasiima, Tricia 194
Twitter 162, 221
Tyler, Imogen 147

UAE 82
United Nations (UN)
  education and child marriage 72, 77
  female genital mutilation or cutting (FGM/C) 104–5
  honour killings 102
  honour and marriage to rapist 97
  Inter-Agency Working Group on Violence Against Women Estimation and Data (VAW-IAWGED) 88–9
United Sex Workers 62–3
unpaid care work/domestic labour
  and sex work, comparison of 183–5
unreported sexual violence 97
USA
  19th century 143, 175
  abortion ban 11, 45
  Boston Women's Health Club Collective 59
  Evangelical Christianity 10, 94–5, 122–3
  Muslim women: makeup and beauty salons 168, 199–200
  premarital sex, attitudes to 60, 114, 123–4, 162
  rape culture 94–5
  sex education, abstinence-based 10–11, 45, 61, 105, 106
  sex workers and domestic workers 184
  sex workers rights movement 181
  virginity pledge/chastity clubs/ purity balls 61, 106–7
  virginity testing 101

vaginismus 110–11
Valenti, Jessica 61
veiling and headcoverings 120, 122, 123
  bans 208, 209–10
  elites 141
  female labour force participation, UK 86
  history of 25–6, 28, 29–30, 32, 35–6, 37, 63
    colonialist perspective 54
    great unveiling 54–6
    Korea 39–40, 55
    and seclusion 33, 35–6, 132, 133, 136
  internalised 'male gaze' 216–17, 165, 195
  as protection 149
  re-veiling 10, 61–2, 155, 164, 167–8
  unveiling and political activism 86–7
  in Western societies 100
Venus figures and images 21, 34
Vestal Virgins 29
victim blaming 93–100
Victorian era
  accounts of ancient civilisations 22, 30
  accounts of matrilineal societies 129–30
  colonialism 53–4, 175
  masturbation 108
  virtue/moralism 49–53, 169, 170–4
Virgin Mary 33, 40
  see also Madonna
virginity
  and history of 25–6, 29, 32, 33–4, 140–1
  testing 119
    and hymen repair 101–2
  see also premarital sex/virginity; *and entries under* USA
von Stuck, Franz: *The Sin* 20